Divorce in Japan

STUDIES OF THE EAST ASIAN INSTITUTE,
COLUMBIA UNIVERSITY

The East Asian Institute is Columbia University's center for research, publication, and teaching on modern East Asia. The Studies of the East Asian Institute were inaugurated in 1962 to bring to a wider public the results of significant new research on Japan, China, and Korea.

Xiaobo Lu, *Cadres and Corruption: The Organizational Involution of the Chinese Communist Party.* 2000

Victor D. Cha, *Alignment Despite Antagonism: The United States–Korea–Japan Security Triangle.* 1999

Joan Judge, *Print and Politics: 'Shibao' and the Culture of Reform in Late Qing China.* 1997

Paula Harrell, *Sowing the Seeds of Change: Chinese Students, Japanese Teachers, 1895–1905.* 1992

Hiroshi Ishida, *Social Mobility in Contemporary Japan.* 1992

Ronald Toby, *State and Diplomacy in Early Modern Japan: Asia in the Development of the Tokugawa Bakufu.* 1991

Theodore C. Bestor, *Neighborhood Tokyo.* 1989

Divorce in Japan

FAMILY, GENDER, AND THE STATE,
1600-2000

Harald Fuess

Stanford University Press
Stanford, California
2004

Stanford University Press
Stanford, California
© 2004 by the Board of Trustees of the
Leland Stanford Junior University
Printed in the United States of America

Library of Congress Cataloging-in-Publication Data

Fuess, Harald
  Divorce in Japan : family, gender, and the state, 1600–2000 / Harald Fuess.
      p.   cm. — (Studies of the East Asian Institute)
  Includes bibliographical references and index.
  ISBN 0-8047-4357-6 (alk. paper)
    1. Divorce—Japan—History. 2. Domestic relations—Japan.
  I. Title. II. Series.

HQ937 .F84   2004
306.89'0952—dc21   2003024487

This book is printed on acid-free, archival-quality paper.

Original printing 2004
Last figure below indicates year of this printing:
13   12   11   10   09   08   07   06   05   04

Designed and typeset at Stanford Univesity Press in 10/12.5 Sabon

For Rika

Contents

Acknowledgments   xiii
Note on Japanese Names   xv

1. The Forgotten History of Japanese Divorce   1

   When Japan Led the World in Divorce, 1   Competing Interpretations of Traditional High Divorce Rates, 6   A New History of Japanese Divorce, 9   Changing Definitions of Marriage and Divorce, 11   Sources, 15

2. For the Sake of the House: Edo-Period Patterns, Perceptions, and Precedents   18

   Divorce Across Status and Domain Boundaries, 21   "No-Fault" Divorce in Popular Plays, 25   Magistrates in Support of Household Authority, 29   Merciful Buddhist Temples: An Alternative Venue for Divorce Negotiations, 39   Household Status Versus Sex, 44

3. Testing a Spouse: The Trial Marriage System   47

   Meiji Marriage Ambiguities, 48   The Frequency of Divorce in the Meiji Era, 57   Multiple Remarriage Opportunities, 67   The Trial Marriage System and Household Survival, 72

4. Unsuitable to the Family Tradition? Popular Divorce Customs in the 1870s   75

   Obtaining a Customary Consent Divorce, 76   The Terms of Customary Consent Divorce, 82   Life After Divorce, 96   Evidence of Female Divorce Initiatives, 96   Early Modern Divorce Revisited, 98

5. Between French Law and Japanese Customs: Codifying
   Divorce in Meiji Japan   100
   Intellectual Interpretations of Divorce in the 1870s and 1880s, 102
   The Napoleonic Code and the Early Codification Process,
   1873–1887, 105   The Backlash Against "French" Divorce, 1887–
   1892, 109   Reaffirming the Dual Divorce System, 1892–1898, 110
   The Civil Code of 1898: Divorce, Family, and Gender, 114

6. When Marriage Was on the Rise: Declining Divorce Rates,
   1898–1940   119
   Legislation and the Precipitous Drop in Divorce, 1897–1899, 120
   The Gradual Decline, 1900–1940, 128

7. Forward to the Past: A Historical Perspective on Japanese
   Divorce After World War II   144
   Legislative Reform During the American Occupation, 145   The
   1960s Revolution in Japanese Divorce Behavior, 152   The Return of
   the Divorcing Society in the 1990s, 161

   Appendix   169
   Notes   175
   Bibliography   211
   Index   223

Figures, Tables, and Maps

Figures

1. Divorce Rates in Japan, 1882–1943 — 3
2. Divorce Rates in Five Industrialized Societies, 1900–1940 — 4
3. The Out-of-Wedlock Childbirth Rate in Japan, 1900–2000 — 53
4. Urban and Rural Divorce Rates, Japan, 1907–1960 — 59
5. Correlation of the Divorce Rate with Marriage Age by Prefecture in the 1880s — 62
6. Correlation of Out-of-Wedlock Childbirth with Duration of Marriage Before Divorce at the Prefecture Level, Average 1919–1921 — 67
7. The Civil Status of Men and Women by Age in Yamanashi Prefecture in 1879 — 69
8. Divorced Persons in the Population by Age in Yamanashi Prefecture, 1879, 1920, and 1935 — 123
9. The Marriage Rate in Japan, 1882–1943 — 126
10. Correlation of the Divorce Rate with Patterns of Cohabitation at the Prefecture Level Around 1920 — 133
11. Divorce Rates in Japan, 1947–2002 — 145
12. Child Custody Arrangements in Japan, 1950–2000 — 157

Tables

1. Commoner Divorce Rates in the Edo Period — 23
2. Divorces in Mantokuji and Tōkeiji by Province of Marriage — 40
3. Changes in Prefectural Divorce Rate Variations, Divorce per 1,000 People — 61

4. Divorce Indicators in Yamanashi Prefecture, 1879, 1920, and 1935	122
5. Divorce and Marriage by Age Group in Japan, 1900–1940	136
A.1. Japanese Divorce Rate by City Size, 1910–1935	169
A.2. Prior Status of Newlywed Brides by Age in Japan, 1919	170
A.3. Index of Divorce by Age Group in Japan, 1919–1940	170
A.4. In-Marrying Husbands Among Newlyweds and Spouses Departing After Divorce, 1905–1935	171
A.5. Court Divorces, 1900–1940	172

Maps

1. Japanese Divorce Rates, 1883–1887	60
2. Average Household Size, 1888	63
3. Illegitimate Children, 1899–1900	64
4. Divorce Within One Year of Marriage, 1920	66

Acknowledgments

"You trashed us all, but what will you replace us with?" replied Lawrence Stone, an eminent history professor, to my criticism of the scholarship on the Western family that I wrote as an undergraduate student at Princeton University. Little was I aware then that my quest for an answer would inspire my research during the following decade. By now, I have published on various topics related to the family in Japan. Divorce, however, held a special appeal since it appeared to provide a window into the personal and emotional lives of people from all classes. Although the source material did not lend itself to the daily family life history that I had originally envisioned, it did lead to a new set of questions on the connection between family, gender, and the state, which this book explores. Recently, while I was still looking for ways to write a history of family and spousal relations in Japan, I was surprised to discover that my former teacher had published three excellent books on divorce in England.

From the beginning in my graduate school days until today this project has received much financial, institutional, and personal support in the United States and Germany, as well as in Japan. The History Department and the Edwin O. Reischauer Institute of Japanese Studies (RIJS) at Harvard University, the Japanese–German Center in Berlin (DJZB), and the German Institute for Japanese Studies (DIJ) in Tokyo granted essential fellowships. Professors Toshitani Nobuyoshi and Banno Junji sponsored my stay at the Institute of Social Science of the University of Tokyo from 1992 to 1995. The German Institute for Japanese Studies tolerated that, conforming to American practice but contrary to German academic tradition, I rewrote the Ph.D. prior to publication while working there as a Research Associate. With great pleasure I express my gratitude to the many scholars who have encouraged me over the years. My Ph.D. advisor Albert Craig set high academic standards and never failed to respond to my appeals for help while in Japan. Hayami Akira graciously invited me to join the Eur-Asian Project on Population and Family History at Nichibunken, which taught me much of what I now know about demography. Ann Walthall, Margret Neuss-Kaneko, and two anonymous referees closely read the manuscript, and offered insightful suggestions. I also benefited from comments by and discussions with Harold Bolitho, Regine Mathias, Wada Mikihiko, Maruyama Satoshi, Kurosu Satomi, Hiroshi Kitō, Sheldon Garon, Richard Gardner, and Peter Duus. The History Study Groups at DIJ and the Modern Japanese History Workshop, now at Waseda University, were always a source of stimulation and inspiration, and encouraged reflection on what it means to be a historian of Japan in Japan. I especially want to thank Carol Gluck whose enthusiasm and energy were a key driving force behind the publication of this book, and Kate Wildman Nakai, who consistently supported my research over the years, first as a teacher and now as a colleague.

Note on Japanese Names

Following East Asian practice, Japanese surnames precede given names, except those whose English-language works have been cited. Japanese who have authored English-language works have been cited with the personal name first. Macrons have been omitted in well-known Japanese place-names such as Tokyo, Osaka, and Kyoto when they appear in the text, in translations of Japanese titles and organizations, or as places of publication.

Divorce in Japan

1

The Forgotten History of Japanese Divorce

When Japan Led the World in Divorce

Divorce has come to symbolize modern change in marriage, family, parenthood, gender, and the workplace. Most believe that frequent divorce originated in the United States and parts of Europe in the 1960s and then spread to the rest of the world. It is thus quite understandable that the majority of analysts have focused on the geographical epicenter of what scholars have often called a "divorce revolution." But elevated divorce rates are neither limited geographically to the United States and Europe nor restricted to the post–World War II era. Several traditional societies, especially those not influenced by Christianity, have recognized and permitted divorce in various forms for centuries. Sometimes it was only under the influence of Western-inspired sets of values and beliefs, mores and morals, policies and institutions that older indigenous forms and frequencies of divorce disappeared in non-Christian cultures.[1] Probably unknown to many, including most Japanese, is the fact that Japan traditionally had a high divorce rate until the turn of the twentieth century. The social function and meaning of divorce in the context of Japan's traditional high-divorce society and its subsequent evolution is at the heart of this study of divorce laws, practices, and perceptions.

Japanese divorce customs were long a constant source of surprise and astonishment to foreign visitors. Before the Japanese government closed the country to all Europeans except Protestant Dutch merchants in 1639, the famous Jesuit Alessandro Valignano noticed casual polygamy and easy divorce: "The men have as many women as they wish, although they usually regard only one of them as their true and proper wife. They can renounce her whenever they please, by divorcing her and taking another woman, without offending any of the people concerned."[2]

Even after the opening of Japan to international diplomatic relations in 1853, foreigners continued to make similar observations. The British envoy A. B. Mitford remarked caustically that Japanese disposed of their wives "like old shirts," underlining both the informal nature of divorce and its widespread occurrence.[3] In the 1890s, a French engineer simply marveled at how often Japanese divorced,[4] and Basil H. Chamberlain, a respected scholar of Japan, admitted that divorce was "common," estimating that the ratio of divorce to marriage was nearly one to three.[5] Justifying their own zeal in reforming Japanese beliefs and behavior, foreign priests paid close attention to the frequency of divorce. In 1925, a missionary complained: "Japan needs a social and religious sanction to marriage to overcome the many trial marriages which if numbered with her divorces would make her stand out more than ever."[6]

Faced with foreign disapproval, and wanting their country to be respected in the civilized world, Japanese intellectuals were increasingly critical of indigenous divorce practices after the 1890s. In 1893, a Japanese diplomat defended the "statistically alarming number" of divorces in his native country to a British audience. He conceded that members of "the lowest classes" might "separate as easily as they unite" but said that "some Western writers," whose knowledge of the subject was "generally confined to the practice of the lower classes of the nation," exaggerated the frequency of Japanese divorce.[7] Japanese domestic perceptions were increasingly influenced by access to foreign demographic statistics.[8] Both the mainstream media and specialized magazines seized on such comparative statistics, with typical headlines proclaiming: "First in Divorce Among All Nations" (1902); "Japan Leads the World in Divorce" (1916); "Most Divorces in the World" (1917); and "Japan's Divorce [Rate] the First in the World" (1921). Subheadings such as "Let's Liberate Women" and "Most [Divorces] Are Within One Year of Marriage" suggest that writers were not proud of this kind of leadership role for Japan.[9] At the same time as public awareness of high divorce rates spread, divorce became construed as an important social and political indicator of the happiness of family life and the health of the state.[10] The emerging unease about the frequency of divorce in Japan was captured in the rhetorical question, posed in 1936, of why there was so much divorce "in our country, proud of its beautiful family customs."[11]

Official divorce statistics published by the Japanese government since 1883 also testify to the high frequency of divorce in Japan in the nineteenth century (fig. 1).

The Forgotten History of Japanese Divorce / 3

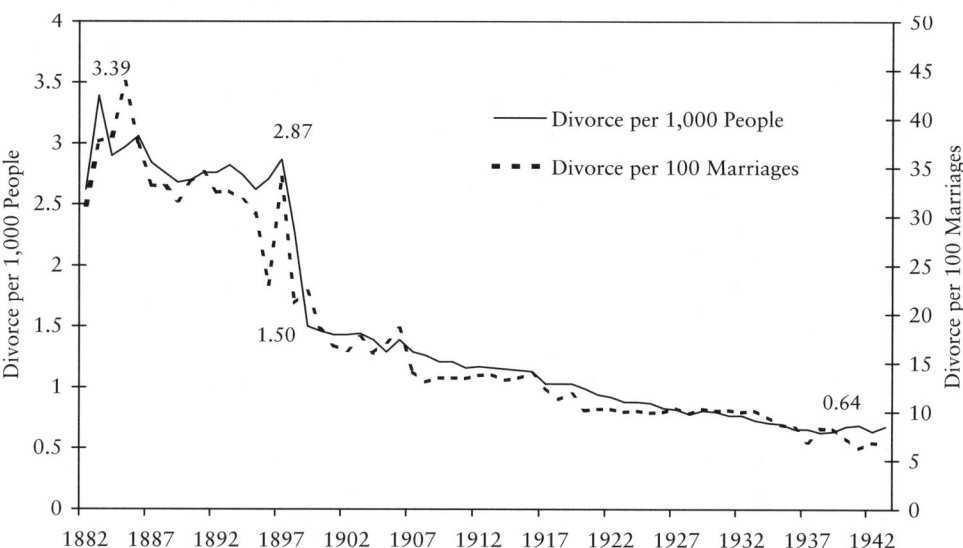

FIG. 1. Divorce Rates in Japan, 1882–1943. (Source: Yuzawa Yasuhiko, "Rikonritsu no suii to sono haikei," in *Kōza kazoku*, vol. 4, *Kon'in no kaishō*, ed. Aoyama Michio et al. [Kōbundō, 1974], 332–33.)

All the statistical indicators show a high divorce rate during the 1880s and 1890s, followed by a sudden change around 1898, when the national Diet passed a civil code and new laws on family registration, and then a gradual decline until the 1940s. Even by today's standards, the prevalence of divorce in the late nineteenth century appears extraordinary. In the twentieth century, the divorce rate in Japan peaked at 1.98 in 1999, which contrary to popular belief is not "low" but mid-range when compared with the countries of western Europe and way below the nineteenth-century record mark of 3.39 in 1883. Japan's nineteenth-century peak overshadows the divorce rates of European countries during the twentieth century and has been eclipsed only by the divorce rate of the United States since the 1970s. Some regions in nineteenth-century Japan, such as the northeast, had divorce rates similar to those of America in the 1980s.

Just as astonishing as the frequency of divorce in late-nineteenth-century Japan is the subsequent change. The divorce upheaval in 1898 suggests that the new laws had a significant impact on divorce, or at least on the way it was recorded statistically. If the slump in the total number of divorces from 124,075 to 66,417 within two years indeed reflects altered practice, this may have been one of history's greatest moments of instant social engineering. The gradual decline afterward, until World War II in-

4 / The Forgotten History of Japanese Divorce

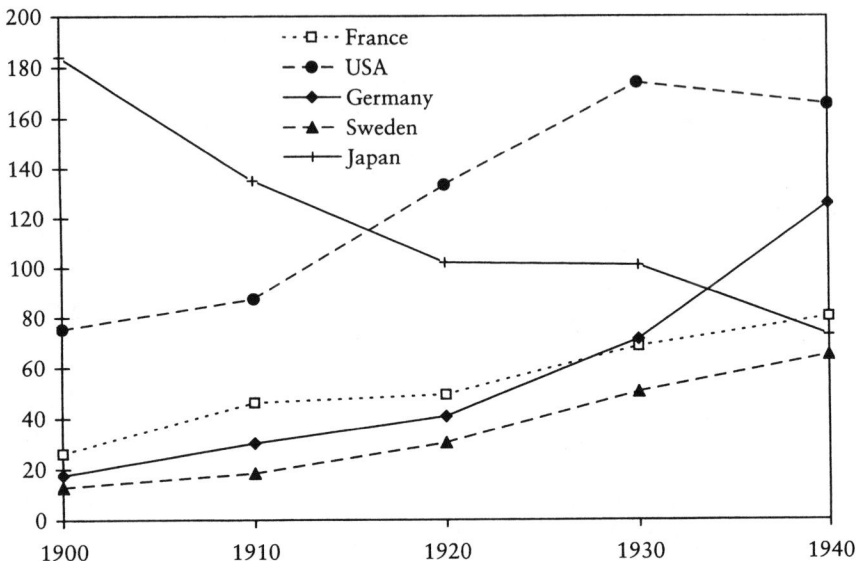

FIG. 2. Divorce Rates in Five Industrialized Societies, 1900–1940. (Source: William J. Goode, *World Revolution and Family Patterns* [New York: Free Press, 1963] 82.)

terrupted the recording of divorces, is also remarkable. As Japan's divorce rate sank after the turn of the century, the rates rose in the United States and most European countries (fig. 2).

By 1940, the Japanese divorce rate had converged to a level between those of Sweden and France. Industrialization, urbanization, and modernization, broad trends often blamed for an increase in divorce, had the opposite effect in Japan during the first four decades of the twentieth century.

European and American visitors to prewar Japan were startled, not only by the high divorces rate, but by the simplicity of the divorce procedure, which did not require the involvement of a court. In an influential book, Sir Rutherford Alcock, a British diplomat, interpreted divorce proceedings in Japan as a sign of cultural backwardness; not yet having "arrived at such a pitch of civilization as to require the assistance of a court" to settle conjugal differences, he observed, Japanese simply wrote "letters of divorce" instead.[12] More than half a century later, William Erskine criticized the fact that "mutual consent or supposed mutual consent" was deemed sufficient to obtain a divorce.[13] In a book on Japanese women published in 1891, Alice Bacon, a long-time resident of Japan, described Japanese marriage as "dissoluble at the will of either party." Social stigma inhibiting divorce seemed almost absent, regardless of social status; among "the lower classes," many men married and divorced several wives in succession, and divorced women were willing and able to marry a second or even a third time. While members of "the higher classes" felt somewhat restrained by scandal and gossip, divorces were so common that she had met "numerous respectable and respected persons who have at some time in their lives gone through such an experience."[14] The critical conclusion of L. W. Küchler, a European diplomat, in 1885, "The knot is loosely tied and may be easily unfastened,"[15] still echoes in the succinct summary of the sociologist Yasu Iwasaki in 1930: "Japan is known as the land of quick marriage and quick divorce."[16]

Despite foreign criticism of the divorce procedure, it found prominent Japanese defenders. The influential legal scholar Hozumi Shigetō argued for the preservation of a loose system of divorce, because spouses should have the choice of dissolving their marriages at their own volition. He acknowledged that being able simply to register a divorce without "anybody knowing" might be what led to Japan's high divorce rate, but argued that prohibiting divorce would limit couples' mutual freedom of choice and impair their happiness by forcing them to remain married against their will. The Japanese system of divorce conformed, after all, to the will of the people. The reason why Western countries treated divorce so restrictively was that Christianity looked on it as a sin.[17] The ease of divorce in Japan was considered beneficial to family life by Toda Teizō, the Japanese pioneer in family sociology. Divorce rates in the United States and Japan were comparable, he argued, but Japanese marriages were happier because there were no barriers to divorce.[18]

In contrast to the drastic change in the divorce rate, divorce procedures have shown a conspicuous continuity over the past few centuries in the marginal role played by courts in divorce. In the Edo period (1600–1868), few divorces were settled by the magistrates, who also functioned as judges, as is revealed in the insignificant numbers of extant divorce cases and by other sources. Even after the government started establishing a modern judiciary system in the 1870s, courts decided only a tiny fraction of all divorces, since their involvement was not mandatory. Between 1876 and 1898, the lower courts handled only 5,273 divorce suits, and the higher courts only 376.[19] Given that there were over 1.9 million divorces from 1882 to 1898, the proportion of judicial divorces before 1898 thus amounted to roughly 0.002 percent. Court involvement in divorces barely increased after the implementation of the 1898 Civil Code. Divorces by judicial decision never exceeded 1 percent of the total between 1900 and 1940. After World War II, despite the establishment of family courts to help settle domestic disputes, the overwhelming majority of divorces, usually around 90 percent each year, took place by simple registration at a local office without involving either courts or family courts.[20] This continuity speaks for spouses' preference to dissolve their marriages outside of the gaze of the judiciary. The important question it raises, however, is why the state gave the population the opportunity to opt out of court divorce when the countries that served as models for other aspects of its modern civil law required courts to act on divorce. Divorce by registration, called "mutual consent divorce," as first codified in 1898, was not even under scrutiny in the civil code revision process started by the government in January 1991, and it has survived into the twenty-first century.

Although the role of courts in divorce in Japan remains marginal, the country's high historical divorce rate prior to 1900 has left few traces. Most Japanese are neither aware of nor care about their ancestors' frequent divorces. Aside from simple lack of information, this probably has something to do with the current Japanese association of the prewar "family system" (*ie seido*) with family stability, which the high historical divorce rate calls into question. What is nevertheless surprising is the government's conscious effort to present Japanese students with an ahistorical view of divorce rates. In June 1997, for example, the Japanese Ministry of Education rejected four new domestic science textbooks for high school students because they allegedly overemphasized rising divorce rates, which contradicted "traditional Japanese values."[21] By defining traditional Japanese values as anti-divorce, the ministry not only rewrote history and reinvented tradition; it also elevated the problem of divorce rates to an issue comparable to the controversies surrounding Japanese atrocities in World War II. The history of divorce, in the eyes of this Japanese government institution, is a political question bearing on national identity.

Competing Interpretations of Traditional High Divorce Rates

Recent scholarship, in English as well as Japanese, has examined Japanese divorce in selected localities and institutions or explored aspects of divorce demography, sociology, and law in particular historical periods. While some of these articles provide excellent insights, as a whole this body of knowledge appears fragmented and sometimes even contradictory, especially when scholars restrict themselves to one set of sources, whether more qualitative information or more quantitative data. One of the many issues still under dispute is how to explain the existence of high historical divorce rates in Japan and interpret their implications for society and the family.

The most divergent views appear in the scholarship connecting the incidences of divorce to changes in spousal relations or the political, legal, ideological, economic, and social position of wives. On one hand, high divorce rates are seen as a sign of the insecure position of the easily divorced wife, but on the other hand, they are interpreted as evidence of the independent position of the wife, who could likewise easily leave. A decrease in divorce rates could thus be interpreted in almost exactly opposite ways, as either the strengthening or the deterioration of women's position in family and society. Depending on their assumptions about the Edo past and subsequent development, scholarly interpretations of the impact on wives of modernity, that is, decline in divorce rates, range from "liberation" almost to "restriction." Interpretations of the position of wives based on frequent divorce alone could thus range from multiple conclusions to the outright meaningless. Although a complex issue, difficult to resolve in all its social, regional, and individual nuances, this has nevertheless been at the center of attention of much scholarship on Japanese divorce, whatever the language.

The modernity-as-liberation view led throughout most of the twentieth century. Ishii Ryōsuke, a legal historian whose opinions on divorce are still widely referred to, showed in the 1970s that no safeguards against divorce had existed for wives, in the Edo period, whose legal right to initiate a divorce was limited. Although the government later enlarged the legal rights of wives to initiate divorce proceedings, wives remained without protection against divorce. As a result, Ishii thought that in the nineteenth century, divorces were frequent because husbands could, and did, arbitrarily divorce their wives.[22] Although he did not explicitly discuss the reasons for the subsequent decrease in the divorce rate, according to Ishii's assumptions, restricting husbands' power to obtain such arbitrary divorce should have been an important factor in the decline. Besides stressing the importance of laws, the modernity-as-liberation school often emphasized how family ideology sustained high divorce rates. Takeyoshi Kawashima and Kurt Steiner, who wrote the first influential post–World War II English article on Japanese divorce, argue that in Japan, the family ideal was traditionally constructed around the sacred, basic institution of lineage, not marriage. Marriages served no other purpose than to continue the lineage, and there was no moral stigma attached to replacing a wife in the interests of the house. In this interpretation, divorce declined because eventually "the individual person emerged from the kinship group. Marriage came to be viewed to a great extent as an individual affair." As the ties of the lineage weakened, "the importance of the conjugal tie between husband and wife increased." The decrease in divorce reflects a national shift in family ideology from lineage to marriage.[23]

A view less convinced of progressive linear history has recently gained adherents. Instead of laws, legal divorce procedures, and family ideology, its proponents examine popular divorce practices, often in local case studies. In a study of the socioeconomic consequences of divorce for women in an Edo-period village, Laurel Cornell has argued that previous scholarship overestimated the impact of divorce on peasant wives in the past. In the longer term, she sees a correlation between female labor force participation and the divorce rate, both going first down, then up.[24] In her study of an Edo-period divorce temple, Diane Wright, pointing to the emergence of textile production and sericulture as an economic force, suggests that women's expanding economic power was the "most important factor" in the evolution of "formal female-initiated divorce procedures."[25] Similarly, Robert Smith, in his analysis of village research conducted in the 1930s, links frequent divorce and easy remarriage to a rural household economy marked by a sexual division of labor in which "wife and husband were absolutely interdependent." He nevertheless attributes the decline in divorce not mainly to economic developments but to value changes fostered by local government agencies, such as schools.[26]

The coexistence of divergent interpretations reveals that a high divorce rate by itself conveys no clear message about gender relations in the past, and that the angle from which divorce is examined has a disproportionate influence on the subsequent findings. Depending on whether the focus is on laws and legal procedures, local practices, or intellectual discourse, the reader almost gains the impression that the authors are discussing divorce in distinct societies. So far, these various viewpoints have not been bridged through a more inclusive approach to Japanese divorce. This social history of Japanese divorce, the first book on the topic to appear in English, draws on a multitude of primary and secondary sources to present an analysis of the long-term legal, social, and intellectual changes surrounding divorce over the past four hundred years, focusing primarily on the Meiji period (1868–1912).

A New History of Japanese Divorce

To create a social history of divorce in Japan, this book explores shifting customs and patterns of divorce with due consideration for intellectual and popular perceptions and with awareness of the development of legal norms and their applications. Two simple basic questions drive this inquiry: Why was divorce initially high, and why did divorce subsequently become less frequent? These questions provide a framework for exploring a further set of questions into the social significance of divorce: What did divorce mean, to whom, when, where, and why? To what extent did position in a household, gender, social status, age, locality, source of income, and profession influence attitudes, inclinations, and opportunities for divorce and its subsequent impact? How is divorce connected to marriage and family customs and to ideas about these? This study combines three common approaches in order to answer these questions.

The first approach analyzes divorce law to show the overall institutional and ideological framework government authorities created for divorce, which clarifies elite thinking on gender relations and the family and is of particular interest to students of comparative law.[27] Since the vast majority of divorces in Japan were settled outside a court system, divorce laws and legal procedures there have been less important than in countries where judicial divorce was mandatory. In the case of Japan, an exclusive reliance on the development of law resembles examining the tip of an iceberg to determine the shape of the vast masses of ice below the water's surface. This does not, however, justify ignoring divorce law altogether, inasmuch as it partly influenced and in turn was shaped by prevalent ideals and popular interpretations of divorce behavior.

The second approach examines demographic and survey data to outline popular practices and complement and counterbalance the natural elite bias of the law. This distinguishes idiosyncratic behavior from common patterns, especially of the large inarticulate masses of the population that were neither involved with the law nor participated in public discourse. Sometimes popular behavior appears to fly in the face of the ideologies and values codified in the legal system. The main weakness of more statistical and survey data is its silence as regards peoples' motivation and individual contexts.

The third approach scrutinizes social and ethnographic commentary and personal writing on divorce behavior and divorce cases, real and imagined, to elucidate popular and intellectual interpretations of divorce practices. This shows what divorce meant for divorce participants in the context of their social and family environments. These documents include the most interesting accounts of marital strife and also provide insights into values and attitudes to marriage and gender relations, as well as actual spousal (mis-)behavior. This kind of material is rather sketchy prior to the Meiji period but becomes abundant by the second half of the twentieth century.

This study crosses the two most important political divides of modern Japanese political history, the Meiji Restoration of 1868 and the end of World War II in 1945. The reason for venturing as far back as the early Edo period is to trace divorce practices that were still in wide use in the Meiji decades and closely connected to the high divorce rate. The main chapters recreate divorce patterns, cultures, and legal debates across the Meiji period, the high tide of divorce in Japan. While most features of Japan's high divorce society began to fade by the middle of the twentieth century, some elements persisted until the 1960s and even beyond. In terms of divorce, 1945 was far less of a decisive break with the past than is commonly assumed.

Chapter 2 looks at traditional divorce as revealed in the patterns, precedents, and perceptions during the Edo period, focusing on agency in divorce and the variables of household position and gender. Chapter 3 argues that traditional divorce was a corrective to initial mate selection in a customary system of trial marriage. Not limiting itself to an examination of the occurrence of divorce, it locates divorce in the trajectories of individual life cycles and strategies for household survival. Chapter 4 investigates popular divorce practices in the 1870s. It explores socially recognized grounds for divorce and their ramifications, including property arrangements, child custody, and remarriage. By contrast, Chapter 5 explores the provisions for divorce in the 1898 Civil Code to shed light on the views on gender, marriage, and the family that informed the legal experts and politicians who defined the modern institutional framework of divorce in Japan. Chapter 6 suggests reasons for the huge drop in divorce rates between 1897 and 1899 and the steady decline in divorce rates over the first four decades of the twentieth century. Finally, Chapter 7 puts divorce after World War II in comparative perspective, tracing both historical legacies and discontinuities in Japan in the broader context of the postwar "divorce revolution" in other industrialized countries to show that Japan, at least in terms of divorce, was not simply a "follower country."

Changing Definitions of Marriage and Divorce

Divorce is usually understood as the legal dissolution of a marriage. Without an official marriage, there can be no divorce, but only the dissolution of a union of cohabitation. What seems clear in theory was more ambivalent in the historical past, since the rules of what constituted a marriage were subject to changing and competing customary and legal definitions overlapping with each other during the period under study. It is only in the modern period that the Japanese government defined marriage and divorce for the entire population by a uniform national law. Previously and, for a while concurrently, a wide range of social and regional variations existed on the issue of how and when a community recognized a union between a man and a woman as a marriage, ranging from written contracts between families, sake-drinking ceremonies, the start of cohabitation, or the birth of the first child. Some local communities attached importance to visual marks of wifely status, such as certain hairstyles, blackened teeth, and depilation of the eyebrows. The facial signs must have been very pronounced. Isabella Bird, who traveled through Japan in 1878, remarked on the physical transformation of young women: "The girls marry at sixteen, and shortly these comely, rosy, wholesome-looking creatures pass into haggard, middle-aged women with vacant faces, owing to the blackening of the teeth and removal of the eyebrows, which, if they do not follow betrothal, are resorted to on the birth of the first child."[28] The Meiji government repeatedly attempted to eradicate such popular customs and to homogenize marriage practices throughout the land. The family registration law of 1871 had already required that the authorities be notified of a marriage, but it was not until the 1898 Civil Code that marriage was finally defined exclusively in terms of registration.

The population as a whole took a long time to accept this legal definition. As described later, families in the early Meiji era often postponed reporting a union of cohabitation as marriage to the authorities until it had proved durable and/or children had been born. In the following Taishō era (1912–26), registration of a marriage was also frequently delayed until the relationship had matured. According to the first modern census in 1920, the proportion of common-law marriages (*naienkon*) was estimated at around 16 percent, which had declined to 7 percent by 1940.[29] By the 1950s, however, formal legal marriage had gained unchallenged social and cultural hegemony. This postwar national consensus on marriage still holds, as is seen in the negligible number of common-law unions (around 1 percent of all "marriages").³⁰ Despite the long tradition of recording vital events in Japan, made compulsory with the creation of the system of surveying religious affiliations in the 1670s,³¹ one of the reasons it took so long for registration to be popularly accepted as the exclusive definition for marriage was the wavering endorsement of the government and the courts during the Meiji era, discussed in more detail later.

Families and communities were expected to control mate selection, with some consideration of the views of the future spouses. Laws and regulations reiterated this ideal, especially for the nobility, even before the Edo period. The Tosa daimyo Chōsokabe Motochika, in his famous 100 Article Code of 1597, restricted the freedom of marriage of his retainers:³² "It is strictly prohibited for samurai who receive over 100 *koku*³³ to arrange a marriage without the lord's approval. Supplement: Whether one's status be high or low, matters of marriage must not be broached at any time if the understanding of both families has not been arranged."³⁴ Besides controlling the choice of vassals' spouses, the code reinforced the authority of families over their younger members, emphasizing the need for consent by the families prior to marriage, implying that this may not always have been the case. The Meiji state similarly stressed the importance of family agreement. In one of the early civil code drafts, it spoke of consent between families and the spouses and explicitly called for the presence of a go-between (*baishakunin*) in marriage.³⁵ Still, in the actual 1898 Civil Code, men under thirty and women under twenty-five needed parental consent for marriage.³⁶ These laws reinforced the customary values and practices of large parts of the population. In a national survey of local customs in the 1870s, headmen and village elders considered the presence of a go-between crucial for community recognition of a marriage. Mentioned explicitly for fifty-three districts, without a single reference to the contrary, it was one of the most frequently cited customs of the survey.³⁷ Among segments of the lower classes in the cities and the countryside, however, cohabitation and marriage were often simply embarked on based on an agreement between two individuals. So-called love marriage, in which spouses choose each other after a period of personal dating, remained a rare occurrence in the period before World War II.³⁸ As late as the Taishō era, they amounted to only 3 percent of marriages; 38 percent were marriages arranged with the future spouses at least seeing each other before the betrothal (*miai*), whereas 40 percent were contracted sight unseen.³⁹ One of the reasons for this predominance of arranged marriages was that, in contrast to marriages in northwestern

Europe, marriage in Japan was so nearly universal that the anthropologist Laurel Cornell asked, "Why are there no spinsters in Japan?"[40] While the case for men is less clear than that for women, few Japanese men born after the 1830s seem to have forgone marriage either, as the very low percentage of bachelors recorded in surveys shows.[41] Since the 1970s, the phenomenon of near universal marriage has weakened, as attested by the rising proportion of men and women who reach their fifties without having been married. But as late as 1990, only 4.6 percent of women and 6.7 percent of men between forty-five and forty-nine years of age had never been married.[42]

Anthropologists have classified marriage in Japan according to various factors, such as locality of residence.[43] The most important distinction relevant to divorce, in both custom and law, however, was based on the position of the newlyweds in regard to their natal families. The Civil Code of 1898 used a definition also often found in later official population statistics, which are an important source in this study. The code recognized three kinds of marriages: normal (*futsū*), *nyūfu*, and *muko yōshi*. It defined a normal marriage as a bride marrying into her groom's family. Both the latter kinds of marriage were marriages in which a groom entered his bride's family. *Nyūfu* and *muko yōshi* marriages were distinguished by the legal position of the groom in relation to his new household head. A *nyūfu* was a husband who married a female head of a household, whereas a *muko yōshi* was a husband also adopted as a son by his bride's parents.[44] For a man to become a *muko yōshi* often meant that he was entitled to receive economic and social benefits from his bride's family. These could be the use of property, succession to a samurai stipend, or bearing of her family name. It is possible that *nyūfu* brides were on average older than *muko yōshi* brides, since they had acquired the status of a head of household. The crucial commonality between all three kinds of marriages was the expectation that through marriage, a couple continued a family line and did not form a new independent legal entity of equal partners. These legal definitions influenced and conformed to social realities, although spouses did not exclusively see their marriages within the framework of lineage ideologies. Still today, Japanese, especially of the older generation, sometimes describe marriage from the perspective of the family, for example, by using such phrases as such as *yome ni iku* (go as a bride) or *yometori* (take in a bride), but terms for marriage lacking the family nuance are more common, such as *kekkon* or *kon'in*, a term found especially in academic writing.

There was a long-term decline in the proportion of marriages with husbands marrying into their brides' families. During the Edo period, they probably constituted 20 to 25 percent of all marriages.[45] Depending on the prefecture, 5 to 15 percent of new marriages were registered as such in 1905. The largest proportions were in the northeastern region of the main island, Honshū, and the smallest in prefectures on the islands of Kyūshū and Shikoku. Usually, more *muko yōshi* than *nyūfu* marriages existed in any locality. The proportion of both forms of marriage declined gradually to virtual insignificance until 1940. Although some men still continued the social practice of marrying into their brides' families after World War II, as can be seen when they took the woman's last name, the New Civil Code, effective from January 1948, recognized only one form of marriage. The fact that by 1975, a mere 1.2 percent of husbands took their wives' last names upon marriage reveals the postwar marginality of the adoption of *muko yōshi* husbands, a practice that seems most widespread among families with single daughters and/or with property.[46]

Just as the basic legal and social distinction in marriage was between normal marriages and those with in-marrying husbands, the corresponding grounds and procedures for divorce differed. The Meiji Civil Code distinguished between divorce (*rikon*) and dissolution of an adoption (*rien*), but recognized the possibility of a connection between the two. The dissolution of an adoption could be a legal ground for divorce (Article 813.10), and after divorce, the adoption of a *muko yōshi* could be dissolved (Article 866.9).

Since the Edo period, *rien* had meant the separation of family ties. Like other popular terms for divorce, such as *ribetsu, fuen, enshō,* and *sabetsu*, this word was rather ambiguous, since it did not clearly specify which family tie was dissolved. By contrast, *rikon*, a word of Chinese origins, still in use today for divorce, clearly denotes the dissolution of a marriage. The Meiji government's first divorce decrees in 1873 called divorce either *rien* or *ribetsu*. Only two years later did a notification distinguish for the first time between divorce (*rikon*) and the dissolution of an adoption (*rien*).[47] As the state continued to use *rikon* in its legal directives, the term spread into popular discourse during the Meiji era, whereas the other terms increasingly had the connotation of a divorce by which the wife was repudiated. By the 1910s, popular discourse often employed *rien* as a term for divorces initiated by husbands, whereas wives also took an active role in *rikon* divorces.[48]

Divorce, like marriage in Japan, meant more than the termination of a conjugal relationship, since it involved cutting ties with a wider family. In popular usage, the separation of a widow from her husband's family was also sometimes called a "divorce." This form of "divorce" does not conform to general English usage of the term, but it reflects the Japanese reality that marriage also involved the families of the respective spouses. In contrast to the remarriage of a divorced woman, there were several legal and social obstacles to the remarriage of a widow of any age, as is testified by the numerous inquiries by prefectures to the Meiji central government on that issue. The act of "divorcing" a widow was sometimes justified as facilitating her remarriage.[49] In an 1879 directive, the Army Ministry allowed the "divorce" (*rikon*) of a widow who was not eligible to receive a widow's pension because she had been married less than a year. This permission for "divorce" enabled the widow to marry again.[50] Besides showing a lack of precise terminology, this example reflects a widespread belief in Edo and Meiji Japan that marital rights and duties did not cease with the death of the spouse but might linger on until formal termination or a new marriage.[51]

Sources

This study draws on Japanese and European-language material, basing its arguments on the findings of previous research and a wide variety of original sources. Among the primary sources are court records, plays, newspapers, magazines, government minutes, diaries and memoirs, and an abundance of survey and statistical data. An important primary source for early Meiji divorce practices is an 1875 survey of local customs that social historians have often neglected so far. This survey, albeit difficult to use because of its lack of specificity and depth, reveals practices both corroborating and contradicting Meiji intellectual discourse. As an aid to drafting a civil code, the Ministry of Justice sent twenty commissioners around Japan in 1875, who interviewed 601 town and village officials listed by name. The results of the survey survived in abridged versions published in 1877 as *Minji kanrei ruishū* and in 1880 as *Zenkoku minji kanrei ruishū*.[52] The content of both publications is called "the 1875 survey" in this study.[53]

Another little known primary source from the 1870s is a trial census in today's Yamanashi Prefecture.[54] In 1879, researchers went door-to-door to check residency against the information from the family register, asking for familiar legal designations, such as the legal head of the family. The result was a survey influenced by the legal terminology of the family registration law that partly ignored actual patterns of cohabitation, for example, registering servants and maids in their natal families and not where they worked.⁵⁵

According to the preface of the published results, people who "lived as a couple" were designated as husband and wife.⁵⁶ The preface did not explain how it determined this marital status. About marriage registration, the entry in the 1875 survey for the area's Yamanashi district said: "As soon as the go-between contracts the marriage, it should be announced to the relatives and five-family group. After the marriage ceremony, it is registered orally with the headman and reported to the temple. If somebody comes from another town or village as a bride, the transfer of registration could take up to two or three months."⁵⁷ Statistics based on marriage registration in this area would have been closer to patterns of co-residence than data for other localities in which marriages were reported with some delay. The 1879 Yamanashi census is the most reliable extant statistical source on marriage and divorce practices in Japan at the dawn of the Meiji era.

Japanese government offices published demographic statistics under changing names during the subsequent decades. After 1898, the annual vital statistics publication was called *Nihon teikoku jinkō dōtai tōkei;* in 1932, it became simply *Jinkō dōtai tōkei,* under which name it still exists today. After 1920, the government conducted enumerative population censuses every five years, which were published in a multivolume series called *Kokusei chōsa hōkoku.*⁵⁸

The demographer Carl Mosk assumes that the statistics became more reliable after the population adapted to the family registers, first introduced in 1872.⁵⁹ Unfortunately, a surge in rural emigration after the 1890s probably contributed to a decrease in the accuracy of national population estimates.⁶⁰ By contrast, the registration of mortality seems to have gained in precision after the Graveyard and Burial Regulation Act of October 1884, which required the reporting of death and stillbirth prior to receiving a burial permit.⁶¹ As with mortality, every other statistical indicator of family life, such as family size and composition, marriage, divorce, and birth, has an individual history. Shifting definitions compound the problem. For example, marriage could variously mean "a unit of cohabitation," "a socially legitimized union," or "a marriage as registered in the family register." Despite the fact that the Meiji Civil Code defined a marriage exclusively in terms of the act of registration, competing definitions continued to be in use even in government surveys.⁶² The official marriage rate in the early twentieth century contained only registered marriages, whereas the first modern national census in

1920 subsumed both the common-law and the legal form under marriage.⁶³ Newspapers reported in 1920 on the decision to record "a mistress" (*mekake*) as "a wife" (*honsai*) in the census. The confusion and discrepancies in the statistics and surveys are both symptoms and part of the larger story of the modernizing, homogenizing, and nationalizing of marriage and divorce in Japan.

2

For the Sake of the House
Edo-Period Patterns, Perceptions, and Precedents

DURING THE EDO PERIOD (1600–1868), shogunate or domain authorities showed no interest in controlling divorce by stipulating reasons for divorce, supervising the process, or regulating its consequences. Moreover, there were no national laws regulating marriage and divorce and no official institutions such as courts of law were required in order to obtain a divorce. In that sense, the state took a laissez-faire attitude to divorce, much as it did in most other family affairs. When spouses and their families had reached an amicable settlement, they were by and large free to decide divorce on any individual basis they liked, without public interference. It was up to the respective local communities to handle cases of conflict according to their customary practices. Only when personal disagreements got out of control would disputes make their way to the local village or town authorities or, in exceptional cases, be heard by the magistrates of the shogunate.

Divorces, like marriages, occurred in a society stratified by status. The standards and ideals of behavior of the warrior aristocracy differed from those of townspeople, rural landowners, and peasants. Within these groups, there were also differences. Divorce may have been most restricted among samurai, because to control political unrest, the authorities kept an eye on the marital alliances of their retainers. Samurai families often had to obtain permission from their superiors before formalizing a change in household membership, including divorce. A denial of such a request would be based on political expediency, and that possibility sometimes even prevented formal dissolutions of marriages. Such potential barriers to divorce did not, however, diminish the frequency with which divorce occurred, even among the samurai, as is discussed in further detail below.

More than almost any other time in Japanese history, the Edo period, when male-dominated warrior society was in full bloom, is seen as a dark age for women. Among others issues, divorce practices have come to be seen as representing the repression of women. Legal and popular debates in the nineteenth and twentieth centuries often used such images of women to show subsequent "progress" in curtailing the power of husbands to divorce and enhancing the wife's ability to do so. Such visions of feudal society have ever since provided a useful backdrop against which to argue for the strengthening of women's rights. Frequent divorce without court interference appeared to disadvantage wives in particular. Not only nineteenth-century foreign visitors but contemporary scholars have argued that husbands separated from their wives at will, whereas wives neither could refuse such divorce requests nor possessed the right or ability to initiate divorce on their own.

Usually, the Chinese-inspired seven Confucian grounds for divorcing wives, already part of the Japanese legal tradition since the eighth-century Taihō code, are cited as proof of the humble position occupied by women, who were easily discarded under various allegations.[1] *The Greater Learning for Women*, a famous Edo text for female moral instruction, usually attributed to the Confucian scholar Kaibara Ekiken (1630–1714), enumerates these seven reasons, which have reinforced the image of unilateral divorce:

1. A woman shall be divorced for disobedience to her father-in-law or mother-in-law
2. A woman shall be divorced if she fails to bear children, the reason for this rule being that women are sought in marriage for the reason of giving men posterity . . .
3. Lewdness is a reason for divorce
4. Jealousy is a reason for divorce
5. Leprosy, or any like foul disease, is a reason for divorce
6. A woman shall be divorced, who, by talking overmuch . . . disturbs the harmony of kinsmen and brings trouble to her household
7. A woman shall be divorced who is addicted to stealing . . .[2]

These injunctions construct the ideal of a virtuous woman as obedient to her in-laws, fertile, faithful, unquestioning, healthy, reserved, and honest. In true Confucian spirit, the authority of the husband's parents is accorded first place, whereas the husband is not mentioned explicitly, and the main aim of marriage is postulated to be producing progeny. Most other points stress forms of submissive and passive female behavior supposedly conducive to family harmony. With disease included as a reason for divorce, these seven grounds differ from the Christian ideal of marriage "for better or worse" until parted by death. Apparently, spouses are not bound together for a lifetime, and the wife is at the mercy of her in-laws, disobedience to whom is construed as "misconduct." That no comparable seven Confucian grounds for divorcing men existed further leaves the impression of a divorce system strongly biased against wives.

By the early nineteenth century, *The Greater Learning for Women* formed part of the canon of texts for training young girls of elite samurai background who were instructed in reading *kana*.[3] The extent to which these and similar ideas reached the masses of the population or even informed the behavior of the aristocracy is open to debate. The peripatetic moralist Hosoi Heishū, who claimed daimyo support and large crowds of listeners, also talks about divorce and depicts the ideal woman as a paragon of endurance. He praises a wife who cared for her ailing mother-in-law while enduring her abusive husband. When the wife finally returned to her parental home after the death of her mother-in-law and a divorce from her husband, her deeds had so enhanced her reputation that she was rewarded with a marriage offer by a wealthy man. Hosoi stressed the wife's obligation toward the helpless mother-in-law and the benefits of divorce to the wife.[4] Filial piety was praiseworthy, and maintaining a marriage does not appear as a value in itself. There is little sense that divorce needed to follow any of the seven Confucian reasons for divorce nor that this woman was harmed in the long term.

Convenient though they are for depicting the submissive position of young brides, the seven Confucian reasons do not accurately reflect Edo divorce practices, as this investigation of patterns, perceptions, and precedents during the Edo period reveals. An analysis of social and regional patterns of divorce incidents will provide the background to a review of images of divorce in popular plays and legal precedents. The examination of an exceptional institution of the Edo period, the divorce temple, also shows that the case for women's disadvantage in divorce negotiations has been overstated. To the authorities, the gender of the initiating spouse mattered in divorce, but the respective positions of seniority in a household were often just as crucial in determining the outcome of divorce disputes. In the most extreme case, parents and in-laws had the power to divorce spouses against their mutual determined effort to remain married to each other.

Divorce Across Status and Domain Boundaries

Like other population groups, samurai preferred to choose spouses with backgrounds comparable to their own, an inclination supported by abundant domain decrees. Amounting to about 6 to 8 percent of the population, the samurai were a rather numerous nobility by European standards. Within the samurai class, there were wide discrepancies of rank, status, and wealth, ranging from powerful daimyo to lowly foot soldier. Aware of the samurai's potential for political disruption and for challenging their hegemony, the Tokugawa shoguns instituted a system of supervising marriages among their retainers. Samurai needed the approval of the shogunate before exchanging betrothal gifts and holding a ceremony.[5] Social practices and attitudes also hindered marriage between samurai houses with different stipends. The famous enlightenment thinker Fukuzawa Yukichi in his later life criticized the rigid hierarchies of the feudal system of the Edo period in his native town of Nakatsu in Kyūshū.[6] There, he claimed, strict social boundaries between lower and upper samurai prevented their intermarriage: "The upper samurai . . . regard such marriages with secret disgust. Neither have the lower samurai any wish for such marriages. On the contrary, they flatly reject them, saying that anyone brought up in an upper-samurai family, whether man or woman, is of no use at all in practical life and that marriage with such a person would mean an end of any future hopes of making a living."[7] Not only were status distinctions an obstacle to such marriages, but so were very practical considerations of whether such a person could fit into the new environment and be productive in the new family. Since Fukuzawa himself had married into a samurai house of higher rank, his emphasis on barriers of status, which he crossed, also served to advertise his own ability.

If marriage among the samurai had a political function and seems to have been confined to samurai of comparable rank, what does this imply about samurai divorce? If marriage is considered an important political affair, shouldn't divorce be too? If so, shouldn't it be difficult to divorce without offending the other party, and wouldn't the long Tokugawa peace create incentives for marriage stability? Divorces, if they happened at all, should have been rather exceptional among the ruling samurai elite, but they occurred. What is more, during the Edo period, marriages of high-ranking samurai were dissolved just as frequently as marriages in some villages.

Studies of samurai houses estimate that about 10 to 11 percent of the marriages of samurai wives ended in divorce. Records of 125 samurai families in Mikawa (in the eastern part of Aichi Prefecture), governed by a Tokugawa collateral house with the surname Matsudaira, show a marriage dissolution rate of about 10 percent.[8] Using a broad definition of "divorce," including the separation of widows from the houses of their in-laws and dissolutions of a betrothal engagement, whether purposefully or by death, the historian Asakura Yūko found that among high-ranking samurai wives from 100 daimyo and 100 bannerman (*hatamoto*) houses, 11 percent of all marriage alliances were terminated before death between 1600 and 1800.[9] Counting only divorces in the sense of dissolution of marriage reduces the above percentage by almost half, at least for daimyo.[10] Still, both studies confirm that family alliances were dissolved even at the highest levels during the long Edo peace.

Within this national sample of high-ranking samurai, divorce varied in three ways: by social status, over time, and by region. Status differences were related to the likelihood of dissolution of marriage alliances. Divorce in the broad sense was more common among daimyo (13%) than among the lower-ranked bannermen (8%). The difference is especially striking in the seventeenth century: almost no bannerman divorce was recorded then, but about one-third of daimyo divorces fell into this period. Higher rank, however, did not automatically lead to more divorce. Among daimyo, for example, divorce decreased progressively with rank. The lowest group of daimyo, with domains under 20,000 *koku*, had the highest marriage and betrothal dissolution rate, 15 percent.[11] "Divorce" became more common as the Tokugawa peace progressed. From the seventeenth century to the eighteenth, marriage alliances ending in divorce jumped from about 7 to 19 percent.[12] Among the daimyo, at least, there was a shift from marriage dissolution to betrothal dissolution. In both centuries, the same number of daimyo marriages was dissolved, but betrothal dissolutions were on the increase, creating the impression of a "divorce" increase. It is noteworthy that most daimyo marriage dissolutions took place in the second half of the seventeenth century when the political system seemed most stable.

Regional variations in daimyo divorce come as a surprise, considering that after 1633, daimyo wives were all required to live in Edo, where they were only visited by their daimyo husbands in alternating years. This being the case, rather homogeneous national divorce practices among the daimyo might be expected. Dissolution of marriages and betrothals by daimyo were about twice as likely in the regions of Tōhoku and Kantō, however, as in the regions of Shikoku and Kyūshū.[13] What makes this

TABLE 1
Commoner Divorce Rates in the Edo Period

Location (and province)	Divorces as a percentage of marriages	Divorce rate per 1,000 people
Yokouchi (Shinano), 1671–1871	11	1.07
Nakahara, 1716–1823	10	
Yubunezawa (Shinano), 18th century	15	
Komagaya (Kawachi), 1694–1749	16	
Nōbi villages (Owari/Minō)	16	
Takayama (Hida), 1773–1871	31	
Minami Ōji (Izumi), 1830–63	40	

SOURCES: Laurel L. Cornell, "Peasant Women and Divorce in Preindustrial Japan," *Signs: Journal of Women in Culture and Society* 15, no. 4 (1990): 717–19; Thomas C. Smith, *Nakahara: Family Farming and Population in a Japanese Village, 1717–1830* (Stanford: Stanford University Press, 1977), 106; Kitō Hiroshi, *Nihon nisennen no jinkōshi* (Kyoto: PHP kenkyūjo, 1983), 105–6; Miyashita Michiko, "Nōson ni okeru kazoku to kon'in," in *Nihon joseishi*, vol. 3, *Kinsei* (Tōkyō daigaku shuppankai, 1990): 49–50; Yōichirō Sasaki, "Urban Migration and Fertility in Tokugawa Japan: The City of Takayama, 1773–1871," in *Family and Population in East Asian History*, ed. Susan B. Hanley and Arthur P. Wolf (Stanford: Stanford University Press, 1985), 142; Dana Morris and Thomas C. Smith, "Fertility and Mortality in an Outcaste Village in Japan, 1750–1869," in ibid.: 242.

NOTE: Divorce rate per 1,000 people = divorces/population/years * 1,000.

east-west division in daimyo divorce so interesting is its similarity to the regional divorce pattern among commoners in the 1880s, the first decade for which national statistics were compiled. Regional cultures of divorce seem to have transgressed social boundaries.

During the Edo period, the rate of marriage dissolution among commoners in various localities varied widely, ranging from 10 to 40 percent (table 1). On the average, rates of divorce were higher among commoners than among the high-ranking nobility.

The first five locations listed in table 1 were agricultural villages, Takayama was a town, and Minami Ōji was a village inhabited by outcasts. Among the agricultural villages, Yokouchi and Nakahara had the two lowest percentages of marriages that were terminated by divorce. Yokouchi might not be representative with respect to divorce, however, since scholars have cited it as an example of a place where marriages lasted unusually long.[14] For Komagaya and the Nōbi villages, the actual percentage was higher than shown in the table. In Komagaya, registers survive only for every other year, and some divorces must thus have eluded researchers. The demographic historian Kitō Hiroshi argues that in the case of the Nōbi villages, it is often hard to tell whether death or divorce ended a marriage, so the actual divorce rate may even have been higher than indicated.[15]

In Takayama and Minami Ōji, divorces were much more common

than in any of the agricultural villages. The high marriage dissolution rate in Takayama may be connected to marriage customs in Hida, today's Gifu Prefecture, since the 1880s, the divorce rate for Gifu Prefecture was slightly above the national average. Nevertheless, Takayama's high rate of marriage dissolution points to the possibility of greater frequency of divorce in towns of the Edo period than in the surrounding countryside. The high divorce rate in the outcast village of Minami Ōji is attributed by Dana Morris and Thomas Smith to family strategies influenced by poverty and almost universal wage work, which encouraged a large number of children, early marriage, and frequent divorce.[16] Whether the fact that the sample from the nonagricultural locations excludes data before 1770 also explains the high rates of marriage dissolution is a topic for further research, since at least in the previously mentioned national samurai study, marriage and betrothal dissolutions increased from the seventeenth to the eighteenth century.

When mortality is added to divorce, the average length of marriages in village Japan appears short in comparison, for example, with that in early modern England, which prohibited divorce and had lower mortality rates. Ochiai Emiko believes that in high-divorce northeastern Japan (for the years 1716–1870), 60 percent of marriages were terminated within twenty years by divorce or death, in contrast to estimates for birth cohorts of 1826 in England of about 30 percent.[17] Divorce was a major factor in shortening the average marriage duration in early modern Japan.

Statistical records confirm that divorce was a common feature of life in the Edo period. From about 6 percent to 40 percent of marriages ended in divorce. Divorce was least likely among samurai in western Japan and most likely among village outcasts. Although the evidence is not conclusive, there is a hint that the frequency of divorce rose during the Edo period. No national estimate for a divorce rate per 1,000 people is possible from the given figures, but the Edo period crude divorce rate must have exceeded the 1.03 calculated for Yokouchi, a village at the low end of the spectrum of marital dissolution. Even if this divorce rate is adjusted upward, it still seems lower than the official crude divorce rates of more than three divorces per 1,000 people recorded from 1882 to 1898. Even before the Meiji period, Japan should be considered a society with a rather high divorce rate across social and regional boundaries.

Scholars have often attributed the ease and frequency of divorce in Japan to Confucian gender ideology that emphasized ideals of submissive femininity. As women were considered relatively weak, there was no serious ideological barrier to their husbands' expelling them and taking a new bride. The above statistical sample questions this view. However prevalent Confucian concepts may have been, they were absorbed most by literate elite groups that also by any measure exhibit the greatest discrepancies in authority and power between spouses. As we have seen, samurai did divorce, but not nearly as often as poorer segments of society with more equal gender relations. Confucianism may have facilitated divorce, but it was not by any means the only reason for the prevalence of divorce, which seems to have been affected just as much by the existence of regional cultures condoning divorce and the socioeconomic environment.

"No-Fault" Divorce in Popular Plays

Despite the seven Confucian grounds for divorce, the active and thriving urban popular culture did not adhere to these rules when portraying divorce. Theaters with large-sized puppets (*jōruri*) and male actors impersonating women (*kabuki*) had been among the popular forms of entertainment for townspeople since the eighteenth century. Although certainly limited as a window onto society, since "censorship eliminated any possibility of writing plays of real social or political significance,"[18] plays nevertheless suggest issues of popular interest and reveal social norms within the culture of the theater.

Avoiding recurrent bans against the use of contemporary events or persons, theater plays were often repositioned to the previous Kamakura or Ashikaga period with certain stock substitutions, such as Kamakura for Edo, or the Inase River near Kamakura for Edo's Sumida River. For moral reasons, the government also repeatedly condemned certain depictions of male-female relationships. It proscribed depiction of activities with sexual connotations in interactions with courtesans in the pleasure quarters, which as urban centers of social life and entertainment provided the settings for the most flowery scenes in many plays. Double suicide by lovers was another popular theme; this topic was effectively banned for only a few years, in a futile attempt by the government to discourage imitation.[19]

Divorce, a recurrent subplot in historic and domestic plays, introduced further drama into the stories. Just as in actual life, instances of divorce knew no status boundaries, as divorces are shown among samurai, townspeople, and peasants. To capture the attention of the audience and to heighten the tragic element, personal guiltlessness, especially of the wife, was a prominent feature of divorce scenes in plays. By giving the wife the role of the tragic hero, these plays also reinforced images of social hierarchy.

The most straightforward plot was of a husband divorcing his hapless wife. In the famous tale of the forty-seven masterless samurai, divorce scenes also serve to illustrate the overarching conflict between honor, duty, and human feelings. The 1748 puppet play *Chūshingura*, which is considered the most popular rendition of the story of the forty-seven masterless samurai,[20] presents the character of Gihei, a merchant in the town of Sakai, who divorces his wife Osono, although neither of them is dissatisfied with their marriage.[21] Cornered by his father-in-law, Gihei hesitantly issues a divorce notice to protect the samurai conspirators who trust in him. The wife does not participate in the verbal exchange leading to her divorce; in fact, she is not even present when the divorce decision is taken. Against her stated wishes, her father announces her remarriage "on the same day" to a "certain distinguished person." Openly confessing merely to covet the "wedding money" from the groom, the father justifies his greedy, inconsiderate behavior as being his paternal prerogative.[22]

Osono, calling herself a "blameless wife," attempts to revoke her divorce by appealing to her husband's love for their infant son, accusing her husband of cruelly intending to put their son under the care of a stepmother.[23] In defense, her husband describes at length how heartbroken he feels, because without a mother, their son is unable to sleep. Nevertheless, he overcomes his emotions and refuses to accept the divorce notice that his wife has stolen from her father. In the end, she escapes immediate remarriage and eventually is assured of a reunion with her husband through the interference of a masked "bandit," who not only steals her purse containing the divorce notice but cuts her hair at the roots like that of a Buddhist priest, making her undesirable as a new bride.[24] During all these scenes, Gihei never explains to his wife why he sent her back to her family in the first place. Despite her loyalty, his wife, as a woman, cannot be trusted with important secrets. Gihei emphasizes the difference between men and women in this respect. Unlike "a woman or a child," who may confess under pressure when a hostage is taken, "Gihei of the Amakawaya is a man."[25]

In these divorce scenes, divorcing husband and divorced wife act as paragons of male and female virtue. To keep secret the plans of his samurai conspirators, the merchant Gihei proves his samurai-like determination by putting his concern for his wife and children in second place. Osono stresses her son's need for a mother, not her own interest, as an argument against her divorce. Conjugal love is also mentioned in the context of parenting. Gihei claims to have no affection left for a wife willing to desert him, the father of her child, to marry another man.

The theme of the virtuous wife is also found in other plays in which fathers or male guardians force husbands to divorce their wives. To protect her personal material resources, but against her stated wishes, a father requests and receives a divorce for his daughter Osan in one of the most famous love-suicide plays written during the Edo period.[26] Since her carpenter husband has neglected his business and family affairs because of his desperate love for a prostitute, Osan has plenty of reasons for discontentment. She remains devoted, however, pawning her clothes to redeem her husband's lover and resisting to the very last moment the divorce request put forward by her family. Again, she phrases her opposition as concern about her small children losing their mother. In contrast to her meek and ineffectual husband, whose only decisive action is his suicide, she appears as a resourceful character, but everyone ignores her views on divorce.

The plays do not restrict the divorce initiative to men. Mothers-in-law are also shown in a position of strength similar to that of fathers and husbands, again vis-à-vis virtuous, innocent wives. In another scene from *Chūshingura,* a mother-in-law, Oishi, dissolves her son's marriage engagement to the daughter of another samurai house. The mother-in-law justifies the divorce in terms not of the words and deeds of the bride but of the shameful behavior of the bride's father.[27] The divorced bride's family, however, criticize Oishi's forceful act as overstepping her position, since she has consulted neither her husband nor her son, the groom. "I've never heard the like—a mother-in-law divorcing her son's wife," the mother of the divorced bride complains.[28] Only the dramatic threat of suicide by the bride and her mother induce Oishi to revoke the divorce, but as a precondition she asks for the head of the father. That cruel demand is satisfied by the father's death shortly thereafter.[29] Though the mother-in-law has acted by herself in initiating the divorce, her family later supports her decision.

Plays portray husbands, when they are also adopted as sons, in a position of helplessness resembling that of the blameless, virtuous wife. Induced by the machinations of the husband's adoptive mother, husband and wife commit suicide together in a 1722 play by the popular writer Chikamatsu Monzaemon. Hanbei was adopted into the house of a vegetable shop owner in the city of Osaka and is later married to Chiyo, her third husband. He gets along well with his wife, and they have a child.

When Hanbei attends the memorial service for his biological father in the town of Hamamatsu, his adoptive mother sends Chiyo back to her natal family under the pretense that she needs to care for her sick father, a prosperous farmer in the village of Ueda. On his way home from Hamamatsu, Hanbei visits Chiyo's natal family and discovers Chiyo's expulsion. Too weak to stand up for his wife to his adoptive mother and unable to keep his promise to his father-in-law to restore the marriage, he dissolves his adoptive ties (*rien*) and he and Chiyo commit the kind of love suicide usually performed by those unable to marry.[30] The mother-in-law, who has initiated the divorce of her daughter-in-law and forced dissolution of the adoption of her son, never reveals the reasons for her antipathy toward her daughter-in-law. Her adopted son Hanbei is nevertheless depicted as unable to preserve his marriage against her will.

In the above scenes drawn from well-known plays written in the first half of the eighteenth century, no obvious legal or customary restrictions prevent divorce. Whether driven by a sense of duty or by selfish interest, divorce initiators and decision-makers, who in these plays are predominantly parents and husbands, do not always specify grounds for terminating marriages. Parents could be fathers or male guardians of either groom or bride; mothers usually were either mothers-in-law or adoptive mothers. Even when coerced, husbands appear to have had the final say in the divorce process when issuing a divorce notice. While the divorcing party may have more or less honorable motivations, the party being divorced, whether wife or adopted son, is overwhelmingly portrayed as virtuous, innocent, and blameless. The presence of infant children in the above marriages, probably meant to increase the sense of tragedy and pity for the divorced party, because children have to be left behind at divorce, also suggests that the spouses have married only recently and partly explains the prominent role of parents in the plots.

According to the plays, a power imbalance existed whereby senior members of a house, male and sometimes even female, were able to use and abuse the possibility of repelling a new member who had entered the house by marriage, adoption, or both. The rejected junior member, whether young wife or adopted son, had no ability to prevent a divorce, even when guiltless. The fault of the party being divorced boiled down to an inability to please senior members of the new household, regardless of what their particular expectations might have been. While evoking sympathy with the plight of junior household members, these plays reinforced the social hierarchy by reminding the audience that it was the senior house members, especially the men, who ought to hold the position of power in family affairs.[31]

Magistrates in Support of Household Authority

The tiny number of extant cases in the legal record shows that shogunate officials rarely interfered with divorces during the Edo period. When they became involved in a divorce case, they were often the last resort in arbitration, as can hardly be overemphasized. For a magistrate to consider a family dispute, members of the five-family-group, a local headman, and domain authorities had to support the suit first.[32] The *Bunden sōsho,* a legal collection compiled in 1673, expected magistrates to forward disputes on the dissolution of adoption to the relatives or the five-family-group.[33] The procedure for divorce cases must have been similar to those for other family disputes or adoption cases. The settlement document certifying a private settlement (*naisai*) had to contain the seals of a go-between, members of the five-family group, a trade association leader, landlords, and those of other participants in the case. Many steps had to be taken before magistrates took up family disputes. The settlement of disputes was only one of the many duties of the town magistrates (*machi bugyō*) and the temple and shrine magistrates (*jisha bugyō*),[34] the magistrates who appeared most frequently in divorce cases of the Edo period. Magistrates rarely decided divorce cases outright. The salient feature of their approach to family disputes was their avoidance of a judgment and support of a private settlement. In guiding the parties in the disputes, they referred to previous court cases and recent ordinances.

Magistrates in the Edo period distinguished between ordinary divorce and the divorce of a *muko yōshi* (a groom adopted into the bride's family). In the collection of Edo legal customs published in 1934, the *Tokugawa jidai minji kanreishū,* the cases were listed respectively under the headings of ordinary divorce (*rikon*) and *muko yōshi* divorce/dissolution of adoption (*rien*). Edo magistrates did not follow that linguistic terminology, and neither is it used in the 1875 survey, but in practice they nonetheless distinguished between the two kinds of divorce. Whether the divorce was of a bride who had entered the household or of a *muko yōshi* was crucial in determining the respective duties of plaintiff and defendant.

Ordinary Divorce

From the magistrate's point of view, an ordinary divorce was the least problematic kind. According to 1668 administrative guidelines for the territory under direct administration of the shogunate, a husband had the complete right to divorce his wife provided he returned her dowry goods (*dōgu*) and dowry money (*jisankin*).[35] It is probably more than mere coincidence that no record of a case remains in which a husband's right to divorce his wife was disputed in principle, although in several instances there was objection to his withholding the wife's personal possessions. By contrast, to what extent authorities granted a wife a legal right to divorce her husband in an ordinary divorce is subject to interpretation. A wife could not legally divorce her husband under any circumstances, some scholars argue.[36] Others qualify this view, suggesting it may have been possible for a wife to request a divorce, but the ultimate decision rested with her husband.[37] The *Jikata* collection recognized several grounds on which a wife could divorce her husband. Unlike her husband, however, a wife could not obtain her divorce right away. She first had to either return home to her parents or, less commonly, seek sanctuary in a temple. The *Jikata* urged magistrates to reject a husband's request for recovery of his wife if she had returned to her family and stayed there for longer than three years. Even if she had remarried without obtaining a divorce notice, the husband could not sue. The fact that after three years, the husband forfeited the right of recovering his wife implies, however, that he had the right to reclaim her before that.

The Sayo divorce case may be interpreted as an example of the differential abilities of a husband and a wife to divorce. Since the case reveals other aspects of divorce by magistrates, it is recounted here in detail.[38] The dispute involved thirty-three-year-old Hanbei, a tenant in Edo's Honchō district, and his twenty-one-year-old wife, Sayo. According to the defendants' final testimony, Sayo, "with a go-between properly witnessing, was given in marriage a few years ago" to Hanbei. Upon receiving a message about the illness of her father, Tsunejirō, Sayo returned home without asking her husband's permission.[39] Prior to the final testimony, Sayo's father had offered a different version of the length of her marriage and the reason for her separation:

I gave my daughter Sayo, . . . in marriage, in the tenth month of the last year of the dragon, to Hanbei; . . . but because of a bad relationship between husband and wife, I received her back in the twelfth month of the same year. In the third month of this year, Hanbei sued to recover Sayo . . . and the case came to trial. But on my restoring Sayo to Hanbei, we petitioned for dismissal of the case.[40]

According to Tsunejirō's version, Sayo's married life had lasted for about three months.[41] She did not adapt to her new environment, and her father's illness was something of a pretext to escape an unwelcome marriage. Whatever the reason for Sayo's departure, her husband failed to approve of it.

Since Sayo remained with her parents, her husband Hanbei eventually went to the town magistracy to recover his wife.[42] Despite the regulation that a husband had a right to recover his wife within three years of separation, Hanbei could not by himself persuade his wife to return. His motivation for retrieval of his wife remained unstated, but Hanbei persevered doggedly. After Hanbei sued, negotiations were encouraged by the town magistrate. The two sides finally petitioned for a private settlement under which Sayo was to return to Hanbei's house. The magistrate granted the request and dismissed the case on the twenty-first day of the fourth month of 1845.[43] The following events suggest the possibility that Sayo felt forced into this agreement, even though she may have changed her mind afterward.

After reaching the private settlement, Hanbei left Sayo in the charge of his relative Eizō, since it was already evening. Why he returned home alone, having just recovered his wife, remains one of the unexplained mysteries of the case. He may have been considerate to his reluctant wife, but it seems more likely that he feared she might run away in the night. His decision to leave Sayo with a relative, however, facilitated her subsequent desertion. On the following day, Sayo sent for her mother because she was afraid to resume married life with Hanbei. Sayo's pleading persuaded her mother to let her return home. Eizō prudently insisted on obtaining Hanbei's permission, however, and Uncle Denjirō, who lived at the mother's place, therefore went to Hanbei and asked for his approval of Sayo visiting her home before being returned to Hanbei.[44] Hanbei, distracted by his business, consented and permitted Denjirō to draft a letter in his name stating that urgent matters had prevented Hanbei from coming in person and authorizing Eizō to deliver Sayo to her mother and uncle.[45] To the magistrates, Hanbei explained later that rather than agreeing to release Sayo, he had only consented to the trifling matter of her meeting her mother.

Sayo's decision to leave her parents and take refuge in Mantokuji, a divorce temple in Kōzuke Province, added to the complications of the divorce case. Hanbei became furious once he discovered that his wife had run away from her parents. He then accused his father-in-law of forging a letter to abduct his wife. Involving a town magistrate for a second time, Hanbei claimed to be victim of a conspiracy, and he again demanded the restitution of his wife.[46]

In his defense, Sayo's father first declared that his daughter had disappeared from home, but he later admitted that he had taken her to the temple because he felt pity for her when she resolutely refused to return to Hanbei.[47] Sayo's relatives later blamed her for seeking sanctuary at

Mantokuji and invoking its regulations to protect her from her husband. Because she had already promised to return at the first trial, Sayo explained, she was not secure at her parents' house. While she waited in Mantokuji, Sayo hoped that Hanbei would submit to her desire for a divorce.

In the final verdict, the town magistrate ignored Sayo's desire for a divorce. Sayo had to return to Hanbei and resume their marriage. Nevertheless, the case does not prove that wives in general had no right to divorce. The reason why Hanbei in the end succeeded in regaining his wife with the help of the magistrates may have much to do with the fact that Sayo and her family had previously agreed that she would return to Hanbei, in an officially sanctioned promise, and defiance of this settlement questioned the authority of the magistrates.

Cases of In-marrying Husbands and Adopted Sons

As a man who is a present or future head of household, an in-marrying husband (*muko yōshi*) involved in a divorce could cause conflicts between legal views on social hierarchy in the family and proper gender roles. Just like a bride, a *muko yōshi* left his natal family to enter another house upon marriage. From the point of view of his adoptive family, he was an in-marrying member, in a newcomer's position that in some ways resembled that of most young wives. Unlike a bride, however, a *muko yōshi* was likely to succeed to the headship of the family he married into, since mostly men became heads of families. As succession to the headship included control of family assets, divorcing a *muko yōshi* was also a form of disinheritance. What made the divorce of a *muko yōshi* more complicated than divorcing a wife was the need to sever his ties as an adopted son in addition to the bonds of marriage. When conflicts arose as to whether senior members of the house, adoptive fathers or even adoptive mothers, had the right to dissolve the ties of a *muko yōshi* as son and husband, the magistrates usually took the side of senior household members.

In several cases, magistrates ruled against the desire of a *muko yōshi* to maintain the marriage after dissolution of the adoption. The story of a merchant daughter is recounted in a 1789 inquiry to a magistrate. Upon the death of her husband, her father-in-law adopted a new husband for her. The father-in-law then dissolved the adoption of the husband and after negotiations sent the woman back to her natal family. The father-in-law wrote her a divorce notice that included a permission to remarry, since she was blameless. Her second husband, however, refused to do the same and wanted her back explicitly because they were the parents of a child—a request her biological father rejected. The reply by the magistrate upheld the divorce and supported the authority of the father-in-law against the husband, but it proposed light punishment (*karuki togame*) for the father-in-law's failure to procure a divorce notice from the husband.[48] In this case, three men argued over a woman's marriage, but there is no reference to the woman's own wishes. A 1743 case reveals the exceptional attachment of a divorced *muko yōshi* who kidnapped his former wife after she had already remarried, a deed for which the magistrate punished him with middle-distance banishment (*chū-tsuihō*).[49] As in the previous case, the view of the wife is entirely missing from the picture, but it is clear that the magistrates protected the desires of the house, as personified by the adoptive parents, against the wishes of the *muko yōshi*.

A detailed case of 1780 shows the ambiguities and conflicts arising from *muko yōshi* status, especially if the divorcing party was the adoptive mother and the adopted son was the legal head of the household. Money, sex, and power all feature in the suit, in which continuation of the marriage was only of incidental interest to the contesting parties.[50] An important Matsuzaka money-lending family, which counted several branch stores in Edo and Kyoto as well as the domain government among its clients, needed an heir to lead the business. In the beginning, everything seems to have gone smoothly. Apparently childless and single, Chigen first adopted Yuri, the daughter of Sōzen. Then, in 1767, she also adopted Jūrōbei as a *muko yōshi* for Yuri, with Sōzen acting as a go-between. When Jūrōbei succeeded to the headship of the family in 1771, he also took the respectable office of town elder (*ōdoshiyori*) of Matsuzaka.

His adoptive family started to criticize Jūrōbei's behavior during his absence in the fourth month of 1779, when he attended a memorial service for his biological father, honoring his obligations to his natal family in Kyoto. The adoptive mother Chigen and the go-between Sōzen wrote to the head of his natal household, his younger brother Sakubei, asking Sakubei to remonstrate with Jūrōbei, who lately had become dissolute, and demanding a written apology assuring them of a change of behavior. Specifically, they asked that Jūrōbei follow the house regulations (*kahō*) and, in case of disobedience, that he agree to a termination of his adoption and a divorce from his wife, Yuri. Moreover, upon divorce, Jūrōbei was to deliver a divorce notice to his wife without delay. In a letter sealed jointly with his brother, Jūrōbei apologized for his past deeds and submitted to all their demands.

Despite his apology, Jūrōbei was soon informed of the impending dissolution of his adoptive and marriage ties because his adoptive mother had discovered his personal notes, which included a letter revealing Jūrōbei's intimate relationship with a prostitute. Jūrōbei had not only redeemed the prostitute from a brothel with 170 *ryō* of gold, but also supported her at the house of her parents in a village near Matsuzaka. After this discovery, the adoptive mother refused further negotiations with Jūrōbei, even when he came to Matsuzaka in the seventh month. On the sixth day of the tenth month, the Kii domain office granted Chigen's divorce petition, which the members of the money exchange guild had endorsed by affixing their seals.

Once the domain consented to the dissolution of adoption and divorce, Jūrōbei expected the decision to be irreversible, but he nonetheless wanted compensation for his loss. The two sides could not agree on the bargain over money, houses, and the status of the retired head of the house, and eventually they ended up suing each other. To the magistrate, the representatives of the adoptive mother emphasized their efforts at appeasing Jūrōbei:

> Fearing the complication into which we might be drawn by Yasubei's [representative of Jūrōbei and his brother] taking action against us, Chigen had the manager of her Edo branch shop talk with Yasubei, when the latter was in that town, offering 1,000 *ryō* of gold to Jūrōbei as guarantee of his future, if they would consent to bring the dispute to private settlement. This they refused.[51]

It was ironic of Chigen's side to declare private negotiation to be the proper procedure, because the suit had reached the magistrate's office due to their failure to negotiate the divorce earlier, at least according to Jūrōbei's accusations.

Everybody was at fault in the opinion of the magistrate. If Jūrōbei was not acceptable to his adoptive mother Chigen and all the relatives, and the domain office had granted the divorce petition, Jūrōbei was irrevocably divorced. The adoptive mother did not need to justify her reasons, so whether Jūrōbei was dissipated was irrelevant. The magistrate affirmed that an adoptive mother was capable of divorcing a *muko yōshi*, even if he was the legal head of the house. This *muko yōshi* case should have been negotiated between the involved parties, the magistrate insisted, criticizing the unreasonable arbitrariness of the decision. The criticism was especially warranted, the magistrate said, since Jūrōbei had apologized for his dissolute behavior and Chigen had forgiven him. Moreover, the magistrate found no evidence for the allegations that two men had initiated the divorce against the wishes of the adoptive mother

Chigen, namely, the biological father of Jūrōbei's wife, who was the go-between in his marriage, and the shop assistant who took over the business after Jūrōbei's divorce. The magistrate granted the adoptive mother the independence to make up her own mind. Jūrōbei lost the suit, failing to resume his *muko yōshi* status or to even obtain his goal of material compensation.

Throughout the entire suit the divorce between Jūrōbei and his wife Yuri was not an issue of contention. Yuri's adoptive mother Chigen, when she initially reprimand Jūrōbei, asked for his pledge to issue a divorce notice promptly should his adoption be dissolved. The issue did not reappear later, probably because it was not disputed. Since Jūrōbei had been involved with prostitutes, he probably did not care much about his wife, and the records present no hint of Yuri's character. Strangely, the documents lack any reference to children from a marriage of about a dozen years, but childlessness was never mentioned as an issue in this case. Jūrōbei's primary concern was to regain his financial position, not to maintain his marriage.

In a 1796 *muko yōshi* case in which the in-marrying husband, Heihachi, had been asked by his mother-in-law, Masu, to leave his adoptive family after the death of his wife, the adoptive mother's decision to dissolve their ties was also endorsed by the magistrate.[52] Heihachi's insufficient consideration and care for his terminally ill wife had upset Masu, so she asked his brother, a peasant, to take Heihachi back. Together with the go-between, the brother apologized for Heihachi's misbehavior but refused Masu's request.

The adoptive mother Masu justified her suit in terms of Heihachi's dissipation, which, as in the earlier Jūrōbei case, meant squandering the family fortune and frequenting brothels. Within two years of the death of his adoptive father, Heihachi had spent 94 of the 2,250 *ryō* constituting the family's business capital on debauchery. To add insult to injury, Heihachi once even returned home to his seriously ailing wife with his topknot cut off by a prostitute to punish him for his faithlessness toward her. The magistrate fully sanctioned Masu's decision to separate from Heihachi, against his objections and despite his family's offer to repay the ninety-four *ryō* Heihachi had squandered. If Heihachi mended his ways, Masu might readopt him in the future, but the magistrate affirmed Masu's ability to dissolve the adoption.

Recurrent arguments erupted around the issue of whether an adoptive mother could dissolve ties with an adopted son. The shogunate issued numerous injunctions for the protection of adopted sons (*yōshi*) from too easy a termination of adoption, suggesting how common these dissolutions must have been. A document from the *Bunden sōsho* collection says that after the adoptive father's death, an adoptive mother could not retract the adoption contract in ordinary circumstances; this contrasts with a memorandum from the same collection that permitted a parent to divorce a *muko yōshi* and have the daughter remarry.[53] According to a document from the *Jikata kōsairoku* collection, a widow forfeited the right to manage the family property if she adopted an heir after her husband's death, even if the adopted son proved to be a failure.[54] The shogunate in principle tried to protect an adopted son from disinheritance by his adoptive mother.

When an adoptive mother wanted to divorce her daughter's *muko yōshi*, belief in male supremacy clashed with the belief that the wishes of senior members of the house should take precedence over those of junior members. In several extant *muko yōshi* cases, magistrates supported social hierarchy and seniority in the household against a husband's prerogatives. The house, even if represented by a woman, was able to divorce *muko yōshi* husbands.

Even if he was unable to prevent the dissolution of his adoption, a *muko yōshi* had the power to cause trouble in a divorce from his wife. Refusing to grant a divorce notice was one way of hindering divorce, as shown by several articles in the *Jikata* treating these recurrent problems with *muko yōshi* divorces. One suggestion was to withhold the personal possessions of a *muko yōshi* until the receipt of a divorce notice, essentially to trade formal consent to divorce for property. Another article in the same *Jikata* censured adoptive fathers who failed to secure a divorce notice by a *muko yōshi*. If there were a dispute over dowry money, the article said, the government should confiscate the money. Another memorandum declared that a magistrate should ignore the suit of a divorced *muko yōshi* to retain his wife, even if no divorce notice existed.[55]

Divorce Precedents and Social Status

The Confucian social hierarchy of samurai, peasants, craftsmen, and merchants also affected divorce. Legal documents generally allude to the importance of social distinctions between samurai and commoners in civil cases and to differences in legal procedures, without describing them in detail.[56] Magistrates disapproved of commoner practices among the samurai. In 1835, Kita Yasuo claimed remuneration of more than one hundred *ryō* for her role as go-between in an adoption between two samurai families. The magistrates rejected the suit, because no precedent among samurai existed for a complaint by a go-between for unpaid fees. Instead, the magistrates applied the analogy of servants' wages and cited an order from 1766 stating that no suits on servants' wages in arrears should be taken up by the magistrate's office.[57] On the pretext of status distinctions, Kita Yasuo was thus cheated of the fruits of her labor.

In the Jūrōbei *muko yōshi* divorce case mentioned above, the magistrate took note of a side incident. Kinbei, a former employee of Jūrōbei's younger brother, denounced the legal inquiry in a written complaint to the magistrate, arguing that in Kyoto, there had never been a divorce of an adopted son of a good family just because of his dissipation. The magistrate sentenced Kinbei to be flogged for his lack of respect in daring to question a magistrate.[58] In so doing, the magistrate affirmed that it was indeed possible to divorce a *muko yōshi* of a wealthy family for dissipation, but Kinbei's action shows that the grounds for divorce were thought by at least some people to differ according to social status.

The issue of social status arose in an 1847 divorce quarrel in a retainer family in the domain of Matsudaira Genbanokami.[59] Since the family were samurai, not commoners, the inquiring official doubted whether it fell under the heading of misconduct (*furachi*), and he was reluctant to involve himself. Parental desires collided with those of their own son in this case, phrased by the official as a problem of the mother-in-law with her daughter-in-law. Despite a previous reconciliation, the official reported, the parents became exasperated with their daughter-in-law and began negotiating for her divorce, but their own son objected and attacked those in charge of the negotiation, thus preventing its completion. At this stage, the argument came to official attention, but unfortunately we are not told how it was resolved. The reason why officials took notice was the son's rejection of his parents' plan; in other words, as a result of his misconduct in terms of filial piety. An outcome in which the son and husband could have retained his wife against his parents' wishes seems unlikely if concepts of social hierarchy were also applied in this case.

Divorce and Punishment

While magistrates preferred mediation to adjudication, they sometimes made clear and final decisions, including the imposition of corporal punishment, even in family disputes. In 1780, a magistrate ordered house-confinement (*oshikome*), severe censure, handcuffing, and flogging in the Jūrōbei divorce case.[60] The magistrate punished the defendants for a failure to negotiate with the plaintiff's family before divorcing Jūrōbei.

He sentenced the adoptive mother, Chigen, to house-confinement for thirty days, and Sōzen, the go-between, to handcuffing (*te-jō*) for thirty days.[61] For the members of the exchange guild, who had attached their seals to the divorce petition without informing Jūrōbei, the magistrate proposed a severe censure (*kitto shikari*). Kinbei, the audacious former employee of Jūrōbei's younger brother, was flogged for lack of respect.

In the Sayo divorce case, there were also penalties for the main participants.[62] An unnamed official remonstrated with Sayo that she should have acted with more prudence if she had no hope of reconciliation and desired a divorce. She was culpable because she had invoked the "temple law of divorce" instead of going through the ordinary negotiations. Her parents should have prevented her from going to this extreme. Sayo and her parents had misbehaved (*furachi*) toward Hanbei. The court ordered Sayo and her parents handcuffed (*te-jō*) for fifty days. The plaintiff Hanbei did not fare any better. The magistrate also sentenced him to the same punishment of fifty days' handcuffing, as his careless consenting to Denjiro's letter permitting Sayo's return had caused a grave misunderstanding on both sides and he had brought suit on erroneous grounds. The verdict closed with a reminder to the ward officers in charge: "Let the above orders be observed." Enforcement became localized. Not only the go-between, but plaintiff, defendants, witnesses, house-agents, five-family-group representatives, and headmen all sealed the document of settlement, proving that keeping an agreement relied on community enforcement.

The final verdict in the Sayo case also raised the issue of the relationship between private arrangements and court decisions. As the case was resolved privately, there should have been no further need for a verdict. The clerk's minute stated accordingly, "The case was dismissed on recovery of the wife by the husband." Nevertheless, the participants in this divorce case were punished because they had bothered the town magistracy twice with their dispute instead of negotiating privately from the beginning. More important, Sayo's flight to the temple defied the previous settlement mediated and guaranteed by a town magistrate. She had attempted to shield herself from official jurisdiction, and sentencing her became a matter of maintaining the authority of the office.[63]

From the point of view of a plaintiff, there was little incentive to solicit the engagement of magistrates as opposed to less formal agents of arbitration. Magistrates tried to facilitate a private settlement in family disputes anyway, instead of judging a case. This means that participants in a divorce could probably have reached a similar agreement through the intervention of a person with recognized social standing. In addition, magistrates could always punish divorce participants by severe censure, house-confinement, flogging, jail, handcuffing, or banishment. This threat was real and unpredictable, more serious than the penalties a community could enforce. Contestants in a divorce turned to a magistrate only if they had exhausted all other options of mediation.

Merciful Buddhist Temples: An Alternative Venue for Divorce Negotiations

Some Buddhist temples became, as divorce temples (*enkiridera, kakekomidera,* or *kakeiridera*), a symbol of the inequality in divorce between men and women in the Edo period. "In a social context where women had no legally recognized ability to initiate divorce," a recent study explains, such temples "offered a state-sanctioned mechanism whereby women might . . . sever their marital ties."[64] Other scholars even went further, arguing that divorce temples were almost the only places where wives could get divorces on their own during the Edo period.[65] Divorce temples justified their policy as an act of mercy to protect battered wives from their abusive husbands. Without fundamentally challenging the relationship between husband and wife, temples provided a safety valve within the existing system of marriage and the family.

The absence of similar divorce institutions for husbands does suggest a difference in the bargaining positions of the spouses in a divorce but, given the exceptional character of the divorce temple, this inference should not be exaggerated.[66] As a proportion of all divorces, the number of temple divorces was almost as insignificant as that of divorces by magistrates. Very few divorce temples existed in the Edo period. After 1762, only Tōkeiji and Mantokuji retained their rights of divorce, argues Takagi Tadashi, an authority on Edo divorce.[67]

Both were located on the Kantō plain, but neither Tōkeiji in Kamakura, Sagami Province, nor Mantokuji, in Kōzuke Province, served as a national mecca for divorce-hungry wives. The majority of the applications for divorce came from the regions adjacent to the temples, as shown in table 2. The numbers for the two temples in table 2 are for different periods. A conflagration in 1809 destroyed the records of Mantokuji, so only later cases remain. Among the Mantokuji cases, about 80 percent were from the three adjoining provinces of Kōzuke, Musashi, and Shimozuke. Most wives came from Kōzuke, the province in which the temple was located. During the last 150 years of the Edo period, divorce ap-

TABLE 2
Divorces in Mantokuji and Tōkeiji by Province of Marriage

	Mantokuji	Tōkeiji	Mantokuji (%)	Tōkeiji (%)
Kōzuke	46	1	43	0
Musashi	27	143	25	31
Shimozuke	14	0	13	0
Edo	9	139	8	30
Shimōsa	2	14	2	3
Awa	1	1	1	0
Sagami	0	156	0	34
Kazusa	0	5	0	1
Other	2	5	2	1
Unclear	6	0	6	0
TOTAL	107	464	100	100

SOURCE: Takagi Tadashi, *Mikudarihan to enkiridera* (Kōdansha, 1992), 165.

plications from the adjoining provinces of Musashi, Edo, and Sagami amounted to 90 percent of the total at Tōkeiji. The largest number of wives came from Sagami, Tōkeiji's home province.[68] A Tōkeiji priest, Inoue Zentei, estimated that about two thousand women must have sought refuge in Tōkeiji over the same period, for not all cases were recorded.[69] Even if the records were incomplete, selective preservation is unlikely to lead to a regional bias. Both Mantokuji and Tōkeiji had a role in divorce that was limited to the provinces around the urban center of Edo.

Sanctuary in a temple was attractive for a woman when neither she, her go-between, nor her relatives could persuade an obstinate husband to grant a divorce. In 1806, the flight of Nui from her husband, Hyōgorō of Kawasaki, presented such a case. When she visited her paternal home after the wedding ceremony, Nui refused to return to Hyōgorō. She must have feared that her parents would submit to Hyōgorō's desire to recover her, because she sought refuge in Tōkeiji while private negotiations were still under way. Her anxiety that Hyōgorō would not relent proved justified when he appealed to a magistrate for a return of his bride, but she finally obtained a divorce through the help of the temple.[70]

More than just seeking help in acquiring a divorce, wives took refuge in a divorce temple to alter the terms of divorce. In 1857, Iku, daughter of a village headman in Kawachi District, went as a bride to Kijūrō, son of the association head of a village in Yūki District, in Shimōsa Province. This was a conventional marriage between two elite families of their respective villages. Iku was unhappy, and Kijūrō struck her crazily. In the end, he threw a divorce notice at her and kicked her out, threatening her with a short sword.

Iku's father, with the help of the go-between, tried to negotiate for a divorce by agreement (*wakai*), but Kijūrō refused this as unreasonable, using abusive words. He claimed that the previous divorce had been invalid and failed to return the dowry Iku had brought into marriage. After her father had thus exhausted every other means, Iku went to obtain the aid of Mantokuji. The temple retainers expressed Iku's desire for a divorce notice and return of the dowry to the officials of the husband's village. By official notification, the village officials tried to persuade Kijūrō and his father. The final agreement was: (1) the return of two-thirds of the engagement money (*yuinōkin*) to the groom's family; (2) the return of Iku's dowry clothes and other goods she had brought into marriage; and (3) the naming of Sukugōemon, a temple official, as guarantor of the arrangement.[71] In Iku's case, the help of Mantokuji increased her family's bargaining power, and she eventually reached the desired private settlement.

Divorce temples submitted to the state completely. They did not base even their privilege of sanctuary on divine right, but rather on the mercy of the shogunate. This is demonstrated in an 1805 memorandum of Ōmura Yosōemon, a Tōkeiji retainer, addressed to the temple magistrate, in which Ōmura emphasized the temple's pedigree and its historically good relations with the shogunate, recounting the history of its founding. The wife of Hōjō Tokimune (1251–84) had established Tōkeiji in Kamakura and obtained the right of sanctioning divorce for it. The shogunate renewed this right on several occasions during the following centuries, and the noble Ashikaga house supplied the temple with its daughters as head priestesses.[72] The temple felt the need to remind shogunate officials, such as the temple magistrate, of its previous rights so as to reaffirm Tōkeiji's privileges, with which the officials may not have been familiar.

Ōmura specified that those rights were to authorize the divorce of any wife who escaped to Tōkeiji from a husband she disliked. The temple granted divorce out of mercy for a woman who was subjected to the misery of living with a bad man. If there was no charge that she had violated any laws of the shogunate, the temple requested a divorce notice from her husband. The wife in return had to stay in the temple for two years. She then was permitted to return to her parents and remarry.[73] Ōmura failed to explain why two years was the appropriate term for a wife to remain in Tōkeiji. He might have justified it in terms of earlier customary practice in exchange for the temple's support, as a period of purification away from contact with other men, or to settle the issue of possible conception, but in the last case, two years would be an unnecessarily long time.

Since previously cited legal precedents also mention that a husband forfeited the right to his wife after they had lived apart for three years, a general notion that long-term separations were evidence of the breakdown of a marriage and gave the wife a right to divorce seems to have been popularly accepted, and not only divorce temple practices. Also, when women wanted to remarry after their husbands had absconded, regulations by the shogunate sometimes suggested that an appropriate waiting period was from one to three years.[74] Thus, remaining in a temple for two years would not seem unusual. Compared with privately negotiated divorces, however, wives were worse off. According to popular divorce culture, discussed in chapter 3, wives were able to remarry the day after receiving a divorce notice. Although sojourn in a temple protected a wife from her husband, it limited her choices, at least temporarily, compared with a divorce negotiated otherwise. Later in the Edo period, most temple divorces were by private settlement (*naisai*), including the acquisition of a divorce notice that would permit a wife's early dismissal from the temple.[75] According to an early eighteenth-century decision by a temple magistrate, Ōmura explains, the temple was required to obtain divorce notices from husbands to avoid confusion.[76] In an 1839 case, Tōkeiji retainers tried without success to coerce a go-between to sign a divorce notice in place of an absconded husband. When the town magistrate backed the go-between's refusal, the temple resigned itself to following the regulation that a wife would return to her parents after staying in the temple for twenty-four months.[77]

Ōmura's definition of a woman in terms of her status as wife in the memorandum is interesting. An adult woman was either a previous or a future wife interrupted in her status by a transient visit to her parental home. Ōmura compared even her stint of celibacy at the temple to her marital duties, as if in the service of her husband.[78] Although a woman might escape a particular marriage, she could not escape notions of adult women being married.

Divorce temples received their privilege from the state and relied on the magistrates for enforcement of their divorce rights. In 1806, seeking the return of his wife, Nui, Hyōgorō of Kawasaki appealed to the finance magistrate, Matsudaira Hyōgonokami, but the magistrate upheld the temple's divorce rights and Nui obtained a divorce.[79] Hyōgorō's suit had challenged the right of Tōkeiji to protect his wife. In 1844, another husband, Yūkichi of Asakusa, questioned the privileges of Mantokuji, the other divorce temple. The officers of Mantokuji enlisted the support of the temple magistrate, Matsudaira Izuminokami, to divorce Yūkichi's wife, Moto.⁸⁰ The temple was unable on its own to enforce its provisions in the face of resistance. The opposition of these husbands indicates a lack of general acceptance or awareness of the function of the divorce temple.

In the battle between the town magistrate and Mantokuji over jurisdiction in the Sayo case described above, the temple clearly lost.⁸¹ The temple magistrate, Naitō Kiinokami, tried to protect the temple's privilege against the town magistrate, Tōyama Saemonnojō. Although both magistrates paid lip service to the principle of joint jurisdiction and cooperation, they fiercely competed for the responsibility of supervising the Sayo case.⁸² Because the case centered on the divorce request by a woman taking refuge in Mantokuji, the temple magistrate, Naitō Kiinokami, explained, it was all about the temple regulations and therefore the case belonged to his jurisdiction.⁸³ The town magistrate in turn claimed priority. He argued that the parties to this case had originally appeared before a town magistrate, and he believed that the defendants had forged a letter disregarding the decision of his office. Regarding Sayo, the wife and main defendant, Tōyama said, it would be intolerable for a wife so lacking in conscience to remain in the temple.⁸⁴ "This headstrong woman, who by forging a letter . . . deceived even her own parents, should be summoned and put on trial," he emphasized.⁸⁵ Finally, Naitō relented, but only because of the external circumstances of the case, and he maintained that if the case turned out to be merely about divorce, he should assume responsibility. In the meantime, he notified the officers of Mantokuji to deliver Sayo to the town magistrate, where she was to remain in custody until the trial.

Timing was crucial in settling the jurisdiction, the scholar Igarashi Tomio argues, and depended on whether a wife arrived at Mantokuji before her husband appealed to the Edo town magistrate's office. In the Sayo case, Hanbei, the husband, was two days faster than his wife, so the town magistrate took precedence, forcing Mantokuji into a defensive battle. Mantokuji's retainer Mine Sōhei appealed to the temple magistrate, Naitō Kiinokami, for help on the tenth day of the seventh month. After the town magistrate had received Sayo in custody, Mantokuji heard that he had tried to coerce Sayo into resuming her marriage. Because this meant a total disregard of temple regulations, the temple protested at the office of the temple magistrate and dispatched a retired priest to petition the town magistrate. Despite Mantokuji's efforts, Sayo eventually agreed to return to her husband, Hanbei.⁸⁶ That the temple tried to protect itself from the encroachment of the town magistrate by means of the temple magistrate is a sign that the temple did not have power on its own and ultimately depended on the benevolence of a state agency for the survival of its divorce prerogative.

The verdict raised several other issues. A controversy over jurisdiction between town and temple magistrates preceded the Sayo verdict.[87] The judgment punished Sayo and her family for trying to settle a divorce dispute by ignoring the town magistrate and seeking the protection of Mantokuji. It is possible that the temple magistrate would have been more protective of the temple's prerogatives and granted a divorce. The town magistrate, however, had already in his correspondence with the temple magistrate invoked precedents for circumstances under which temple rights of sanctuary could be broken, leading to the surrender of a woman taking refuge, for example, by Tōkeiji.[88] Temples could provide shelter against husbands but not against the state.

The divorce temple was a special institution that did not outlive Edo society. The new Meiji government rejected the idea of this special divorce privilege granted by religious institutions. At Tōkeiji, the last woman was divorced in the twelfth month of 1870. Tōkeiji then officially stopped being a divorce temple when the Meiji government failed to renew the divorce privilege. At Mantokuji, the last divorce petition was also granted in 1870. In 1872, the temple ceased functioning for lack of money.[89] The government also abolished the surveys of religious affiliation that certified the non-Christian affiliation of each Japanese around the same time. Temples lost their positions both as nationwide custodians of family registration and as local refuges of last resort for distressed women. The government thereby diminished the role of Buddhist temples in marriage and alliance.

Household Status Versus Sex

Edo period divorce is still most often associated with Confucian male prerogatives and the institution of the divorce temple. It is commonly assumed that husbands could and did divorce their wives without any form of legal or ideological restraint, whereas battered wives were only able to resort to the rare institution of the divorce temple. This widespread view, however, is somewhat misleading. It is true that legal precedents failed to explicitly grant wives a general right to divorce under any circumstances, but neither do documents issued by shogunate authorities prohibit wives from initiating the dissolution of their marriages or divorcing reluctant husbands. As long as these conflicts remained within the respective communities, the authorities had no interest in interfering or setting broader norms of conduct in marriage and divorce. The fact that divorce was common across status and regional boundaries tells us little about agency in divorce or its causes and effects. But by looking at the social distribution of divorce frequencies, which appear lower among high-ranking samurai than among the poorest status groups, we come to suspect that Confucian gender ideals may have facilitated divorce among the elite, but probably do not suffice to explain why divorce permeated every part of Edo society.

Popular puppet or theater plays frequently included divorces as examples of tragic conflicts between duty and human feelings. What these depictions have in common is the guiltlessness of the divorced party, whether a young bride or an in-marrying husband. Reasons for divorce were not spelled out or restricted to a particular canon of accepted reasons, such as the seven Confucian grounds. Senior household members, whether male or female, seem to have had the power to decide divorce against opposition from junior relatives. Senior household members are not always portrayed as acting arbitrarily or in their own selfish interest, as when relatives forced a divorce to protect a wife from a profligate and incompetent husband. Despite accusations of individual misbehavior, what is almost absent from these plays is the notion of a guilty party. Dissolution of a marriage, especially when pushed through by senior members, was shown as very distressing, but it may not have conveyed the same sense of a moral failure attached to divorced wives in those early modern European societies that restricted divorce to cases of adultery.

Social hierarchy according to the sex of the spouse and to position in the household figures largely in Edo divorce cases depicted in popular plays, shogunate regulations, and divorce temples. Young wives and *muko yōshi* husbands often appeared in a vulnerable position with respect to senior members of the household into which they had married, whether those senior members were husbands or parents-in-law. This image of inferiority was reinforced by the frequent appearance of parents, parents-in-law, or legal heads of natal households in the divorce negotiation process. The in-marrying member was presented as nearly defenseless, even against the divorce wishes of his or her own family.

Magistrates of the Edo period especially adhered to concepts of social hierarchy when dealing with family issues. Depending on the position of the husband in the house, the rights and duties of the divorce participants varied. From the authorities' legal point of view, the divorce of a young bride was the least troublesome, since she was both a woman and in a junior position. Although this was a minority form of marriage, most conflicts involved divorces of in-marrying husbands (*muko yōshi*) who were also adopted as successors to the household. A *muko yōshi* husband was often in an unstable position similar to that of a new bride, which may sometimes have been difficult to bear for the groom, considering male prerogatives in society at large. Noticeable are cases by which the house, represented by a senior woman, divorced an in-marrying husband. Since only a fraction of houses had a female head, these instances should not be considered typical examples of divorce at large.[90] Their prominence in the legal record is to be explained by conflicting notions of gender ideology and social hierarchy. What is surprising is that, like a man in the same position, a woman who was the senior member of the house could dissolve the adoption of a *muko yōshi* and divorce him from his wife. To officials, seniority and one's position in the house were at times more important than one's sex in determining divorce. Even when conflicts arose between lineage prerogatives and the maintenance of marriage ties, officials sided with senior members against husbands wishing to continue their marriages.

3

Testing a Spouse
The Trial Marriage System

JAPAN'S HIGH DIVORCE RATES in the past occurred in the context of a nuptial and family system that facilitated and condoned divorce because it treated marriage as conditional. In certain regions, this conditionality was sometimes formalized by temporary or trial unions, practices still encountered by ethnographers in the early twentieth century, although their historical significance is often discounted because they were mainly discovered on faraway islands and in the remote countryside and are seen as the result of socioeconomic seclusion.[1] While the prevalence of such customs may be open to debate, like marriage practices in the more distant past, they rest on the idea that the strength of a union between a man and a woman has to be tested through the experience of life and work together. The evidence presented in this chapter shows that such ideas of testing a spouse must have been rather widely accepted by the masses until the Meiji period and formed a crucial part of the early modern system of marriage.

Spousal testing manifested itself demographically in two forms: (1) delay of official notification of marriage to the community and authorities until a union proved "stable," often resulting in vague distinctions between marriage and cohabitation, and (2) high incidences of divorce soon after official registration of marriages. Because of its conditional nature, especially in the early stages of shared life, this early modern system of popular marriage with late registration and frequent divorce is here referred to as a trial marriage system. Its characteristics varied, but in relative terms, "spousal testing" was most likely to take the form of informal unions of cohabitation in western Japan and among the urban underclass, and of official marriages in eastern Japan and in the countryside. Remarriage was possible for both men and women of all classes and regions.

Meiji Marriage Ambiguities

Modernizing Marriage Regulations

In the well-known Charter Oath of April 1868, the emperor Meiji promised policies breaking with "the evil customs of the past" and "seeking knowledge throughout the world so as to strengthen the foundations of imperial rule." Concrete measures to stabilize the land after years of civil war together with far-reaching reforms terminated or transformed many social institutions of the Edo period (1600–1868). The new central government abolished class restrictions on professions and trade in 1869 and in the following year permitted commoners to assume family names. In 1871, outcast groups were given full legal equality. Samurai continued to be classified separately from commoners, but by 1876, they had lost their main privileges, such as government stipends and their prerogative to carry two swords. Universal compulsory education and national conscription further contributed to blurring former status distinctions among samurai, peasants, artisans, and merchants.

As part of its reform policies to create a uniform nation-state, the new leadership abolished all the legal obstacles to marriage with people from different classes or localities that domains had maintained. Moreover, it went further by proposing a legal definition of marriage valid throughout the entire land, namely, the act of registration according to the Family Registration Law (*kōseki-hō*) of 1871. But it did not apply this definition consistently in later years. The 1882 Criminal Code accepted unions as marriages when they were recognized by the community. After controversial public debate and shifting policies, the Japanese government finally settled, in the 1898 Civil Code, on the definition of marriage as the act of registration. Although lawyers repeatedly challenged this definition in the early twentieth century, the 1948 Civil Code, which is still valid today, also defined marriage in the same way.[2] By establishing and emphasizing a legal definition for marriage, the government began to marginalize other forms of relationships between men and women, which were declared to be common-law unions (*naien*) in defiance of government policies. To what extent this was done before 1898 is a matter of conjecture, but the 1875 customs survey and population statistics indicate some of the dynamics of defining marriage exclusively by registration.

By the 1870s, the Japanese population had been exposed to about two centuries of policies checking on their religious affiliation, which incidentally also recorded their social position vis-à-vis the household head, such as "wife." Unlike parish registers in Europe, whose purpose was to ascertain vital status such as birth, baptism, marriage, and death, the Japanese surveys do not seem to have served as certificates of matrimony to the population. Population registers in the Edo period reveal loose attitudes toward marriage notification. In the Okayama registers of western Japan, marriage was only recorded when a couple's first child was expected.[3] By contrast, in the registers of the village of Nakahara on the Nobi Plain, marriage was recorded before pregnancy and childbirth.[4] In nearby Yokouchi, registration of marriage and first birth were also independent events.[5] These differences in notification of marriage practices were expressions of local domain priorities and regional customs.[6]

Annual surveys of religious affiliation stopped in 1873, but they had become so entrenched that the national customs survey of 1875 still used them as a point of reference in describing the ideal procedure by which local officials became aware of a new marriage: "After the ceremony [*shiki*], a marriage [*kon'in*] is usually reported orally to the local office, and at the time of the religious survey [*shūmon aratame*], it is recorded in the register [*sekimen ni kanyū*]; the procedure is the same as that for births."[7]

Unlike samurai, who in the Edo period were supposed to petition their authorities before a marriage, commoners began living together as man and wife, sometimes marking the occasion with a ceremony, before informing the local authorities. Registration was a post facto administrative act, not the definition of marriage itself. There are examples in which families announced marriages in the neighborhood and only told the village officials at the time of the annual religious survey.[8]

In the 1870s, various attitudes to marriage notification existed, ranging from immediate notification to total inattention. Negligence was not the only reason for non-notification or a delay in notification, since families sometimes consciously chose to delay notification until the union was considered stable and children were born. The delay reflected the common belief that the first stage of living together was a period of probation, and that registration was a further step in sanctioning a marriage.

Some provinces required rapid formal registration, such as a written report sent to the headman and the temple within three days of a ceremony.[9] In quick, casual examples of notification, a barrel of sake was sent as a present to the village headman during the wedding.[10] The village headman was expected in some places to attend every ceremony. As the ultimate guest of honor, he was seated above the go-between, incidentally familiarizing him with new marriages.[11] In Mino Province, a family announced a marriage to the local community of relatives, neighbors, and officials by walking through the village two or three days after the ceremony.[12] Depending on the ruling house, practices varied in Shinano Province. On domain territory, marriage information was first collected in a petition book of the temple magistrate before being entered in the temple register, whereas in areas under direct management of the shogunate, marriages were recorded directly in the temple register.[13]

Custom, especially in western Japan, explicitly recognized living together before registration as a period of probation. In Mikawa Province, Nukada District, a wife was taken temporarily to her husband's family before formalizing the union, a practice called "entering one's feet" (*ashi-ire*), a term also often found in later anthropological literature on Japanese trial marriages.[14] In Yamashiro Province, registration was linked to the ritual of a bride's return visit to her parents after the wedding (*sato-gaeri*).[15] In three other provinces, women entering the households of their husbands without either report to a local office or even ceremony were designated "wife by courtesy" or "daughter by courtesy" (*tsuma-bun* or *musume-bun*).[16] The common delay in reporting a marriage not only stemmed from negligence but at times was a conscious family decision. One explicit reason was to confirm the durability of the marriage.[17] A marriage was announced to relatives and neighbors in Suō Province at the time it took place, but it was only registered formally when "domestic harmony was certain."[18] Similar references to living together in domestic harmony (*kanai wajuku, kanai kyōgō*) as a precondition for notification were stated for the provinces of Mikawa and Izumo.[19] In another province, the larger family group had to be on good terms with the bride before a marriage was registered. A certain degree of mutual empathy (*shinboku no jōjuku*) was expected between the parents and the married couple.[20]

Pregnancy and childbirth, besides proving fertility, showed that a relationship was worthy of formal marriage notification, especially in eastern Japan. "In the old days" in Uzen Province, marriage was reported to the headman after the first conception, but in 1875, this information was required immediately after the wedding, suggesting implementation of changed regulations.[21] In some places, official notification was reported to have been delayed for more than three years until the first pregnancy.[22] When the first child had been born, "a year or two after the marriage," the transfer of the register was expected elsewhere.[23] Testing the bride's fertility was not the only reason to postpone registration, but the birth of a child was considered synonymous with a mature relationship. Chikugo Province officials saw in childbirth a sign of the durability of a marriage.

In Mii District, "registration was delayed for two or three years until a child was born and the relationship of both sides had matured" (*ryōhō jukuen*).²⁴

Marriage notification was not practiced at all in some provinces in western Japan, suggesting that the authorities there did not require such information. Though a marriage might be registered at childbirth, this was not required in Awa Province. Often people were cancelled from the registers as "missing since marriage" (*kon'in-mushuku*).²⁵ In Bitchū Province, similar practices resulted in the registration of children but not the wife.²⁶ Enforcement of registration in Bingo Province was just as casual, with few people bothering to register, although it was required. In Mitsugi District, it often happened that a wife with several children was buried in the temple of her own family because the registers had not been transferred.²⁷ There was no need to register a marriage at all in Buzen Province.²⁸ Marriage registration was insignificant in Hokkaidō's Oshima Province, Kameda District. A marriage there was only announced in the neighborhood.²⁹ Moreover, references to nonregistration of marriage were often linked to the "lower classes" and "common people."³⁰

Legitimate and Illegitimate Children

Related to the ambiguities in marriage were conflicting definitions of out-of-wedlock childbirth, which may also serve as an indirect indicator of common-law unions and sexual relations outside of marriage. Despite the severe punishments for illegitimate childbirth threatened by the Chinese-inspired criminal code (*shinritsu kōryō*) promulgated on 16 February 1871, there is ample evidence of it. One of the important explanations for the existence of illegitimate childbirth in the 1875 survey was the opposition of a family to marriage. "When a child is born to a father and mother before their parents have given their consent to the marriage" was a typical definition in several localities.³¹ Children born out of wedlock were thus, in part, the result of failed marriage arrangements. There is no direct evidence to prove that cohabitation in these cases preceded childbirth, but it seems rather likely in light of delayed marriage registration practices. There were several ways of registering children born outside of marriage as legitimate. The most straightforward way was to overcome family resistance by finding a go-between and getting the relationship approved by the parents.³² Otherwise, the child's family and legitimacy status was often altered at registration with the connivance of the authorities. In Yamato Province, for example, "An illegitimate child is brought up in the father's family and is usually registered as the younger brother or sister of the natural father."³³ Besides registering a child as the child of the (paternal) grandparents,³⁴ a common strategy was to find foster parents.³⁵ Legitimate and illegitimate statuses were often not even distinguished in the official records.³⁶ Similar ambiguities are also seen in national statistics.³⁷

Even the central government sometimes acknowledged children born out of wedlock as legitimate. In some cases, central ministries required that the parents be married as a precondition for legitimacy. An 1891 reply to an inquiry by a prefecture insisted on recording as an illegitimate child (*shiseiji*) the offspring of parents who had married by "normal custom" but had not registered this union in the family register.³⁸ In other cases, however, paternal recognition was deemed sufficient. The very ambiguity in the ways in which the legitimacy of children was defined reflected the ambiguities in the definitions of marriage.

Parental marriage and paternal recognition were also the twin factors in defining a child's legitimacy in the 1898 Civil Code. A child born during marriage was a legitimate child (*chakushi*). Paternal recognition, however, made a difference in the status of illegitimate children: the law distinguished between those recognized by their father (*shoshi*) and those without such recognition (*shiseiji*). A *shoshi* automatically became a legitimate child upon the parents' marriage. By contrast, a *shiseiji* needed to be especially recognized by both parents if they married.³⁹ After 1898, government statistics listed *shoshi* and *shiseiji* separately.

By the twentieth century, the birth of children out of wedlock certainly seems partly related to delayed notification of or failure to report marriage. A 1940 census shows a strong correlation between the ratio of illegitimate children and the percentage of common-law marriages at the prefecture level. Regions tolerant of common-law marriages presumably also accepted illegitimate children, and some of these were born in common-law marriages. By Japan's standards after 1960, when illegitimate childbirth remained under 1.5 percent nationally, the local figures for the last two decades of the nineteenth century appear high, ranging between 5 and 25 percent at the prefecture level. The prefectures north of Tokyo had the lowest ratios, and towns and cities, especially the commercial center of Osaka, had the highest.⁴⁰ The delays in marriage registrations found in the 1875 survey appear to correspond broadly to the statistics on illegitimate childbirth compiled in later years. Late or non-notification of marriage presumably also went together with more children born out of wedlock in the early decades of the Meiji period and before.

Just like common-law marriages, rates of illegitimate childbirth de-

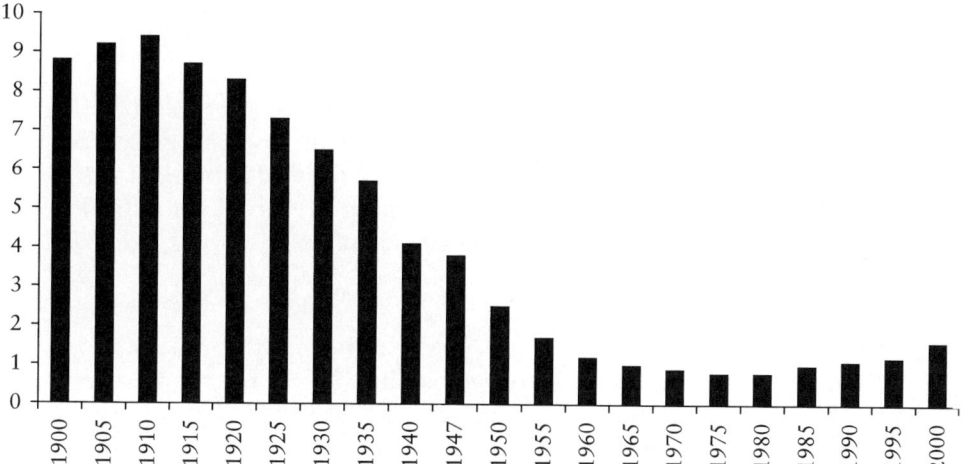

FIG. 3. The Out-of-Wedlock Childbirth Rate in Japan, 1900–2000 (percentage of births). (Sources: Masaoka Kanji, *Kazoku: Sono shakaiteki hensen to shōrai* [Gakubunsha, 1981], 201, for 1900-1940 data; Kōseirōdōshō, *Jinkō dōtai tokei Heisei 12nen* [Kōsei tōkei kyōkai, 2002], 1:119, for 1947–2000 data. The prewar rate is as a percentage of total births, whereas after 1947 the rate is as a percentage of live births.)

clined during the first half of the twentieth century and remained low thereafter (fig. 3).[41] The official rate for illegitimate children peaked at more than 9 percent around 1910 and gradually declined thereafter, reaching its twentieth-century low point of 0.8 percent in the 1980s.[42]

In contrast to the official concern for children's legitimacy visible in population statistics, no comparable interest existed in distinguishing between official and common-law marriages prior to the 1898 Civil Code. The code, however, reasserted previous policies of defining marriage exclusively by registration. During the decades after 1898, Japan's population gradually accepted this legal definition of marriage. Modern census counts, first implemented in 1920, give estimates of common-law marriages of about 16 percent in 1920 and 17 percent in 1925, declining to 7 percent in the 1940 census. No later national surveys exist, but the figure of around 2 or 3 percent for Kyoto in 1962 indicates that common-law marriages continued to decrease after World War II.[43]

The population's acceptance of the state definition of marriage is best seen in the narrowing time gap between the marriage ceremony and marriage registration after the 1898 Civil Code was passed. Whereas only 60 percent of marriages were registered in Toyama Prefecture within a year of the ceremony in 1927, the percentages rose steadily after World War II for all of Japan: 75.5 percent in 1950, 86.7 percent in 1960, and holding around 95 percent since the 1970s.[44]

The early modern practice of testing a spouse through premarital cohabitation had faded out of existence even among the poorer segments of the urban population by the 1950s. The government's definition of marriage rose to an unchallenged prominence during the period when the divorce rate declined for decades, suggesting common factors at work to strengthen and lengthen marriage.

On Wives and Concubines

Another Edo period legacy of the ambiguities of marital status was related to the fact that besides a main wife, a husband was permitted to keep one or more secondary wives. Foreign visitors eagerly reported on strange Japanese customs that flew in the face of Christian moral teachings, especially those they considered licentious. They criticized the existence of concubines and the prevalence of divorce, usually interpreting both as evidence of the insecure position of wives. Some went further and implied an interrelationship between the two practices. A seventeenth-century French trader is quoted as saying: "One Man hath but one Wife, though as many Concubines as he can keep; and if that Wife do not please him, he may put her away, provided he dismiss her in a civil and honorable way."[45] The medical doctor Philipp Franz von Siebold marveled: "Not only may the husband introduce as many unwedded helpmates as he pleases into the mansion over which his wife presides . . . but he has also a power of divorce, which may be considered unlimited, since he is restrained only by considerations of expediency."[46] Even after the Meiji Restoration, foreign observations mentioned both issues in the same breath. "[T]hey have . . . polygamy and concubines . . . and write letters of divorce," a British diplomat explained.[47] "[D]ivorce . . . is permitted by the law, and a semi-official concubinage is quite admitted under the husband's roof," a French account noted, specifying that virtually no concubines existed among the middle and lower classes, and that even among the nobles, "under the influence of Europeans the practice is daily becoming more rare."[48] Nonetheless, in the early twentieth century, the longtime missionary Walter Weston argued for the need of religious sanctions for Japanese marriage, because divorce was rampant and concubinage "to some extent" prevailed.[49] In lumping together the institution of concubines and divorce as Japanese oddities, Europeans correctly noted the social acceptance of both practices, but they overstated the prevalence of secondary wives and partly misinterpreted their status.

Institutionalized concubinage was mostly practiced among elite status groups. For the Meiji period, population records list the number of concubines in Japan by class and region. In 1880, the ratio of concubines to male heads was 4:10 for the high nobility (*kazoku*), 4:1,000 for samurai (*shizoku*), and 5:10,000 for commoners (*heimin*), showing a significant class difference.[50] It is not surprising that the population of registered concubines was the highest in the urban prefectures of Tokyo and Kanagawa, because peers were required to reside in the nation's capital. The 1879 Yamanashi census confirms that the number of concubines (*mekake*) was rather small, amounting to ninety in that prefecture. In the 1880 national list mentioned above, the records for Yamanashi Prefecture, which had one of the highest ratios of concubines to male household heads in Japan, there were seventy-seven registered concubines, or one registered concubine per thousand male household heads.[51] Although the numbers differ between records, they are close enough to show convincingly that concubines were rather rare, even taking into account that most secondary wives may never have been registered as concubines.

Nevertheless, the issue of secondary wives is interesting, because it bears on the problem of modernizing the institution of marriage in Japan based on European legal and moral notions of monogamy and fidelity. Although Edo-period Confucian instructions such as the *Greater Learning for Women* admonished wives not to feel jealous and expressly condoned the practice of keeping concubines, the vast majority of people were monogamous, and the family of the wife considered a husband's exaggerated involvement with a prostitute or his keeping of a concubine to be reasons for divorce.[52] Edo customs were designed to minimize household conflict by distinguishing between the responsibilities and social position of a main wife (*honsai*) and those of a secondary wife (*gonsai, mekake*). The social critic Yamakawa Kikue believed that in the Mito Domain of her samurai ancestors, a man could not change the status of a concubine to that of a wife even if he had no official wife. A concubine in the Edo period, she said, could formally be accepted into the household only upon the wife's consent. The relationship between wife and concubine was comparable to that of master and servant.[53]

Yamakawa captured an ideal; in reality, it was possible for a secondary wife to be upgraded to a main wife, especially among commoners and the lower levels of the elite. An ordinance of 1724 forbade making a concubine (*mekake*) into a wife (*tsuma*) "without permission from superiors" and required strict observance of the period of mourning for the main wife.[54] This regulation reveals the permeability of wifely status. An 1848 inheritance case also suggests that such a transition was conceivable. The master carpenter Sawamura Gisaburō had relationships with three women. He first took Gin as his wife. There were no signs of a marital crisis between Gisaburō and his wife Gin until her half-sister Chiyo entered their household. Gisaburō fell in love with Chiyo and induced Gin to return to her parents. Gisaburō did not limit himself permanently to Chiyo, but started an affair with Saku. He then concurrently maintained relationships with Chiyo and Saku, dividing his time between their separate residences. After Chiyo's death, he lived with Saku in a new house. Saku's relationship with Gisaburō was disputed. She declared herself to be his main wife (*honsai*), since she had lived together with him for eight years, but her neighbors believed her to be just a concubine (*mekake*). The official record of the case did not settle the issue of whether Saku should be considered Gisaburō's main wife simply because she lived with him. Her claim alone, however, was credible enough for officials to ask neighbors about her status, showing that among commoners, women could cross the line separating a main from a secondary wife, and community approval was crucial.[55] That marital statuses could be changed is further attested by the fact that in population registers, the same woman was listed in different years as wife, secondary wife, and maid.[56] Even Yamakawa, who argued for a strict status separation between wives and concubines, talks about her grandfather finally registering his concubine Otane as his legal wife (*seisai*), and people called her his wife (*okusan*) after the death of Yamakawa's grandmother.[57]

In the Meiji period, the practice of keeping concubines continued among the highest levels of the Meiji elite. The Meiji emperor himself had several wives, and his successor, the Taishō emperor, was the child of a concubine.[58] The eminent Meiji statesman Matsukata Masayoshi, whose children were so numerous that at one point he allegedly forgot their exact number, consecutively took up relations with three concubines. As in other upper-class elite households, social boundaries were strictly observed here. Matsukata's wife did not permit his concubine Kita to ride in the same train as Matsukata. In order "to observe the proprieties," Kita always followed on the next train. Kita lived in a villa in Kamakura, a seaside resort near Tokyo, and was never allowed into the main residence in Tokyo.[59]

During the Meiji decades, concubines lost in social status compared with main wives. The 1871 Criminal Code put concubines on the same level as wives in their degree of relationship to the household head, a clause deriving from Chinese legal thought.[60] The 1882 Criminal Code, which was inspired by contemporary French law, recognized common-law wives as married but stopped recognizing concubine and mistress registrations in order "to appear civilized."[61] The 1898 Civil Code failed to legally accept concubines and made bigamy a punishable offense and cause for divorce.[62]

The Meiji laws on secondary wives were significant, not because they legally excluded a few concubines from marital status, but because they gave a new ideological emphasis to monogamy and wifehood. By criticizing the practice of concubinage, intellectuals, usually Christians, often claimed the moral high ground, as in the famous example of the essays "On Wives and Concubines" published under the auspices of the Enlightenment-inspired Meirokusha Society by Mori Arinori, later minister of education. By implication, though, the thrust of the criticism was against the social order that supported the old aristocratic elite and their powerful successors. If he were to publicly condemn the keeping of concubines, the long-term diet member Ozaki Yukio (1859–1954) observed as late as 1925, he would be exposing most of his friends, who presumably were also in prominent social positions.[63]

The Frequency of Divorce in the Meiji Era

As already discussed, divorce in Japan cut across social classes and regional boundaries. Nevertheless, three basic fault lines in divorce rates can be identified: class differences, urban-rural distinctions, and regional variations. After varying greatly in the last two decades of the nineteenth century, divorce rates declined during the first decades of the twentieth century, and the divorce rates of hitherto divorce-prone samurai, townsmen, and peasants began to converge.[64]

Social Variations

As in the Edo period, divorce in the following periods was least frequent and is best documented for the very top level of society. The peerage, comprising former daimyo and court nobles, was called *kazoku* in 1871. The peerage law of July 1884 created new peers from among samurai and commoners.[65] The number of peer households grew from 518 in 1886 to 817 in 1908. There were between one and six peer divorces each year. The average crude divorce rate among peers between 1886 and 1898, 0.6 divorces per 1,000 people, was far lower than the national average of 2.74 for the same period.[66] Within the peerage, the likelihood of divorce increased with lower rank, just as divorce among the Edo daimyo did. Among the highest peers, divorce was almost nonexistent. In 1928, only one out of 123 household heads among princes, marquises, and counts had experienced divorce, whereas the percentages of marriage to divorce among the lower-ranked viscounts (7.27%) and barons (7.91%) were on levels comparable to Edo-period daimyo. For the peerage as a whole, the divorce rate was about 6 percent.[67]

While peers had the lowest divorce rate in Japanese society, townspeople and the mostly urban samurai also divorced less often than peasants. In the town of Kanazawa, 16 percent of samurai household heads and 12 percent of commoner household heads were divorced in 1871. By contrast, in Ishikawa Prefecture, where Kanazawa is located, 29,189 marriages and 11,292 divorces were recorded between 1883 and 1887, indicating that some 39 percent of marriages were dissolved.[68] Even though these observations are separated by a decade and compiled from different sources, frequent divorce appears to have been overwhelmingly a rural phenomenon in the 1880s. Other localities show a similar, though less marked, rural-urban distinction. The city of Osaka had a lower rate of divorce per marriage than did the prefecture in 1890.[69] After the turn of the twentieth century, crude divorce rates were generally higher in rural than in urban parts of prefectures (fig. 4). Although the divorce rate gap narrowed during the mid 1920s, the respective rates only reversed after World War II, and they diverged significantly in the 1950s. Crude divorce rates also varied with city size. While divorce rates gradually declined in all urban locations, the pattern of higher divorce rates in small towns than in large cities continued from 1919 to 1933.[70]

Within towns, the cohabitation, marriage, and divorce practices of the poor met with middle-class intellectual disapproval. Suzuki Umeshirō, a *Jiji Shinpō* journalist, visited Myōgyō-chō, a poverty-stricken part of Osaka in 1888.[71] Suzuki explains how the poor in that area married, giving it as an example of their "uncivilized and nonsensical" lifestyle. Parents did not interfere in marriage in the "Japanese style," and children followed a "free style" of life in the "American way." In the poor areas of Myōgyō-chō, when they reached maturity, boys and girls worked side by side as ragpickers, entertainers, or actors. After exchanging a few words once or twice before work in the morning or after dinner, they quickly became intimate. They started living together, without any ceremony, simply informing their parents, who failed to interfere or guide their children's "vigorous youthful passions."[72] The journalist Yokoyama Gennosuke had similar impressions of marriage among the poor in Tokyo in 1897. Yokoyama wrote that few husbands and wives had been brought together by proper go-betweens. When he checked the registra-

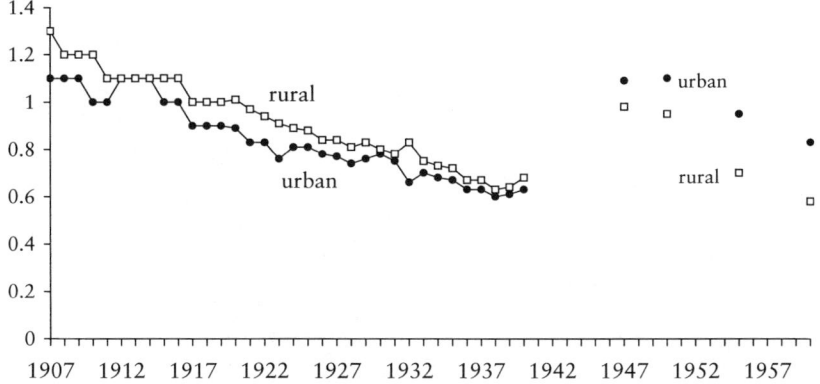

FIG. 4. Urban and Rural Divorce Rates, Japan, 1907–1960 (per 1,000 population). (Source: Tsubouchi Yoshihiro and Tsubouchi Reiko, "Nihon no Rikon," in *Tōnan ajia kenkyū sōsho*, vol. 4, *Rikon* [Sōbunsha, 1970], 150.)

tion reports of a row of ten houses, he found that only two or three couples had been officially registered.[73]

In the countryside, mountain villages were on the lower end and fishing villages on the higher end of the divorce spectrum according to Japanese anthropologists. Between 1873 and 1953, in a village of charcoal burners in Shiga Prefecture, only 4.5 percent of the 174 marriages recorded in the family registers were dissolved. What is interesting about divorces in this particular locality is that the divorce rate for the many (138) marriages with brides from the village was lower than that for the few (36) marriages with brides from outside the village: 1.5 percent versus 17 percent.[74] In a fishing village on the Shima Peninsula of Mie Prefecture, which had above-average divorce rates between 1921 and 1959, divorces were also more likely when a spouse came from outside the village.[75] Other scholars similarly report lower divorce rates for brides marrying into the village than for those marrying outside of it in the Edo period.[76] Familiarity with the locality was a stabilizing force in marriage.

East/West Distinctions

Scholars of the Japanese family have found substantial differences in regional family practices related to social and economic structure and local beliefs. This discussion of regional variation of divorce limits itself to the most basic cleavage relevant to nineteenth-century divorce (and marriage), a phenomenon the eminent demographic historian Hayami Akira once called a "fossa magna," comparing a conspicuous gap in the mar-

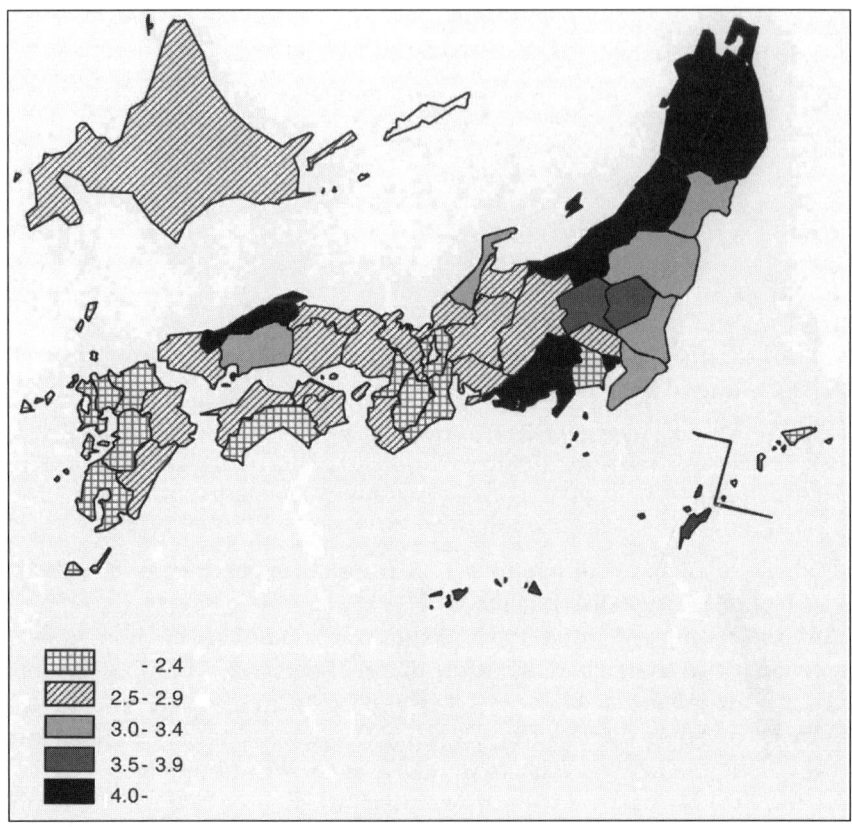

MAP 1. Japanese Divorce Rates, 1883–1887 (per 1,000 population).

riage age to a geographical fault line between eastern and western Japan.[77] In the 1880s, Japan appears to have been divided into two halves, not only by divorce but also by other family practices; the halves were western Japan, comprising the prefectures west of Niigata, Nagano, and Shizuoka, and eastern Japan, comprising all other prefectures except Hokkaidō.

Divorce rates were higher in eastern than in western Japan between 1883 and 1887 (map 1). Almost all prefectures in eastern Japan had a crude divorce rate above 3. Divorce rates above 3.5 were recorded for five Tōhoku prefectures, three Chūbu prefectures, and Tokyo. By contrast, most prefectures in western Japan had divorce rates under three. Many Kansai and Kyūshū prefectures even had divorce rates under 2.5 percent. In western Japan, Shimane was the prefecture with by far the most divorces.[78]

TABLE 3
Changes in Prefectural Divorce Rate Variations
(divorce per 1,000 people)

	1883–1887	1908–1912	1932–1936
Average	3.07	1.17	0.75
Median	2.69	1.13	0.75
Minimum	0.86	0.26	0.16
Maximum	5.41	1.84	1.08
Standard deviation	0.88	0.29	0.18

SOURCE: Calculations based on data from Tsubouchi Yoshihiro and Tsubouchi Reiko, "Nihon no rikon," in *Tōnan ajia kenkyū sōsho*, vol. 4, *Rikon* (Sōbunsha, 1970), 153.

The differences in divorce rates between prefectures and regions subsequently narrowed substantially. The variation between maximum and minimum divorce rates became smaller, and the standard deviation declined. Divorce rates gradually became more uniform across Japan after the 1880s (table 3). Divorce rates dropped by at least 50 percent in all Japanese prefectures between the 1880s and the 1930s. The decline was most precipitous in eastern Japan. It ranged between 75 and 86 percent in Tōhoku and Kantō. It was around 75 percent in the Chūbu prefectures that do not border the Sea of Japan. The decline was less uniform and slower in western Japan. It was more than 70 percent in Kansai and the adjacent prefectures of Okayama and Tokushima, more than 65 percent in the Kyūshū and Chūgoku prefectures, and smallest in the Hokuriku prefectures and Shikoku (excluding Tokushima). With a decline of 76 percent, the Okinawa region had one of the highest drops in Japan.

The relative distribution of divorce rates in the 1930s shows both continuity with and change from the 1880s. Three regions maintained their respective divorce ranks: on the high end, Tōhoku, and on the low end, Kansai and Hokkaidō. All Chūgoku prefectures except Okayama were far above the median in the 1930s, as were Ehime and Kōchi. Kyūshū was no longer a relatively low-divorce rate region. By contrast, Kantō emerged as an area of low divorce.

The leveling out of regional variations in divorce went hand in hand with government efforts toward building a modern nation, which introduced new systems of political, economic, communications, and educational infrastructure. The late-nineteenth-century regional patterns of divorce, however, also suggest related variations in how trial marriages functioned in Japan, testing spouses either after marriage registration or before.

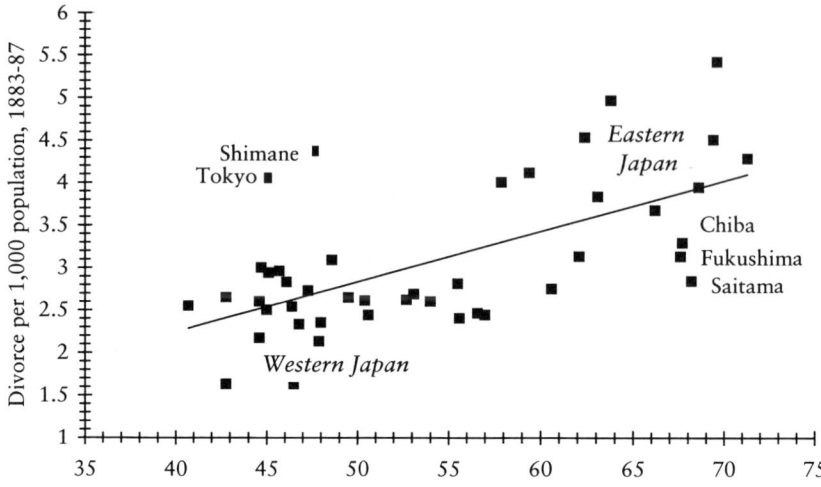

FIG. 5. Correlation of the Divorce Rate with Marriage Age by Prefecture in the 1880s. (Sources: Hayami Akira, "Another *Fossa Magna*: Proportion Marrying and Age at Marriage in Late Nineteenth-Century Japan," *Journal of Family History* 12, no. 1/3 [special issue 1987], 64, for marriage age data; Tsubouchi Yoshihiro and Tsubouchi Reiko, "Nihon no rikon," in *Tōnan ajia kenkyū sōsho*, vol. 4, *Rikon* [Sōbunsha, 1970], 153, for divorce rates. According to the traditional system of counting ages, a newborn child is one at birth and ages a year with the passing of each New Year.)

Exceptionally high divorce rates in the 1880s in eastern Japan correlate with youthful marriage, large average household size, and relatively high rates of in-marrying husbands, to name just a few of the sociodemographic factors also showing an east-west cleavage. In 1886, the marriage age in eastern Japan was conspicuously lower than that in western Japan.[79] The relationship to divorce is striking, but only for eastern Japan, where divorce rates increased visibly with early marriage (fig. 5).

There was an east-west distribution of household size in 1888 similar to that for marriage (map 2). Japanese household size by prefecture varied from under 4.5 to over 6.5 members per household. The largest households were in eastern Japan, where all prefectures except Tokyo and Nagano had an average household size of over 5.25. In eastern Japan, the prefectures of Tōhoku and eastern Kantō stood out with especially large household sizes, with many areas exceeding an average of 6 members per household. In contrast, the majority of prefectures of western Japan had a household size of fewer than 5 people.

Though less conspicuous than for marriage age or household size, the rates for in-marrying husbands among total newlyweds also followed an

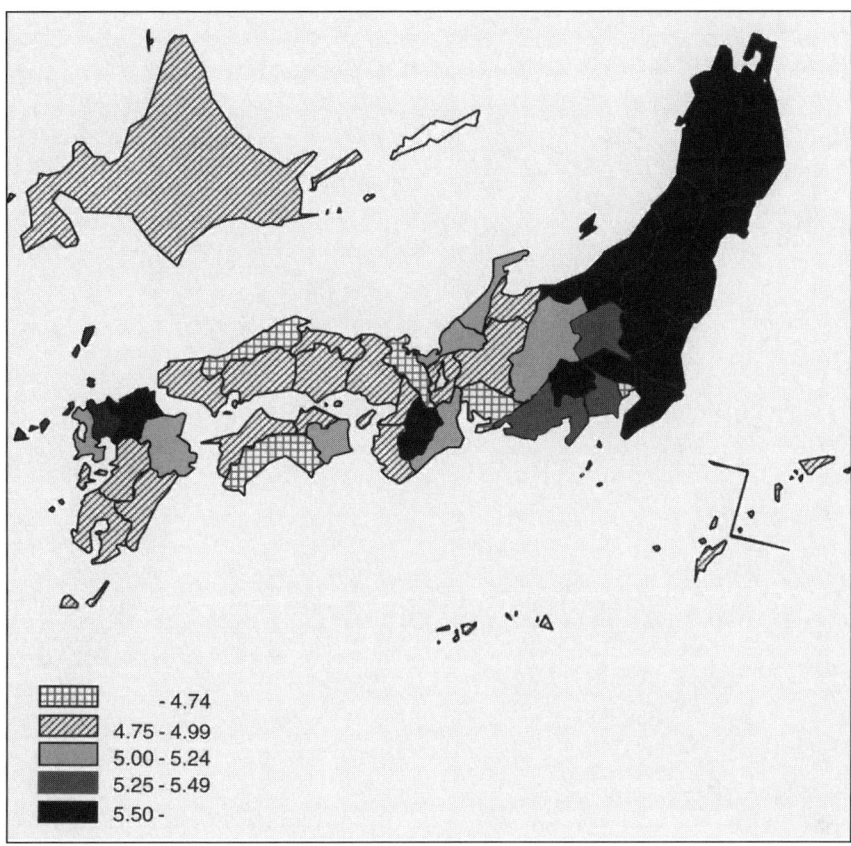

MAP 2. Average Household Size, 1888.

east-west pattern. In 1905, the percentage of marriages with in-marrying husbands was higher in eastern than in western Japan. In eastern Japan, the ratio was almost always over 10 percent. In Tōhoku, Niigata, Ibaraki, Chiba, and Shizuoka, it exceeded 12.5 percent, but it was only between 9 and 10 percent in Tokyo and the two adjacent prefectures of Saitama and Kanagawa. In the majority of prefectures in western Japan, fewer than 10 percent of marriages involved in-marrying husbands. The ratio was particularly low, at less than 7.5 percent, in most of Kyūshū, western Shikoku, and Okinawa. Within western Japan, the Chūgoku region had the most in-marrying husbands.

Japan's western prefectures on the whole had lower divorce rates than those of eastern Japan in the 1880s. To the population of western Japan, the state-sanctioned version of marriage by registration appeared less im-

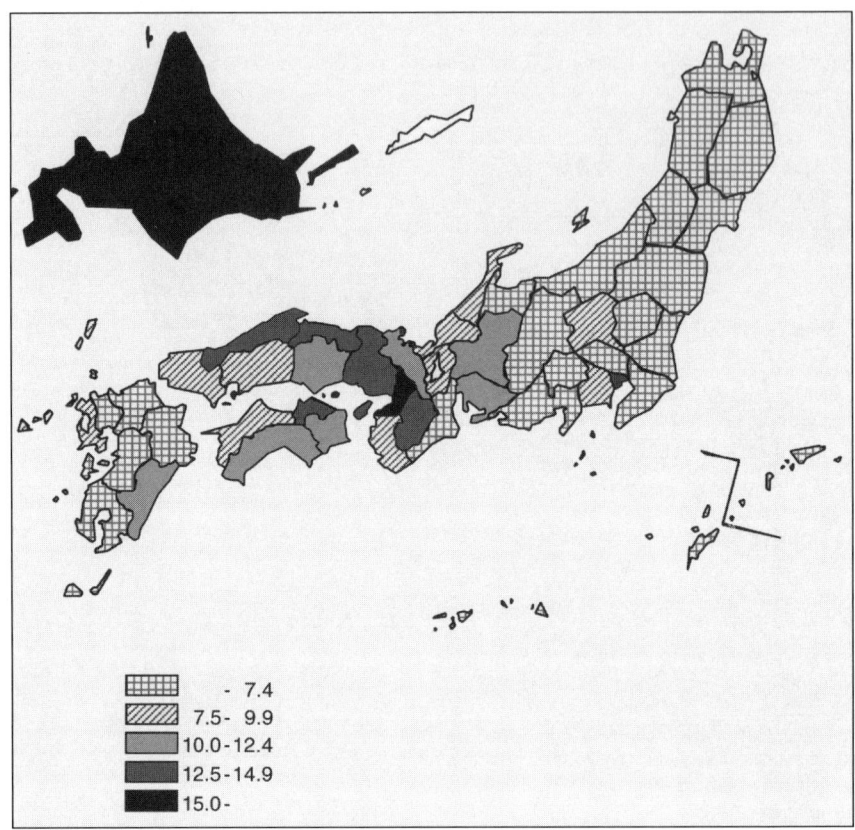

MAP 3. Illegitimate Children, 1899–1900 (%).

portant. The 1875 survey suggests that not only was marriage registration delayed more often, but common-law marriages and illegitimate children were more frequent in some provinces of western Japan (map 3). The greater prevalence of cohabitation in western Japan, one surmises, led to more premarital separations, which then fail to appear as divorces in official statistics. At the prefectural level, a slight inverse relationship between divorce rates and common-law marriages is visible.

The regional variation in divorce rates in the 1880s, with northeastern Tōhoku above and southwestern Kyūshū below average, induced scholars to search for reasons for this difference in the respective family systems. Farming households in northeastern Japan possessed relatively larger farms than those in the southwestern part of Japan and regarded a bride as valuable labor, explains a sociologist, and if a very young bride did not meet expectations, her husband's family expelled her again.[80]

Other authors agree. Distinguishing between strong and weak repudiation divorce (*oidashi rikon*) in the northeast and southwest respectively, they attribute the differences in divorce to varying economic demands shaping rural households in ways not necessarily due to the power of the patrilineal (*fukeiteiki*) house.[81] According to anthropologists, strongly hierarchical family structures in the northeast, compared with the rather egalitarian structure of families in the southwest, influenced not only divorce rates, but whether wives initiated divorce.[82] They say divorce in northeastern Japan was relatively more likely for "family reasons," and divorce in southwestern Japan, for "individual reasons."[83] Indeed, in the Meiji period, the percentage of female household heads, which scholars often use as an indicator of women's social status in a region, was higher in western Japan.[84] All the above explanations seem plausible in general to explain variations in and grounds for divorce, but they share one weakness. Many differences in family and social structure persisted while divorce rates became more similar across the country. The issue of geographical variation deserves further exploration through comparative local studies.

Short Marriages Prior to Divorce

Besides the frequency of divorce, an important feature of the early modern system of marriage was the fact that divorce occurred relatively soon after marriage became official. Around the turn of the twentieth century, almost a quarter of all divorces were for marriages that had not even lasted a year, and nearly half of all divorces ended marriages that had lasted less than two years. Even more noteworthy is the relationship to regional divorce rates. Those prefectures with the highest divorce rates, and the lowest marriage ages, also exhibited the shortest duration of marriage before divorce. The length of marriage before divorce varied according to prefecture, as shown in map 4.

In 1920, the length of marriage before divorce was shortest in eastern Japan. In most eastern prefectures, 17.5 percent of divorces were within one year of marriage registration. The percentage was higher than 22.5 in six prefectures. In the majority of prefectures in western Japan, on the other hand, less than 17.5 percent of divorces were within one year of marriage. The four prefectures of western Japan closest to the eastern part of the country showed shorter marriage durations.

Just as the divorce rate declined, the length of marriage before divorce rose in the following decades. The fastest divorces in the official records occurred in 1899. As a proportion of all divorces, 22 percent occurred within one year, 46 percent within two years, and 58 percent within three

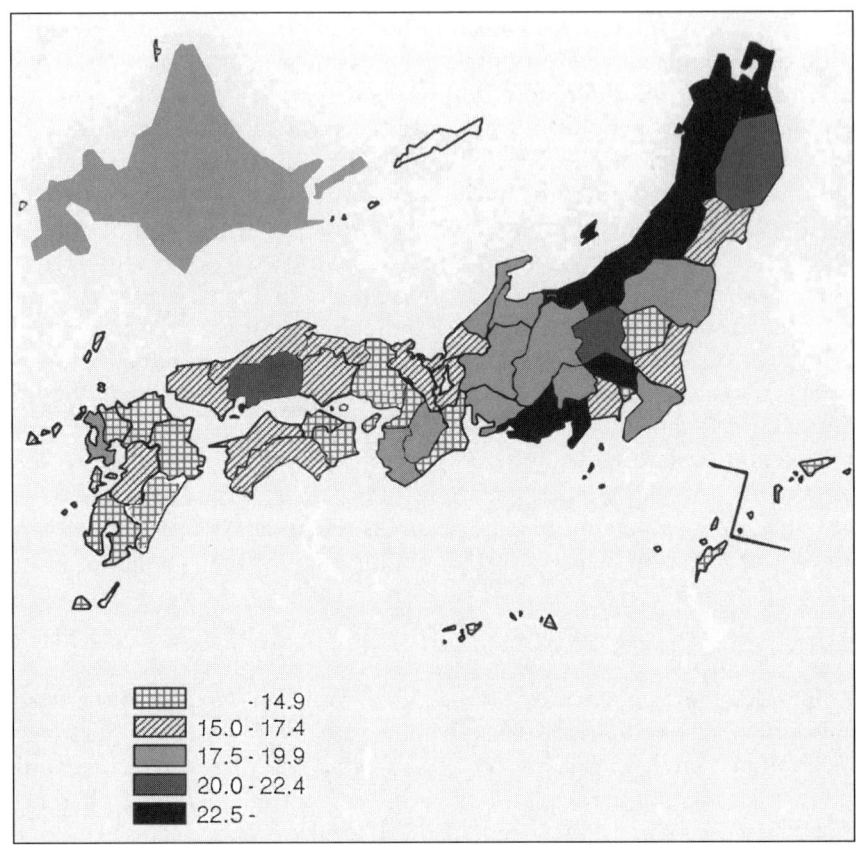

MAP 4. Divorce Within One Year of Marriage (%), 1920.

years. Based on an index of 100 for 1900, the rates for 1935 are 63, 60, and 67 for one-, two-, and three-year-old marriages.[85] In comparison with today's divorce, divorce around the turn of the century occurred at an early stage of marriage, when the spouses had invested less time and energy in their marriage, and at a much younger age. Moreover the ratio of divorces for couples with children was much lower around the turn of the century; extension of the length of marriage before divorce increased the likelihood of childbirth because marital fertility rates remained high until the 1940s.[86]

The duration of marriage and the frequency of common-law marriages relate inversely to other marriages before World War II. Illegitimate childbirth, taken as a proxy for common-law marriage, and the length of marriage before divorce exhibit an inverse relationship at the level of prefectures (fig. 6).

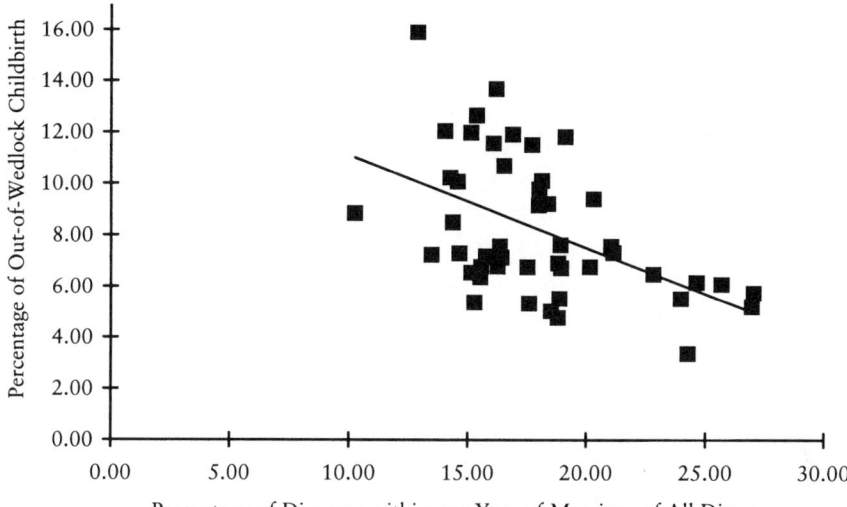

FIG. 6. Correlation of Out-of-Wedlock Childbirth with Duration of Marriage Before Divorce at the Prefecture Level, Average 1919–1921. (Sources: Calculated from Hayami Akira, ed., *Kokusei chōsa izen Nihon jinkō tōkei shūsei* [Hara shobō, 1993], and Takahashi Shin'ichi, ed., *Kokusei chōsa ikō Nihon jinkō tōkei shūsei* [Hara shobō, 1994]. The out-of-wedlock childbirth rate includes children recognized [*shoshi*] and not recognized [*shiseiji*] by their father.)

The cluster points suggest that couples who lived in prefectures with fewer common-law marriages dissolved their marriages faster. This correlation has implications for our understanding of the marriage arrangement and divorce process in Japan. Depending on the region, there were opposite strategies for mate selection. Whereas in eastern Japan, a marriage was dissolved after incompatibility had been assessed during a formal marriage, future spouses had more opportunity for contact before marriage in most prefectures of western Japan, so there was less tendency to divorce afterward. The difference is perhaps explicable in terms of greater control of children by families and patterns of co-residence that made it essential to test a new spouse within the family context. The increase in the length of marriage before divorce may, in other words, have reflected an increased opportunity for prospective spouses to get acquainted with each other before marriage.[87]

Multiple Remarriage Opportunities

Although Confucian moralists in both China and Japan urged that women not remarry, in Japan, remarriage after a divorce was in practice not only possible but almost as likely as not. The criticism of women remarrying after divorce in the Confucian text *Greater Learning for Women* may be interpreted as a sign that divorcées in fact remarried frequently.[88] Some demographers point to the ease with which divorced peasant women remarried in the Edo period.[89] In Mikawa Province, the rate of remarriage for divorced samurai wives was about 50 percent.[90] A remarriage rate after divorce of 59 percent can be calculated from a national sample of daimyo and bannermen. Remarriage rates were higher among daimyo than bannermen, and, unlike divorce rates, the rate of remarriage increased with the size of daimyo holdings, except among the very top daimyo, with domains of more than 250,000 *koku*.[91] Divorced samurai women were economically penalized when they remarried, since, on average, they entered their new households with lower stipends than other samurai brides, but the post-divorce remarriage rate even of samurai wives in the Edo period was probably higher than the low remarriage rate of divorcées in the 1960s. In the turbulent decades prior to the Edo period, there were famous cases of divorce explicitly for the purpose of remarriage when political alliances shifted.[92]

Foreign visitors to Meiji Japan were startled by the widespread acceptance of remarriage after divorce. Gustav Kreitner, who reached the country in 1878 and had many contacts with Japanese of the upper classes, remarked: "The divorced wife again obtains total independence in her actions, and nothing prevents her from contracting a second or third marriage."[93] The 1875 survey anticipated that a divorced wife would return to her natal home. The expectation that a divorced woman would easily reintegrate into her natal family suggests that a young bride had never completely severed the social and emotional connection with her natal home. A wife's strong ties with her home might even have facilitated her divorce when her family encouraged her to leave an unsatisfying marriage. Ties to one's natal family influenced the decision to divorce.[94] Families were more likely to accept returning members if they would not become long-term burdens on the household, and since the eventual remarriage of a divorcée relieved her natal family of that possibility, the easier it was to remarry, the less reason a family had to oppose their daughter's divorce in the first place.

In the 1870s, remarriage was common both for divorcés and divorcées, and the gap between men and women in remarriage was much smaller for the divorced than for the widowed. This shows that the primary function of divorce was to rearrange people in the hope that the new match would be better able to fulfill mutual expectations. The possibility of remarriage then became an incentive to divorce.

The Trial Marriage System / 69

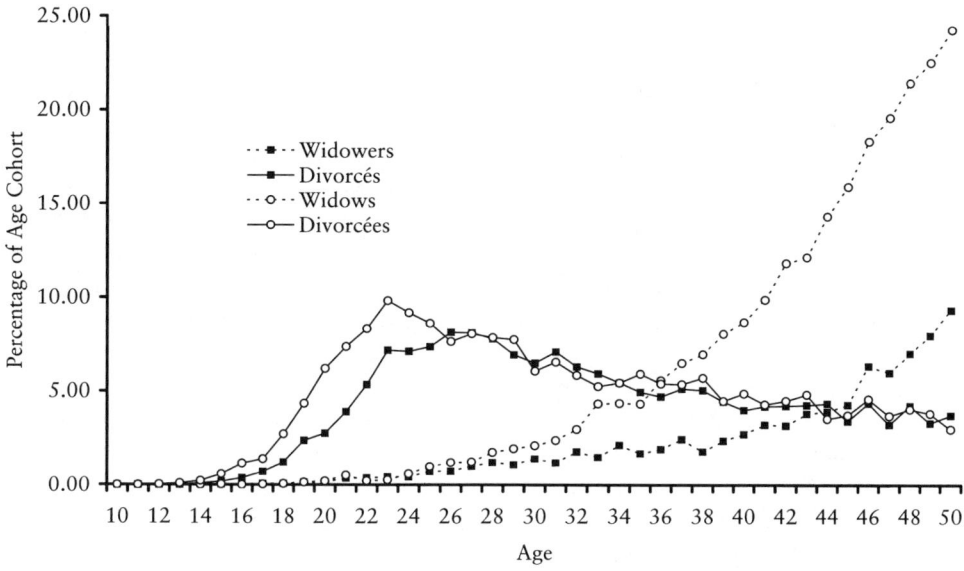

FIG. 7. The Civil Status of Men and Women by Age in Yamanashi Prefecture in 1879. (Source: Tōkeiin, *Kai kuni genzai ninbetsuchō* [Tōkeiin, 1882], 14, 43. Age on 31 December 1879 according to the current system of computation, under which one is zero at birth.)

Figure 7 shows divorcés and divorcées and widowers and widows as percentages of their age groups for 1879 in Yamanashi Prefecture.[95] The curve for divorcées peaks at around 10 percent for twenty-four-year-old women. The line for divorcés plateaus at around 8 percent for men between twenty-seven and twenty-nine. After the age of about twenty-nine, the curves for both sexes decline gradually, following each other closely. After about age forty, the decline stabilizes near 4 percent. There are two possible explanations for the rate stabilization. First, it shows that a certain number of people were unable or unwilling to remarry. Second, it indicates that as many people divorced as remarried.

There was a gender difference in divorce. Women divorced earlier, and the proportion of remarried divorcées rose higher than that of divorcés. The difference between men and women in age at divorce reflected the gap in the marriage age, which was about four and a half years in Yamanashi Prefecture in 1879. The number of divorces must obviously have been the same for both genders, but the peak was lower for men than for women because divorced men probably remarried faster than divorced women. In the total population of Kai Province, there were 5,681 divorced men versus 6,460 divorced women, a male/female ratio of 0.88.

Although divorcés remarried faster, many divorcées also remarried eventually, and after people reached their late twenties, there was no significant gap, suggesting a comparable opportunity to remarry after divorce for men and women.

In contrast to divorcés and divorcées, the discrepancy between the number of widowers and widows widened remarkably with age. There are obvious demographic reasons for an increasing gap among widowed people—on average a husband was older and died before his wife. The difference is still striking. There were 9,006 widowers and 24,812 widows in the prefecture, a male-to-female ratio of 0.36. Differences in remarriage are a further explanation for the gender gap among widowed people. Customs and laws discouraged the remarriage of widows. For example, in the town of Nagaoka in Echigo Province, a widow had to cut her hair at her husband's funeral as a sign of renouncing remarriage.[96] Foreigners also noticed trimmed hair among widows. The missionary Walter Weston reported that: "The orthodox or old-fashioned Japanese widow (however young) . . . rarely considers herself free to marry again. Indeed it has, at least until lately, been usual for a widow to cut off her hair, not as a sign of following a fashion supposed to be attractive, but as rather the reverse!"[97] A. H. Exner observed that a widow who wanted to stay unmarried cut the hair on the back of her head, but a widow who intended to remarry wore a turtle-shaped pin on plaited hair.[98]

Government agencies believed that widows should not remarry. In 1889, the governor's office of Shizuoka Prefecture sent an inquiry to the central government asking whether the widowed mother of the commoner Ide Ushimatsu could remarry. The inquiry argued that although remarriage of a widow was immoral, it should be permitted in this case because of the widow's poverty, which prevented her from supporting herself and her son.[99] In a May 1889 reply, the Ministry of Justice informed Shizuoka Prefecture that a widowed woman with children should remarry only if the head of the house was sick or could not work and if the head of the house and relatives approved of the remarriage.[100] In the government's view, widows with financial support had no reason to remarry.

Gender differences in the rate at which widowed people remarried also arose from their relationships to children. Children posed a stronger impediment to the remarriage of widows than to that of widowers. In part this can be explained by the fact that a widow might lose her children to the house of her deceased husband if she remarried. A gender gap in the remarriage of widowed people also existed in Germany, however, where a widow kept her children at remarriage.[101] In both countries, women married chiefly in the younger age groups, whereas men were also able to marry at later ages. One of the reasons widows failed to remarry as often as widowers was that they were often too old to attract a new husband.

Age is not the only explanation for the difference in the rates at which divorcées and widows remarried. In twentieth-century Japan, there were almost always more divorcées than widows among newlyweds. Not only did more divorcées than widows remarry in the younger age groups, in which there were more divorcées in the population, but, remarkably, at all ages up to seventy, more divorcées than widows remarried.[102] This suggests that a woman was more likely to remarry after divorce than after the death of her husband.

It is puzzling to find that the female-to-male ratio for remarriage after divorce was greater in the 1870s than in the first decades of the twentieth century. When data from the trial census in 1879 are compared with data from modern censuses of 1920 and 1930 in Yamanashi Prefecture, the gap in remarriage appears smaller in 1879 than in more recent censuses. The male/female ratio of divorced people in the population dropped from 0.88 in 1879 to 0.62 by 1920. The increased remarriage gap points to the possibility that divorced women were more likely to remarry in the Meiji period than in the Taishō period.

On the national level, moreover, gender differences in the rate of remarriage after divorce rose continuously after 1910, becoming most pronounced in the period between the 1930s and the early 1970s, as is reflected in the male/female ratio of divorced people among newlyweds: 1.03 in 1910, 1.25 in 1940, missing data until 1.28 in 1968, and 1.11 in 1990.[103] Scholars have found a staggering gap in the rate of remarriage after divorce in the mid 1960s—89% for men as against 46% for women—when divorce rates in Japan were at their historic low.[104]

Assuming an equal preference by men and women for mates with similar backgrounds, divorced people should show similar remarriage patterns, as they more or less do in Japan today. Early-twentieth-century remarriage rates follow that expectation only partly. More than one-third of divorced newlyweds married divorced spouses, but otherwise the rate of remarriage diverged sharply by gender. Divorced men were more likely to take never-married spouses (50 to 60%), whereas divorced women were much more likely to marry widowed spouses (25 to 30%) between 1900 and 1940. This bifurcation in the rate of remarriage widened after the 1910s, possibly because divorce imposed an increasing stigma on women as divorce rates declined.

The Trial Marriage System and Household Survival

Frequent divorce in Japan until the end of the nineteenth century was part of a larger system of trial marriage. Spousal compatibility was tested through cohabitation or marriage, and if the test was unsuccessful, separation or divorce ensued. In either case, marriage afterward was permissible for men and women, and the gender gap for remarriage was probably smaller in the 1870s than in the middle decades of the twentieth century. In its simplest version, the trial marriage model worked this way: marriage or cohabitation at an early age, quick divorce or separation, and a new trial marriage for both men and women.

There were two forms of spousal testing in the last decades of the nineteenth century, namely, in informal unions by cohabitation mainly in western Japan and in official marriages mostly in eastern Japan. In western Japan, trial marriages manifested themselves in the guises of delayed marriage registration, frequent common-law marriages, illegitimate children, and high divorce rates. In eastern Japan, trial marriages were more commonly evident in very high divorce rates and very short duration of marriages before divorce. Relatively more couples living together were registered as husband and wife in eastern Japan, and the dissolution of such unions thus entered the official divorce statistics. This is one reason why the divorce rate in eastern Japan was the highest in the country in the 1880s. There is a slight negative correlation on the national level between the divorce rate and the rate at which illegitimate children were born, showing that there were fewer divorces where there were more common-law marriages. The very simple model of western and eastern marriage patterns can be applied to the geographic divisions between town and countryside. In the early twentieth century, cities showed features that were distinctive of the western Japanese marriage pattern, such as relatively high rates of common-law marriages and illegitimate children. In the countryside, on the other hand, households were larger, people married when they were younger, and marriages did not last as long.

Spousal testing in both forms decreased in tandem with the declining divorce rate. The number of common-law marriages declined between 1900 and 1940. This decrease was more than an aggregate move of the marriage registration date to an earlier period of living together. It reflects the fact that marriage had taken on a new meaning, resulting in changed behavior. Divorce rates should have increased if couples still believed that the first years of living together were a period of probation, but the divorce rate decreased everywhere. It declined at the slowest rate, however, in regions with the highest percentages of common-law marriages. The second form of spousal testing, visible in especially high divorce rates and short marriages before divorce, also became less pronounced. It is not surprising that regions with this form of trial marriage, such as in eastern Japan, also had the highest divorce rates initially. The length of marriage before divorce increased well into the postwar period, but divorce rates in eastern Japan fell faster than those in other parts of the country.

This chapter has argued that frequent and early divorce should be considered in the context of the process of spousal selection and was facilitated by the notion that the beginning of marriage or living together was a period of probation. The subsequent decrease in divorce was caused by increasing abandonment of the practice of spousal testing. The divorce decline shifted the function of divorce. In the early modern period, up to the end of the nineteenth century, the possibility of divorce was taken into account when arranging a marriage. Even around the turn of the century, almost half of all divorces took place within the first two years of marriage. In the early twentieth century, the practice of divorce changed. Divorce was no longer a corrective to original mate selection, but an occurrence in marriages that had lasted for many years.

Historians of divorce like to shock their readers with the casual observation that what divorce does today, death achieved in the past. The average length of time that humans can bear to stay married to one spouse, they imply, has remained roughly constant throughout history. Divorce is a functional substitute for death. This said, they then shyly retreat, suggesting the possibility of differences in the effect of how one loses a spouse, parent, or family member. Exceptional historical periods with unusually long marriages were the ages in between, such as the Victorian age in England.

Since there is no evidence that mortality in Japan was lower than elsewhere, this type of argument does little to account for the high divorce rates in Japan's past—unless one assumes an increase in the ability to endure marriage to the same spouse. The incentive to divorce must be sought elsewhere; probably it was an aspect of a family system prone to shedding family members perceived as less productive or valuable, including the elderly, infants, and new wives, in response to individual and social crises.

Plenty of demographic studies on Japan have scrutinized strategies of household survival, focusing on the crucial relationship between production and reproduction. A central issue in this line of inquiry is the explanation of patterns of household regeneration and economic growth. Of foremost interest are such issues of fertility, marriage age, labor patterns, headship retirement age, and whether families abandoned old people. Despite its obvious frequency, divorce has never taken such a prominent place in demographic theories. The flexibility the possibility of divorce gave families in times of individual and collective crises, however, should become an integral feature of any discussion of the history of the Japanese family. The system of trial marriage not only enhanced spousal compatibility but was one of the regulatory mechanisms to ensure optimal marital fertility and household survival in an age of near universal marriage.

4

Unsuitable to the Family Tradition?

Popular Divorce Customs in the 1870s

As previous chapters have already illustrated, the frequency of divorce varied by social status and locality. An explanation derived exclusively from Confucian ideals promoted particularly for samurai or propertied commoners may not be sufficient to explain a phenomenon that, although universal, was more pronounced among the poorer townspeople and peasants. To account for the frequency of divorce in Japan during the nineteenth century, to clarify the expected role of the participants in divorce, and to evaluate the terms of divorce, there is a need for a broader examination of customary values.[1]

In 1875, to assist in the process of drafting a modern civil code, the government sent out commissioners to explore local customs. Scholars in Japan referred to the results of this survey for a long time without systematic analysis, since the entries for localities are rather vague and without clear social distinctions. Admittedly, it is difficult to recreate actual practices from this rather abstract source, but it is the only survey of its kind during a crucial period of political transition in the nineteenth century, the 1870s. It is not surprising that some aspects of divorce revealed in the survey conform to previously discussed perceptions, the most significant being the low barrier to exit from marriage. In terms of assessing the impact of divorce, it provides a wider context than legal precedents and fiction, enabling us to distinguish more clearly between exhortation and possible popular practices. This chapter, based mainly on the 1875 survey, sketches the popular culture of divorce in the 1870s, which functioned as a kind of normative framework in divorce decision-making, with special attention to sex differences in obtaining a divorce, in the terms of the divorce, and in the impact of divorce.[2]

Obtaining a Customary Consent Divorce

Grounds for Divorce: Acknowledging Divorcing Wives

It is almost impossible to determine the reasons for divorce either on an individual level or in the aggregate. The issues quarreled about at divorce are not necessarily those that lead to the dissolution of a marriage. If divorce can be obtained through a court decision, participants in divorce suits will shape their cases according to the accepted legal norms. Although why and how divorces were obtained varied with each individual case, popular divorce customs reflected preferred ways of obtaining a divorce, such as the grounds for divorce sanctioned by the community.

Contrary to legal precedents or images in fiction, popular divorce customs acknowledged the possibility of either side initiating a divorce. The basic reason for a divorce was mutual incompatibility. In Musashi Province, for example: "There is no single reason for divorce. Lack of harmony between the husband and wife or the two families, imbecility [*hakuchi*], laziness [*randa*], or extravagance [*kyōsha*] on either side may all be grounds for divorce."[3] This Musashi entry is typical in that it mentions examples of grounds for divorce, not restrictions on them. More explicit than most other entries, it stresses that any person connected to a marriage, regardless of sex or household position, might be responsible for dissolution of the marriage. In other places, the failure of mutual compatibility was phrased in gendered terms, according to the sex of the divorce initiator, also showing the possibility of divorce from either side. Divorcing a wife was described in Nagato Province as "she did not fit the family tradition" (*kafū ni iranu*), whereas a wife demanding a divorce was described as "the waters did not mix" (*mizu ga awanu*).[4] Instead of the collapse of a long-term relationship, both sayings pointed to an initial failure of household members and/or the spouses to adapt to each other, which is an overarching theme in the survey's reasons for divorce.

Insufficient adaptation to the members and customs of a new family was a prominent reason for divorcing a wife, which is not very surprising considering that it was brides who most often entered the households of their husbands upon marriage. "When she disregarded the family tradition, opposed the wishes of her parents-in-law, . . . and was not obedient toward her husband," a wife was divorced in Kai Province.[5] A very similar set of reasons was advanced in Shinano Province: a wife was divorced for disobedience to her parents-in-law, disharmony with her brothers-in-law or other relatives, or failure to adapt to family traditions (*kafū*).[6] At first glance, these expressions evoke the common image found in fiction.

The young bride fails to measure up to rigid, demanding family traditions and thus is driven away. An alternative scenario, however, should not be ruled out: the young bride dislikes the new environment and leaves or provokes her own expulsion.

In the case of a wife's mistreatment, popular culture explicitly affirmed the wife's right to demand a divorce. The request was justified in Kai Province by cruelty (*kokugyaku*), dissipation (*hōtō*), or punishment for a crime (*kei*).[7] Dissipation (*hōtō*), insincerity (*fujitsu*), unkindness (*fujiai*) of her parents-in-law, and insincerity (*shin narazaru*) of brothers-in-law were enumerated in Shinano.[8] A husband's misbehavior gave cause to permit the wife's parents, with the help of a go-between, to reclaim even a wife living in another province.[9] How these rather general terms were interpreted in particular cases is left unexplained. Male dissipation was linked in the legal precedents to squandering of family resources and involvement with prostitutes. Despite the vagueness, these cases show popular culture recognizing the possibility of wives exiting unsatisfying marriages.

Examples of grounds for divorce were rarely phrased in a restrictive manner. In Sagami Province, a wife's family was supposed to ask for a divorce only in response to criminal behavior by the husband: "If the husband committed a crime [*hanzai*], the wife could demand a divorce. Where the husband refused, there have been cases when his relatives and the men of the association acted as guarantors and divorced the wife."[10] Although crimes (*hanzai*) were grounds for divorce by either a man or a woman, in the case of a wife, theft (*tō*), laxity in filial obligations (*fukō*), or adultery (*kan*) were further specified. What constituted a crime for a husband is left unexplained, but it was probably a crime for which he was sentenced by the official authorities.

Popular divorce culture reflected a sexual double standard. Husbands were permitted to divorce their wives for adultery, but not the other way around. In several localities, adultery justified the divorce of a wife, but there is no comparable reference to a man's adultery in the 1875 survey.[11] For example, a wife was divorced in the provinces of Kai and Shinano if she was unchaste toward her husband, and a wife's adultery was mentioned as grounds for divorce in several other provinces.[12] When the Meiji Civil Code later included adultery of the wife and excluded adultery of the husband as grounds for divorce, it followed popular divorce customs that judged the adultery of husband and wife differently.[13]

Infertility is conspicuously missing in the 1875 survey as a reason for the divorce of a wife. This is surprising, as it allegedly was a common reason for divorcing a wife in a society that attached great importance to perpetuating the family lineage. *Greater Learning for Women* condoned divorcing a barren wife, since the purpose of marriage was to provide men with progeny. There are two possible explanations why there is no reference to infertility as grounds for divorce in the survey. It could have been subsumed under another category. Unlike other reasons in the survey, infertility was not intentional misbehavior. If childlessness was caused by a wife's refusal to engage in sexual intercourse, it could have been called disobedience to her husband. A bride uncomfortable in her new family might have attempted to prevent a pregnancy that tied her closer to her marriage.

A more plausible interpretation is that mere infertility was not popularly recognized as grounds for divorce if the bride fulfilled all her other wifely obligations. Even *Greater Learning for Women* qualified the rule that barren wives deserved divorce, cautioning: "A barren woman should . . . be retained if her heart is virtuous and her conduct correct and free from jealousy, in which case a child of the same blood must be adopted"; nor should a man divorce a barren wife if he already had offspring from a concubine.[14] Besides offering a justification for keeping concubines, this indicates an alternative to divorce for lack of progeny. Although a family might prefer biological children, adoption was an accepted way of recruiting successors.[15] Like biological sons and daughters, adopted children provided security in one's old age and continuity of the family line. Barrenness existed as an excuse for divorce, but according to popular culture, it was not a legitimate basis for divorce.

The Divorce Notice as a Remarriage Permit

As we have seen, the shogunate encouraged husbands to write a divorce notice. This very fact enhanced the husband's bargaining power at divorce, since it was up to him to issue or withhold a divorce notice. Popular customs reflect the husband's almost exclusive role as the author of divorce notices: "The husband presented a divorce notice to the head of his wife's family," we read, and "The husband gave the divorce notice directly to his wife."[16] Legal precedents and popular plays, however, also accepted the image by which senior members of the wife's family forced husbands, whether *muko yōshi* or not, to hand over a divorce notice. The husband's power to decide divorce by himself was not unlimited. Nevertheless, the divorce notice has become strongly associated with male prerogatives. Much has been made of the unilateral nature of the transaction and wives' lack of protection against such a divorce, even in recent scholarship.[17] A detailed analysis of the use of divorce notices, however, reveals that women often gained more than they lost through the divorce notice practice. The sex difference in the ability to issue a divorce notice is obvious, but its role is often misunderstood. The divorce notice functioned as proof of the termination of a marriage and as a remarriage permit.

The popular Japanese name for a divorce notice was *mikudari-han*, but the 1875 survey mostly uses the term *rienjō*, literally, "letter of divorce." Local names for a divorce notice included *ribetsujō, itomajō, sarijō, temajō, himajō,* and *issatsu*. The term *mikudari-han,* "three and a half lines," described the format of a divorce notice, which was so universal that a piece of paper with three-and a half-vertical lines sealed with the thumb mark of an illiterate husband was sufficient to divorce.[18]

A divorce notice certified that a marriage had definitely been dissolved. This was an issue of utmost importance in the case of remarriage, since a divorce notice protected a divorced wife from a former husband who wanted to prevent her remarriage. In Kii Province, for example, a wife procured a divorce notice for "fear of disputes" (*fungi*).[19] In Bingo Province, the handing over of a divorce notice protected the divorced wife against the evil practice (*akushū*) of her former husband extorting money at the time of her remarriage. Many divorce notices closed with a crucial reference to remarriage. In Shinano Province, a divorce notice stated that the wife could remarry into whatever family she pleased.[20] Actual divorce notices contained a reference allowing remarriage. This common reference was also part of the subsequent examples of divorce notices, which also include an explicit allusion to a demand for divorce by the wife. In 1808, a peasant sent the father of his wife the following divorce notice: "I received your daughter Iho as my wife. She recently asked for a divorce [*hima o negaisorō*], and I have agreed to it. I do not object to her remarriage, no matter to whom it might be." In 1847, a husband addressed the divorce notice directly to his wife Moto, saying: "You have asked for divorce. I grant the divorce you wanted. For future reference, I certify that I have no objections [to your remarriage], whomever you remarry from now on."[21] Another peasant divorce notice, from Kōzuke Province in 1854, addressed directly to a wife and referring to her wishes for divorce, similarly declares: "I certify that I do not mind at all no matter whom she remarries."[22]

The desire of wives for divorce notices is also made explicit in the 1875 survey. Unless "a divorce was requested for some reason by the wife's side," no divorce notice was delivered in Kaga Province. In Tango Province, the wife also asked for a divorce notice if she had initiated the divorce.²³ In Uzen Province, too, it was the wife who desired a divorce notice, since she "feared future disputes [*fungi*]."

When the divorce notice was required by custom, it often became a precondition for remarriage. In about half the localities with divorce by divorce notice, it was also indispensable for remarriage. In Mikawa Province, "A husband wrote and thumb-marked a divorce notice. There had been cases in which a woman could not remarry even after living with her natal family for several years."²⁴ In Chikugo Province, "No matter how many years the couple had been separated, it was the custom that the wife could not remarry without a divorce notice."²⁵ In Tamba Province, officials were to punish women who remarried without a divorce notice.²⁶

A missing divorce notice was a sign of trouble. The husband, for example, might have withheld it as a punishment for the wife's adultery. In Ise Province, Shima District, a divorce notice was refused when the divorce was due to the wife's misbehavior (*furachi*). She was prevented from ever marrying again to chastise her for her sin (*tsumi*). Another reason for the lack of a divorce notice was a runaway husband, who was not there to deliver it. Problems might arise upon his return if the wife had remarried. In the case of an absconding husband, a wife was not supposed to remarry immediately. After some time, the go-between, relatives, or members of the five-family group could hand over a divorce notice in the husband's place.²⁷ Shinano Province had the strictest rules covering a husband's desertion. Neither father nor brother delivered a notice, at least not until three years had passed.²⁸ This practice of withholding a divorce notice made a wife responsible for her husband's whereabouts and punished her for his misdeeds. A husband might not be able to prevent his wife from divorcing him, but by absconding, he delayed her remarriage. A certain Kikuzō ran away in 1839 when the officers of Tōkeiji demanded a divorce notice for his wife, Fun. As a result, his wife could not shorten her stay in the temple and was forced to remain there for the entire twenty-four months.²⁹ If a wife desired divorce, it was thus in her best interest to prevent her husband from absconding, since, unlike in the case of a divorce by disappearance, she could then remarry the next day.³⁰

In the 1870s, the divorce notice was common but not a universal practice. Divorces with and without divorce notices were possible in the same locality, and nationally there were thirty-seven districts that required a divorce notice and thirty-six that did not.³¹ When other means existed to certify the end of a marriage publicly, the divorce notice became superfluous. Just as in marriage, a go-between often settled a divorce. Playing the roles of both negotiator and witness to the divorce proceedings, the go-between in divorce decreased the need for a divorce notice. Typical entries read: "There was no divorce notice if a go-between had negotiated the divorce," and "A divorce was sufficiently guaranteed by the go-between, and there was no need for a divorce notice."[32] The more important alternative to the divorce notice was registration. "Divorce was requested orally by the go-between without a divorce notice," it said for Ugo Province, and "registration at the town office proved it." With a stronger link of causality, in Sado Province: "Because the transfer certificates of the local office and temple were adequate proof of divorce, there was no divorce notice."[33]

Changes in official divorce registration policies forced the divorce notice out of existence. Since samurai had to petition the authorities in divorce, they already felt no need for divorce notices in the Edo period, but the shogunate encouraged the practice for commoners.[34] The family registration system provided a new means to identify marriage and divorce, however, and the Meiji government ceased to endorse divorce notices in the 1870s. The divorce notice disappeared after the 1880s, both from government ordinances and from Supreme Court cases, the legal scholar Numa Masaya argues, seeing this as an indication of the notice's general demise. The last known divorce notice was issued in 1917.[35] By the early twentieth century, registration had replaced the divorce notice and the go-between as the main proof of a divorce.

Wives sometimes responded to a divorce notice with a note of acknowledgement. This receipt of a divorce notice, called *kaeri-issatsu*, is not mentioned in the 1875 survey, but there are copies extant. The dearth of records indicates that the *kaeri-issatsu* played a fairly subordinate role in divorce. The *kaeri-issatsu* was usually shorter than the divorce notice but contained similar information. In 1878, a wife replied to a divorce notice written on the same day that she was grateful for receiving the divorce notice, and she alluded to repeated trouble in her marriage.[36] Rarely did a *kaeri-issatsu* precede a divorce notice. Due to a poor relationship with her parents-in-law, Kei left her husband, Tanaka Gisaburō. At the time of their divorce, Gisaburō and Kei secretly promised to resume their marriage in the future, but Kei started a relationship with another man. A year before receiving a divorce notice, Kei apologized for her faithlessness in a *kaeri-issatsu,* and out of consideration for Gisaburō, she promised not to live close to Gisaburō's residence or to behave disgracefully with her new man in public.[37]

The Terms of Customary Consent Divorce

Besides divorce itself, post-divorce financial and custody arrangements needed to be settled among the respective participants. Dowry and divorce were connected in three ways. First, a suggestive relationship existed between dowry size and the inclination to divorce. Second, retention of the most valuable part of the dowry by the natal family of the bride or *muko yōshi* was common for a period when the possibility of divorce could not be ruled out. Third, the natal family had an interest in ensuring the complete return of the dowry at divorce. In divorce negotiations, the return of the dowry was one of the most important issues, and it was at this point that the sex-differentiated grounds for divorce, described above, had their greatest impact. Popular customs of divorce strongly affirmed the right of the divorced wife to receive her dowry back, but she forfeited her dowry if she was considered the "cause" for divorce.

Dowry Return: A Catalyst to Remarriage

Small Dowries. The dowry of a bride usually included clothes and furniture. The 1875 survey describes the ideal content of a dowry:

> When a woman marries, she brings many chests of drawers [*tansu*] and bridal coffers [*naga-mochi*] in a procession, if from a wealthy family. Whereas if she is from a poor family, she wraps a few things in one piece of cloth, bringing handtools [*tedōgu*] and clothes [*irui*]. If money or land is brought besides the trousseau [*kagu*], this is called the *jisan-kin, jisan denpata,* or *keshōden.*[38]

Obviously, the dowry varied with the absolute wealth and status of the two families engaged in a marriage, but regardless of socioeconomic background, the bride was expected to bring her own clothes into the marriage. Some places went as far as to ask for enough clothes to last for a lifetime, as in Uzen Province.[39] Memoirs by samurai women describe their labor and apprenticeship in providing for the trousseaux of their sisters or their own trousseau.[40] Village women also wove their own kimonos for their dowries.[41] A bride's reputation in her new community often depended on the quality of the clothes she brought into marriage, as they revealed her dressmaking skills.[42] To some extent, the dresses a bride brought into marriage were the result of her prenuptial labor.

In contrast to clothes and furniture, a dowry rarely included money or land, even in wealthy families. Including land as part of a dowry was more common before the 1870s. Villagers in Shimotsuke Province formerly transferred dowry land under the name of *keshō-men*, but ceased the practice by the 1870s. In Kawachi Province, dowry land was more common "in former days."⁴³ According to the 1875 survey, money and land were included in the trousseau as material compensation for the bride's deficiencies in appearance or social standing. "Only one bride out of a hundred may bring money or land; the bridegroom's family regards it as something shameful, and the matter is generally negotiated in secret."⁴⁴ These additions to a dowry showed that the bride was undesirable or that the groom and his family were in financial trouble. Thus, it is not surprising that money and land dowries were hidden from the community.⁴⁵ Differences in social standing were also bridged with money and land. In Noto Province, dowry money was limited to marriages among priestly families and marriages between commoners and priests.⁴⁶ In Mino Province, inferior social status was also redressed with money or land: "When commoners married their daughters to priests or samurai, they always gave some property [*zaisan*], although they considered this a shameful practice among themselves."⁴⁷ Those unequal unions were a means for impoverished families of good lineage to reestablish their economic health through marriage to propertied commoners.

By contrast, dowry land for the establishment of a branch house was a socially accepted endowment in various places. In Ise Province, dowry land combined with a husband's property could be sufficient to establish a new household. In Hōki Province, a family rich enough to provide a daughter with a dowry preferred a *muko yōshi* marriage to let the daughter start a branch house.⁴⁸ In Mutsu Province, people with status brought property into marriage.⁴⁹ In Kii Province villages, it was possible to include cultivated land or forest land in the dowry. Townsmen rarely gave such dowries.⁵⁰

A *yōshi* (adopted son) or *muko yōshi* received a larger share of his family's wealth than did an out-marrying bride. The 1875 survey never mentions clothes and furniture as a part of the *yōshi*'s dowry, but often cites land and money. In the case of a *yōshi*, dowry land and money were not a sign of deficiency. In Yamato Province, a *yōshi* had to bring something valuable, even if it was as little as one yen, but sometimes he received cultivated land.⁵¹ A *yōshi* who succeeded to the headship of an adoptive family brought the largest dowry. In Kai Province, Yatsushiro District, both a *yōshi* and a *muko yōshi* as heirs brought money, or cultivated and forest land, to the adoptive family.⁵² Among the samurai in Yamanashi District, the dowry of a *yōshi* was linked to the stipend of the family to whose headship he succeeded. The appropriate amount was 100 yen for 100 *koku* or 200 yen for 200 *koku*, thus showing a relationship of one yen of dowry per *koku* of stipend.⁵³ In Rikuchū Province, a *yōshi*'s dowry was justified by the fact that a *yōshi* eventually acquired all the property of his adoptive family. ⁵⁴

A common theme among foreign visitors who came to Japan in the mid to late nineteenth century was the small size of a bride's dowry in Japan in comparison with practices in Europe and the United States. They often attributed them to there being less of a need in Japan to set up an independent household at marriage. The retired German-born U.S. general Wilhelm Heine mentioned that the bride received only presents, with nothing comparable in value to a European dowry. The French engineer Lamairesse concurred that girls' dowries were negligible.⁵⁵ The businessman A. H. Exner said that in Japan there was less need for household goods and a dowry for the establishment of an independent household than in Germany. His view was supported by the missionary Arthur Lloyd, a long-term resident of Japan, who spelled out the pattern of residence after marriage: "a newly-married couple in Japan do not set up house for themselves, but go to live with the father or mother of the bride or bridegroom." The Japanese diplomat Daigoro Goh explained to an English audience in 1892 that, while Japanese parents outfitted their girls with trousseaux, parents would not bequeath any fortune in the form of a dowry. Although admitting that dowries existed, he said a dowry system was unnecessary because the newlywed couple lived with parents.⁵⁶

The relative insignificance of the dowry may have contributed to the instability of marriage. Exner perceived a strong causal link between these factors. There was little risk in marrying, he explained, and few financial losses or complications were involved in divorce.⁵⁷ Japanese proverbs also reflect the belief in a decreased likelihood of divorce with greater dowry: "Where there is a dowry, the bride is attached."⁵⁸ If dowries were of low relative economic value, they should have been of little concern to the participants in a divorce negotiation. The principle of dowry return is nevertheless the best-documented aspect of Japanese popular divorce culture in the past, showing that numerous conflicts existed. Even if its material value was low, the dowry appears to have had an ideal or social value.

Preserving a Dowry. Out of fear of divorce, natal families continued to control the most valuable parts of the dowry, money and land, even after the marriage ceremony. The transfer of these in Sado Province was postponed until the marriage seemed secure and the wife had borne several children.⁵⁹ Also in Suō Province, dowry money and land were not delivered until the marriage proved stable and children had been born.⁶⁰ Especially in marriages of a *muko yōshi*, the fear of divorce and the dissolution of adoption induced parents to delay the transfer of ownership. In the provinces of Sagami and Echigo, the adoptive family could only use the income from the dowry until the *yōshi* succeeded to the household headship, when ownership rights were transferred.[61] In Izumo Province, Nogi District, both proceeds and ownership of a dowry were withheld until succession.[62] In Suō Province, natal families only handed out a dowry if a *yōshi* succeeded at once to the headship, since adoptive families often failed to return dowries at the dissolution of an adoption.[63] The reason a natal family transferred ownership when the *yōshi* succeeded to the new household was that this was a sign that the new relationship had matured and was less likely to dissolve. For example, in Mimasaka Province, a *yōshi* only succeeded to the headship when his behavior had been ascertained or he had fathered a child, criteria similar to those for registering the marriage of a bride. In the 1875 survey, however, there was no suggestion of a delay in the delivery of the two most common items of a dowry, namely, clothes and furniture.

The concern of the natal families of brides or *muko yōshi* to retrieve their assets in the event of a divorce is demonstrated by the popularity of dowry lists and prenuptial contracts. In Mutsu Province, the bride's family handed a dowry inventory (*dōgu sōjō*) to the go-between so as to ensure return in case of divorce.[64] In Awaji Province, Tsuna District, a dowry list was usually presented on a favorable-omen day immediately before the wedding. After accepting the items listed, the husband's family returned a receipt.[65] Dowry lists were known in the provinces of Yamashiro, Mikawa, Chikugo, Higo, and Echigo.[66] In Mikawa Province, the amount of dowry money and land was officially recorded: "Dowry [*kashi*] existed in the form of personal property and land [*dōsan fudōsan*] called *keshō-ryō*. Money was registered in the marriage inventory and fields were entered in the land register by the village headman."[67] An 1815 premarital agreement among the father of the groom, Ichibei, the go-between, Gonzaemon, and the brother of the bride, Jōemon, in Shimo-Ujiie Village, Echizen Province, for example, promised the return of twenty-eight *ryō* of gold coins regardless of the reasons for the dissolution of the marriage:

My son Tsurumatsu has received your older sister as a bride. I certify the receipt of the gold coins stated above as the price for furnishing their necessary household goods. I promise to return all of the above coins with the girl you entrusted to me should the marriage break up. In such a case, we shall not protest even if there are various arguments, regardless of the nature of the complaints. For future reference, we deliver this document sealed by the go-between.[68]

A far larger sum of money was involved in an agreement in Aichi District, Owari Province, in 1861, when Kojima Ryōemon promised to compensate his bride-to-be Omura with 1,000 *ryō* of gold if he were to divorce her. When Omura later wanted a divorce, her family asked for the 1,000 *ryō* compensation.[69] These prenuptial agreements show the desire of natal families to protect the money they gave to brides and ensure its return in case of divorce, no matter the reason.

Separating the dowry from common household goods was another strategy for protecting a dowry. In Uzen Province, a new bride could put her trousseau (*naga-mochi*) in the family storehouse once she expected to live with her husband until old age; until then, she was to keep it in her own room.[70]

The possibility of a return of the dowry at the early death of a bride shows the reluctance of natal families to part with the property given to out-marrying members. Depending on the presence of children and the length of marriage, a dowry could be returned when a wife died. In Shinano Province, Saku District, a dowry was to be restored if a wife had died without children.[71] In Suō Province, this occurred if a wife died "soon after marriage" and childless.[72] In Rikuzen, return of the dowry after the death of a wife meant that her natal family also had to bring her body back and bury her.[73] In Awaji Province, a bride's natal family had a right to recover her dowry after her death.[74] In Chikugo Province, the dowry was distributed among the wife's younger relatives after her death.[75] In other cases, a husband married the deceased wife's younger sister in order to retain his wife's dowry after her death.[76]

Negotiating Return of the Dowry. Already in the Edo period, the principle existed that a wife retained control over her dowry during marriage and took it with her at divorce. Legal precedents and popular plays often refer to this ideal. A husband, for example, could not alienate his wife's possessions by sale or mortgage against her will. The eighteenth-century legal collection *Jikata kikigaki* granted a wife's parents the right to decide on a divorce if the husband pawned her clothes and goods without her consent.[77] The divorce failed to return the wife's personal possessions, but the ordinance declared that the husband had to keep his hands off his wife's dowry.

Popular divorce culture in the 1870s was emphatic about the return of the dowry. Almost no reference in the 1875 survey challenged the principle that upon divorce, the bride should receive her entire dowry undiminished.[78] When the wife was accused of being the cause of the divorce, on the other hand, she lost her dowry. At this stage of the divorce process, the grounds for divorce, as described above, became relevant. A double standard of acceptable conduct for a husband and for a wife influenced negotiations for dowry return. If the divorce were due to his wife's adultery, the husband could retain her dowry as punishment. There is no evidence that a wife could divorce her husband for adultery and simultaneously retain her dowry. The 1875 customs survey recognized a wife's demand for divorce to be legitimate when it was for cruelty, dissipation, insincerity, unkindness, or punishment for a crime. The differences in the reasons for divorce between husbands and wives were probably less important in obtaining a divorce, but they influenced the financial settlement.

The principle of dowry return included all parts of the dowry and applied both to brides and to *muko yōshi*. Dowry return is testified for numerous provinces. In Rikuzen Province, clothing and furniture were returned upon divorce.[79] Unless the wife was divorced, money, cultivated land, and house lots brought as dowry at marriage remained permanently in the possession of the husband's family in Kaga Province.[80] In Chikugo Province, daughters-in-law or *muko yōshi* took their dowries and personal belongings with them upon divorce.[81] Similar practices existed in the provinces of Ugo, Uzen, Sagami, Mino, Mikawa, Ise, Izumo, Bizen, Bitchū, Mimasaka, Suō, Sanuki, Iyo, Higo, and Satsuma. However imperfect the eventual recovery of the dowry was, the norm of a dowry return upon divorce was widely accepted.

If she was the cause for divorce, a wife lost her claim to her dowry. In Mikawa Province, a wife had the right to all parts of her dowry after divorce, except when she had committed adultery (*kan*).[82] In Shinano Province, a wife's fault (*zaika*) invalidated the general principle that dowry money (*shiki-kin*), clothes (*irui*), and furniture (*dōgu*) should be returned to her immediately upon divorce. In a divorce caused by the wife's fault, the goods she had brought to the marriage were not to be returned according to the "old law."[83] A wife's fault also influenced the return of dowries in Rikuzen Province: "Upon divorce, the cloth and various effects [*shodōgu*] that the wife brought into the marriage are to be returned to her natal family . . . but for the lower classes [*chūtō ika*] when the divorce was due to the wife's misconduct [*furachi*],[84] the goods were usually not returned."[85] In this exceptional case, the link between misconduct and dowry was limited explicitly to the lower class. The reference can be interpreted in two ways: (1) upper-class women were not expected to misbehave, or (2) upper-class women retained their dowries even after misconduct. Few statements in the survey explicitly granted wives the right to all their personal property regardless of the circumstances of divorce, and thus the first interpretation seems more likely.

Not only being at fault but asking for a divorce could cost the wife her dowry, as only a few examples show. To obtain a divorce, the other party was financially compensated or simply bribed to consent. For a district in Shinano, when a wife divorced "against her husband's consent," she left her dowry at his home.[86] When the wife sought a divorce herself, she left her dowry with her children.[87] In the following two references, the compensation applied to either husband or wife. The person who proposed divorce in Suruga Province, be it husband or wife, had to deliver some goods to the other.[88] More specifically in another province: "If the wife demanded a divorce, the bridewealth [*yuinō*] should be returned to the husband's house; if a divorce request came from the husband, the wife could take with her all the goods she had previously received."[89] What was seen as fault here was not misbehavior but the abandonment of the marriage. Either husbands or wives could leave provided that they satisfied their former spouses financially.

In rare instances, wives might receive allowances in addition to their dowries, again depending on the reasons for divorce. In Shinano Province, Saku District, a wife recovered her dowry (*jisan bukken*), and if she was divorced unjustly, she might receive additional money (*kinsen*) or goods (*buppin*). If she initiated the divorce, though, she received nothing.[90] In Takai District of the same province, a husband reimbursed his wife for her years of service to him at the wages of an employee (*yatoinin*),[91] showing her value (and function) as a laborer. For marriages lasting longer than ten years and with no just cause for divorcing the wife, parents-in-law sometimes gave clothing money (*ifukuryō*).[92]

The dowry return principle also applied to the goods a *muko yōshi* husband brought into a marriage. In 1741, a town magistrate explained that if the adoptive family dissolved its ties to an adopted son (*yōshi*), a position similar to that of a *muko yōshi*, his dowry was to be returned within thirty days, whereas if the request came from his side, the decision was left to private agreement.[93] In response to a 1797 inquiry by a town magistrate, the Chamber of Decisions decreed that suits over the dowry money of a *muko yōshi* should be considered despite a new ordinance over money suits to the contrary.[94] The *jikata* explained that a *muko yōshi* lost the right to his dowry money if he left his adopted house because he disliked his wife. As in the divorce of a wife, the return of dowry money at the divorce of a *muko yōshi* depended on who initiated the divorce and why.

The return of the groom's bridewealth at divorce was a less contentious issue than the return of a dowry, at least in the 1875 survey, presumably because it was both less common and less valued socially and economically. If she or her family demanded a divorce, a wife ought to return the ceremonial dress originally received as a betrothal present in Rikuzen Province.[95] Among poorer peasants in Buzen Province there is also evidence for a bridewealth return principle: "Among lower-class [*chūtō ika*] villagers, large and small amounts of money called *tanomi* (asking money) are sent [as betrothal presents] to be used for purchasing the dowry [*kasō*]. If there should be a divorce, the same sum of money is to be returned via the go-between, except when the divorce has been caused unnecessarily by the husband's family."[96] Underpinning the principles both of the return of bridewealth and return of dowry was a fundamental belief in getting even at divorce, at least in economic terms. The exchange of bridewealth and dowry that marked the beginning of the marriage was erased symbolically and materially with their return. The ideal of a resumption of the premarital (financial) status quo explains in part why references to an allowance for a divorced wife are so few and, more important, why no indication of alimony for a divorced wife is present in the 1875 survey. Alimony, if paid, was at odds with the popular culture of divorce, which assumed a termination of all spousal rights and obligations with divorce.

Interpreting the Dowry Return Principle. Both husband and wife could leave a marriage, but the wife's family mainly supplied the cost of the divorce settlement, and materially the husband had less to lose than his wife. A new wife brought the husband a new dowry, whereas a wife had to rebuild a lost dowry by begging it from her family of birth or through work. In that sense, the economic stakes in dowry return negotiations were higher for a wife than for a husband. Despite suggestions that a dowry was returned "regardless of the reason for divorce,"[97] reasons for divorce were highly relevant in determining the financial settlement at divorce. Unequal grounds in the popular divorce culture did not imply that a woman was unable to divorce a husband, for example, for adultery. She had two options: either she made a convincing argument for his dissipation or cruel treatment, which were accepted causes for divorcing a husband, or she gave her husband her personal possessions. Depending on the cause of the divorce, she thus either lost or retained her effects.

The dowry return principle protected a wife from divorce, scholars argue, an interpretation also proposed for other societies with similar practices.[98] This certainly is an intriguing idea, and indeed divorce was more likely in the lower levels of society. Although we do not know whether the dowry of an upper-class woman was larger as a percentage of her natal family's wealth, it was certainly larger in absolute terms than the dowry of a poor bride, who might even marry without any dowry. These differential divorce rates, however, were certainly not caused merely by a desire to retain dowries; other status-based values, attitudes, and socioeconomic factors must have played a more significant role.

If the return of dowry was meant to protect a woman from divorce, one has to conclude that the safeguard was fairly ineffective at preventing divorce on a large scale. Reversing cause and effect might be more plausible: the custom of returning the dowry existed because families anticipated the possibility of divorce and wanted to secure their wealth. Families would only consent to parting with assets when there were means of ensuring and enforcing their eventual return in case of marital failure. This was in the interest of both the wife and her family, since a returned dowry was recycled at remarriage, whereas its loss would increase the cost of remarriage. The custom of returning the dowry was thus less of an obstacle to divorce than a facilitator of remarriage.[99]

Enforcing Dowry Return. Despite the almost universal acceptance of the principle of dowry return and, less so, a consensus on what constituted just cause for divorce, enforcement depended more or less on community pressure. A go-between was the most likely mediator in a marriage conflict and, if this intervention proved unsuccessful, in negotiated divorce. The go-between was supposed to decide the reason for divorce and then enforce the recovery of the bride's dowry accordingly. As the original link between two families in arranging a marriage, the go-between was expected to be involved in case of marriage trouble or failure. The role of a go-between in the mediation of marriage disputes or divorce was cited in thirty-eight provinces, but in ten provinces, no such obligations existed. In some places, a divorce was unobtainable without a go-between.[100] Contemporary commentators on Japanese marriage and divorce speak of the role of go-betweens in arranging divorces.[101] The go-between often did more than just convey the decision of the husband's family to the wife. In Higo Province, the go-between recognized the interests of both parties "by acting as an impartial judge in any dispute arising between the two families, to maintain amicable relations between them."[102] In Shinano Province, a go-between was given the right of final decision.[103] Mediation was not just a duty, it was often considered a prerogative. In Hizen Province, the go-between protested if someone else meddled in negotiations.[104] This exclusive right to arbitration brought predictability to the arbitration procedure. One of the reasons the go-between was so crucial to a marriage was because of his or her potential role in a divorce. The obligation could go beyond mere negotiations. In Musashi, a go-between had to shelter a wife who had left her husband until the resolution of their dispute.[105]

A go-between was not only mediator and judge in marriage squabbles, but also the strongest protector of a bride's dowry and enforcer of the marriage contract.[106] The 1875 survey summarized the function of the go-between at divorce as follows: "It is the go-between's duty to mediate in marital disputes. When there is a divorce, the go-between is usually in charge of the return of the wife's dowry [kagu]."[107] The latter part of the go-between's duties may have persuaded natal families to grant dowries to out-marrying members, since the go-between acted as an enforcer of retrieval in case of divorce. A marriage without a go-between was a risky marriage for any family with property, because the recovery of a dowry was more difficult.

The high status of a go-between sometimes prevented the formal dissolution of a marriage. The lord of the Mito Domain, Nariaki, had a part in arranging the marriage of his retainer Isamu to Kin. When Kin was sent back to her family on the grounds of her ill health, Isamu had to provide her with economic support for the rest of her life, just as if she had remained his proper wife.[108] A powerful go-between could provide security despite divorce.

Child Custody: From Split to Whole Custody

Two principles of child custody after divorce existed side by side in both custom and law. One legal principle, which first appeared around 1300, expected a parent to take custody of same-sex children after divorce: boys to the father, girls to the mother.[109] Since the children were divided according to their sex, one could call this split custody. The other principle expected all the children to remain in the house in which they had grown up, whether it belonged to their paternal or maternal ancestors. Regardless of sex, the children remained together under the custody of one parent, an arrangement that is here called whole custody.

A battle between these norms for hegemony already existed in the Edo period. The *Chōseidan,* a manual of legal precedents compiled in 1737, considered it wise to divide children by sex. Edo-period literature also reflects this view. *Honchō tōin hiji* says, "Now as for the two daughters, at divorce the 'old law' stated that boys go with the father and girls with the mother." In a work by Chikamatsu Tokuzō, a certain Kichibei yells at his divorced wife, "[B]oys belong to men; leave Kichimatsu and get out."[110] From the second half of the eighteenth century on, there was a shift in legal discourse in favor of whole custody. The *Bunden sōsho* collection of 1763 advised magistrates to disregard popular custom in which the husband was responsible for the boys and the wife for the girls; it urged instead that all children be handed over to the husband.[111] Other legal advice on the disposition of family suits concurred, for example, in *Kōsairoku*:

> People are accustomed to say without any real basis that when a wife is divorced, the male children go with the father and the female children, with the mother, but in the Office of the Magistrate, there is no such regulation. When disputes are brought before a magistrate, he should adjudicate on the basis of the principle that both male children and female children should be taken by the husband.[112]

The *Kōsairoku* referred to a correspondence in the Tenmei-Kansei period (1781–1801) as an example of the legal principle advocating whole custody. A reply to an inquiry by Matsudaira Izu no Kami in 1814, cited in *Shin'en shokaku,* explains that a child born after divorce belongs to the husband regardless of sex.[113] In 1816, an inquiry to the Chamber of Decisions about the disposal of a child custody dispute between a father-in-law and his divorced *muko yōshi,* with the remark that precedents for child custody cases were missing for peasants, was submitted by a finance magistrate. Based on an 1802 samurai precedent, the magistrate proposed to give the *muko yōshi* peasant father custody of all the children, regardless of their sex, suggesting a samurai solution to a commoner problem.[114] Magistrates increasingly opted for whole custody rather than split custody.

Popular culture in the 1870s reveals a similar coexistence of ideals. The 1875 survey claimed predominance of split custody in Japan: husbands took the boys and mothers took the girls. In contrast to the summary of national practice, though, a closer regional analysis reveals both split and whole custody, citing more districts with whole custody. Whole custody existed in thirty-seven districts and split custody in twenty-five. Both principles were found in fourteen districts.[115] The local examples suggest that whole custody was probably more common than split custody.

The issue of child custody is one of the few instances in which the 1875 survey is inconsistent. The guidelines to the survey explain that deviations from the general norm are recorded for the localities. Local examples of child custody both prove and contradict the general norm, but for other customs, the majority of the local examples are affirmative.

Children stayed together after divorce in whole custody, but custodial rights were determined by the kind of marriage their parents had entered into. Unless their father was a *muko yōshi,* children remained with their paternal family, as numerous references testify. Children then experienced the least disruption in their environment, as they continued to be raised in their natal home.[116] Only on the island of Awaji was a wife permitted to take all the children with her even if not married to a *muko yōshi,* and this example was used to support the claim that no fixed rules existed there.[117]

The need for household successors and family continuity supported whole custody arrangements. Even when the parents divided their children, a successor was to remain in the father's house. In Uzen Province, the wife could take any of the younger children but never the eldest son.[118] In Shimotsuke Province, a wife could take all the girls unless the eldest daughter was an heiress, in which case, this girl had to remain in the father's family.[119] In Shinano Province, the significance of the lineage was described in terms of a special blood relationship (*ketsu-zoku*) the children had with their father, justifying why the girls fell under his custody after divorce.[120] Whole custody assured the maximum number of potential successors to the paternal house. Boys were more important than girls in succession, because girls were more likely to eventually leave the household at marriage. A girl could still function as a backup successor by marrying a *muko yōshi.* Whole custody may in part have predominated in Tōhoku because of the special importance attached to lineage continuity (and a need for labor) in that region. The economic positions of the spouses and their respective families also favored whole custody. More than his wife, the husband was able to support his children by his labor or his inheritance.

In contrast to whole custody, in split custody, the kind of parental marriage made no difference to the future of the children, since children were simply allocated to the parent of the same sex. In Echizen Province, for example: "Among the children born during marriage, it is common for the mother to receive the girls at divorce, and at the divorce of a *muko yōshi,* he takes the boys along."[121] Officials also saw split custody as a lower-class practice. In the provinces of Inaba and Mino, for example, only mothers of the so-called underclasses (*chūtō ika, chūnin ika*) took the girls.[122] Already in the Edo period, magistrates considered split custody a less preferable commoner custom in contrast to whole custody, which was especially practiced by samurai. By the 1870s, split custody seems to have been on the retreat. Although it survived in several places as an ideal, it was superseded by the other practice. In Ōmi Province, for instance, "although there is a proverb [*kotowaza*] stating that girls belong to the divorced wife, in fact, girls are more often raised by the husband's family."[123] In other districts, norms also supported split custody, while local officials reported whole custody practices.[124] Officials may have tried to belittle split custody because they associated it with an inferior social status.

Different family ideologies and economic necessities were the reasons for a greater prevalence of split custody among the "poor" parts of the population. Less constrained by the obligation to maintain the continuity of a family line, poorer spouses had more of an option to choose split custody. Moreover, the gap in the economic position of women versus men was smaller among poorer spouses; poorer mothers were better able to provide a lifestyle for their children that was appropriate to their social environment. Issues of material child support were a concern to the participants in divorce; for example, in Kaga Province a mother took the girls if her family was wealthier than her husband's.[125] Split custody only worked if divorced wives supported their children, either alone or with the help of their natal families. While ideals of family continuity and worries about child support encouraged whole custody, a strong sexual division in household labor facilitated split custody. As revealed by nineteenth-century diaries, after infancy, children needed to be trained in their roles mainly by the same-sex parent so as to perform their appropriate work and household tasks. The father was relatively more responsible for boys and the mother for girls. Both parents acted as teachers and role models in their respective spheres.[126] In wealthier households, maids might do part of the rearing and training of daughters, but lower-class families had only grandmothers or stepmothers to substitute for a divorced mother.

Unlike in the case of dowry return, there is no direct evidence that misconduct by either husband or wife had any impact on child custody. It is thus impossible to tell whether a wife divorced for adultery might still be considered fit as a mother. There are several puzzling citations suggesting that when a wife initiated a divorce, she also took custody of her children. In Iwami Province, for example, a wife who requested a divorce received her daughters.[127] In Mino Province, only mothers who demanded divorce could take the girls.[128] This is the inverse of the relationship concerning dowry, in which a wife who initiated a divorce often left her dowry behind. Does this mean that children were seen simply as an undesirable burden, with which the divorce initiator was punished? This was not the case in Sūo Province. When a wife was expelled from her marital family upon her husband's death and had to leave her children, she was compensated with land.[129] A more convincing explanation centers on the nature of the divorce. Unlike in the case of the return of dowries, the 1875 survey did not differentiate between reason and request for divorce in child custody. A wife who asked for a divorce obtained custody of her girls if the other parties to the divorce accepted her reasons as just.

The notion of a final, irrevocable disruption of spousal ties loomed large in child custody, as in the financial arrangements at divorce. Visitation possibilities do not appear as an issue, and there are only a few references to child support contributions. Contact between child and noncustodial parent was discouraged. The mother had full responsibility for the children she took with her in Sagami Province, and the father did not need to care for them anymore.[130] Sometimes a relationship of interdependence continued between the spouses after divorce. When there was no qualified woman to perform the child-rearing role, a temporary arrangement was found in which the former wife raised the children for a certain time, while the ex-husband contributed financially. This compromise could be as short as thirty to fifty days after the birth of a child,[131] but it might also last for two to three years after the divorce.[132] Eventually, the children would be transferred from their mother to their father. In these impermanent child custody cases, the father contributed to educational expenses (*yōikuryō*).[133] In other localities, it was also conceivable for fathers to pay support (*yōikuryō, yōiku no teate, teatekin*) for girls under their mothers' custody, at least until a certain unspecified age, sometimes depending on the judgment of the go-between.[134] An exceptional citation urged that mothers not be prevented from leaving part of their property behind for their children after divorce.[135] Also, when a wife was pregnant at divorce, the husband had the duty of support (*fuji*) until delivery.[136] An important reason for the scarcity of references to child support payments is that the majority of the children were supposed to live with the financially stronger parent, who needed no additional funds for child rearing and education. At least in the form of providing materially for children not in his custody, a father was sometimes expected to have a continuing relationship with his daughters, but on the relationship of the mother with children of whom she did not have custody, there is only silence.

Which custody arrangement was in the best interest of family, parent, or child is difficult to determine in the abstract. Preconceived notions of fatherhood, motherhood, and childhood to a large extent shape our interpretations of what is good for whom. Criticism of custody arrangements points to a mother's loss of her children at divorce as a sign why wives must have experienced divorce as a traumatic episode. Some foreign visitors supported this view. Postwar, mainly feminist, scholarship reflects it rather uncritically in attacking the patriarchal past. The benefit of the child was a contested issue even to Japanese in the Meiji period, as reflected in the records of court custody disputes.[137]

Life After Divorce

Ignoring the possibility of wives working after divorce, the 1875 survey imagined two avenues open to divorced wives: their natal homes and/or remarriage. Commonly, a divorced wife was expected to remarry eventually, after returning to her natal family as her first destination after divorce.[138] After obtaining a proper divorce, the wife (and the husband) was free to remarry at any time without having to endure a waiting period of any form. "There is no problem if the wife remarries the day after divorce," we read, and "The husband can't complain if the wife remarries the day after divorce."[139] Problems only ensued if it was unclear whether the spouses were actually divorced. As discussed in detail above, an absconding husband or the lack of a divorce notice in localities that required them told potential suitors that if they married this woman, who could not really be regarded as divorced, there might be trouble with the previous husband. The divorce culture thus dissuaded women of such unclear marital status from remarrying. The issue of uncertain paternity of children born after divorce or remarriage did not feature in the discussion of divorce culture, and there is thus no indication of a remarriage prohibition on that ground. In the only case in which remarriage after divorce was frowned upon, it affected both spouses: "The husband is prohibited from remarrying for three years, [and] the wife cannot remarry."[140]

Evidence of Female Divorce Initiatives

The numerous references in the 1875 survey, and in various divorce notices, to a woman or her family asking for divorce attest to the ability of women to initiate divorce according to the early modern popular culture of divorce in Japan. As several actual cases show, wives demanding a divorce were more than a mere abstract possibility. Even Edo-period samurai wives sometimes decided to leave their husbands and return to their natal families. Among the six people in a samurai household of the

Mito Domain, for example, there was a younger sister of the head of household who returned home after several unsuccessful marriages. Her divorces were explained by her lazy, inconsistent behavior: "She had been married three times, but lacking the will to persevere, each time had returned home of her own volition even before her husband's family made any move to divorce her."[141] While the other women worked, she spent her days reading popular novels, although she enjoyed making sushi and dumplings. Although her spoiled attitude must have given her a bad reputation, it did not prevent her from finding suitors for a second and even a third marriage.

From the Meiji period, too, there are many examples of wives initiating a divorce. Alice Bacon tells the story of the maid Kiku, who quit her job for marriage but returned to her employer within a month because she found her husband's mother unbearable. Before the marriage, her husband had promised that his mother would live with his older brother, and that he and Kiku would have an independent, separate house. After the marriage, however, the mother-in-law moved in with her younger son. She was attracted by the industrious and good-natured Kiku and left behind another daughter-in-law, who seems to have been lazy and bad-tempered. Kiku found her mother-in-law abusive, however, and she gave up on her husband and asked for and obtained a divorce.[142]

Hani Motoko, the founder and editor of the important women's magazine *Fujin no tomo,* narrated her own experiences as the child of divorced parents and as a divorced wife. After some trouble over the use of family money, her grandfather divorced her *muko yōshi* father. After the divorce, she had little contact with her father, who had remarried, and she was instead raised by her demanding grandfather and dull mother. She was a strong-willed girl who excelled at school, and she chose her own husband, a student who started drifting aimlessly after their marriage. After less than a year, she abandoned him and found employment in Tokyo. Later, she remarried and had three daughters, whom she and her new journalist husband raised. Hani rejected later stock suggestions that her divorce from her first husband had been a typical case of a mother-in-law repelling her daughter-in-law, pointing out that she had never even met her mother-in-law.[143]

Besides showing the real possibility of wives initiating divorce, the above cases also contain some rather typical features of the early modern marriage and divorce system in Japan. No wedding ceremony or marriage registration figures in the narratives. All the wives had very short marriages. The divorced wives returned to their natal households, worked, and above all used the opportunity to remarry, and, depending on the individual, their new marriages either once again ended in divorce or succeeded.

Early Modern Divorce Revisited

The culture of divorce in the 1870s placed no restraints on mutual-consent divorce. Spouses or families who agreed on divorce and the terms of divorce were free to divorce any way they wanted. Compared with a system that required court mediation and divorce according to a set of limited specific grounds, divorce in Japan was indeed easy and there was no suggestion that divorce needed to be prevented. Simple divorce procedures facilitated divorce, but what really sustained divorce rates was the prevalent belief that what humans had voluntarily united, humans could voluntarily dissolve. A failed marriage was a mismatch between spouses and/or their families, not a personal moral failure. When a wife or *muko yōshi* clashed with the ways of a particular house, she or he was permitted to try again with another family. The new match was possibly better able to fulfill mutual expectations. In remarriage, spouses were given a second chance.

The finality of the dissolution of marriage was also an important aspect of the culture of divorce in the 1870s. Since the marital ties were cut, no further relationship or obligation existed between spouses after divorce. This had ramifications for the financial settlement at divorce, child custody agreements, and above all, remarriage. In the material sense, by reexchanging the bridewealth and dowry that they had invested in a marriage, divorcing spouses and their families returned to the financial status quo ante. Only in exceptional cases, such as extremely long marriages, was any form of alimony even considered. After divorce, the spousal duty to provide material support ceased abruptly. Child custody ideals, whether keeping all the children together in the families of birth or granting parents custody of children of the same sex, to a lesser degree also reflect the belief in a termination of family ties through divorce. The scant references to a father paying child support for his daughters in their mother's custody, or to a mother giving property to children remaining under their father's roof, suggest that these kinds of arrangement were rather unusual. The continuation of other bonds of a parent with a child not in his or her custody is not even discussed. Last, but not least, the ability to remarry instantly after divorce conformed to the notion that the relationship between the spouses indeed totally ended at the time of divorce. Surprisingly, there were not even any waiting periods to ascertain a wife's pregnancy before remarriage.

Contrary to perceptions in legal precedents and popular plays of the Edo period, it was customarily possible in the 1870s for either the husband or the wife (and their respective families) to initiate divorce. In 1873, a change in the law also legally recognized demands of divorce from the side of the wife, and the increased scope for wives to initiate divorce may already have influenced answers in the survey two years later. A more likely interpretation is that both state legislation in 1873 and the survey in 1875 reflect a general culture of divorce that was permissive of wives' dissolving their marriages. If this was indeed so in the 1870s, it should logically at least to some extent already have been the case in the Edo period, but then the question arises of why we are still under such a strong impression that Edo wives were disadvantaged when it came to divorce. The answer probably lies, not only in Edo social policy and gender ideology, but in the process of modernization, which justified change by disparaging the past.

5

Between French Law and Japanese Customs
Codifying Divorce in Meiji Japan

ON 15 MAY 1873, Council of State Decree No. 162 permitted a wife and her natal family to sue a husband for divorce in court. "When the husband denies his wife a divorce," the decree explained, "he violates her rights of personal freedom" (*jinmin jiyū no kenri*) and "prevents her remarriage." In such a case, the wife, accompanied by her father, brothers, or relatives, was allowed to sue in court at once.[1] In July 1873, a decree on legal procedure further extended the right of a wife to sue for divorce. Although it required the plaintiff in a divorce suit, whether husband or wife, to obtain two seals of parents, grandparents, or relatives on the document requesting divorce, it permitted the wife to sue by herself in emergencies when "she was unable to inform her relatives."[2] In 1891, the law on legal procedure unconditionally recognized the legal personality of the wife by fully affirming the right of wives to sue for divorce in a court of law.[3]

Scholars now consider the 1873 decrees milestones in the legal history of divorce in Japan, stepping-stones toward greater legal equality in divorce between husbands and wives.[4] Hozumi Shigetō, an eminent prewar scholar of family law, called them "the Meiji revolution in divorce law."[5] This legislation by the group of political leaders forming the new Meiji government thus came to be interpreted as supporting female emancipation by liberating wives from unwanted shackles of marriage. Some scholars even went so far as to attribute the extremely high divorce rates recorded since the 1880s to the wife's right to sue for divorce, obtained in 1873, implying that the new regulations providing for judicial divorce also encouraged more wives to seek divorce outside of the courts.

While no shogunate law prohibited a wife from seeking a divorce through magistrates, the decrees by the new government were the first affirmation of a general right on the wife's side to obtain a divorce through the intervention of a government institution. The very government institution deemed responsible for such divorce suits, namely, the modern court (*saibansho*), was itself a product of the recent political transformation. After the Ministry of Justice was established in July 1871, it slowly claimed control over Japan's various judicial organs, for example, envisioning a national system of courts of five types in August 1872.[6] At first it seemed that Japan was embarking in 1873 on a road leading to a divorce system resembling that of many contemporary Western nations, which not only offered, but required, court intervention in divorce. Instead of simply adapting such foreign models, however, the Japanese government eventually came up with an indigenous solution for settling divorces, enshrined in the 1898 Civil Code. The code distinguished between divorce by mutual consent (*kyōgi rikon*), effective by registration in the family register, and court divorce (*saiban rikon*) according to ten specific grounds, which a court needed to adjudicate before a divorce could be registered. This dual divorce system restricted the role of courts to contested divorce cases.

The dual divorce system subsequently lasted for more than a century, so it is interesting to trace its evolution as a legal construction in the process leading to the civil code. Perceptions of the state's actual and ideal role in regulating, or not regulating, family affairs, and of the nature of family, marriage, divorce, and gender relations, loomed large in the ensuing twists and turns in Meiji codification of the law governing divorce. Debates on establishing a system of divorce were accompanied by controversies over whether, and which, grounds for divorce should be admitted into the codes. By 1873, the government had not yet made up its mind on the issue of grounds for divorce. Decree No. 162, for example, contained no concrete reasons justifying or limiting divorce, for the government condoned the divorce request of a wife simply when the dissolution of the marriage was "unavoidable." While the decree on divorce procedure of the same year required a recording of the reasons (*gen'yu*) for divorce in the documents for the divorce suit, it detailed no grounds needed for such a suit.[7] Decades of debate eventually led to specific grounds for divorce, but prominent members of the committees drafting the civil code promoted no-fault court divorce even after the mid 1890s. Less important in their potential impact on divorce than the system of divorce itself, the grounds for divorce received wider public attention because of their controversial ideological significance in seeking to "teach morality" to citizens.

Intellectual Interpretations of Divorce
in the 1870s and 1880s

In the 1870s, divorce was not a major topic of debate. The enlightened intellectuals of the influential Meiroku Society, many of whom otherwise strongly urged reform of marriage and family relations along Western lines, touched on divorce only somewhat incidentally in their magazine between 1873 and 1875. In his diatribe against concubines, which generated a conservative outcry against his egalitarian marriage ideal, Mori Arinori referred to divorce as an example of the social inequalities between men and women. Lamenting the lack of "national legislation against arbitrary divorce by the husband simply because [the wife] does not please him," he argued for the state to protect women from such divorces.[8] He was not, however, against divorce in principle. In a sequel in which he outlined his belief in the importance of mutual sexual fidelity in marriage, he urged the state to assure the possibility of divorce in case of adultery or "unbearable immoral treatment" by either spouse. The injured party, moreover, should be entitled to "a monetary settlement" of up to "two-thirds of the property of the other party."[9] His divorce philosophy derived from a belief in marriage as an exclusive sexual relationship, infringement of which should constitute the sole reason for divorce. Rather than simply changing the divorce laws, he aimed at transforming public morality to eliminate the double standard for men and women. He criticized the then-current legal system for not guaranteeing wives the power to divorce unfaithful husbands, while letting husbands divorce for reasons of their own choosing (although he in fact did so himself, divorcing his own wife on the grounds that she did not live up to his ideals of modern femininity). But his rather meek demands for divorce reform were symptomatic of the lack of pressure by intellectuals on the government to alter divorce legislation in the 1870s.

These attitudes began to change with the start of the publication of divorce statistics increasing awareness of high divorce rates. An 1881 article in *Kojun zasshi* analyzed divorce in the nation's capital, where 8,667 women married, while a staggering 4,203 women divorced in 1879. A search of causes for the common occurrence of divorce included a criticism of the state of society. The article proposed four reasons: (1) rash marriages, (2) poverty, (3) pressure of the system, and (4) ease of divorce. Divorce due to rash marriage occurred when a man and woman married on the spur of the moment, without consulting even their best friends or parents. Poverty became a reason for divorce when spouses lacked work skills and children were born, or one of the spouses became impaired by disease. Pressure of the system meant the unrestricted authority of adoptive parents, parents-in-law, and husband to expel an adopted child or wife for allegedly not fitting into the family tradition (*kafū*), even when the expelled person was complying with the duty to love (*ren'ai*). The ease of divorce was seen when a person left one house today to marry into another tomorrow.[10] Whether divorce was attributed to thoughtless marriages, lack of earning potential, uneven distribution of authority in the family, or low barriers to exit, the popular acceptance of divorce was the overarching theme. More important than the analysis is the conclusion drawn from the article: there was no call to prevent divorce by law.

Fukuzawa Yukichi, a famous figure of the Japanese enlightenment, participated in the search for causes for divorce, which was "common and frequent in this country," and in 1886, he singled out insufficient social interaction between men and women. Many spouses met each other for the first time when they exchanged sake cups at the marriage ceremony, he said, even forgoing the superficial trial meeting (*miai*), so "marriage is like a lottery." Given this method of choosing spouses, "it is the long-lasting union that is rare." Moreover, spouses communicated little after marriage and thus failed to become close, resulting in "many divorces." After divorce, men could remarry without satisfying the needs of their wives, who were "driven out into the world, forced to wander about as their youthful features quickly give way to wrinkles, indicating the passing of marriageable age. With any chance to remarry gone, they will spend the rest of their lives in misery."[11] Despite his gloomy scenario of the causes and consequences of divorce, Fukuzawa ruled out restrictive divorce legislation in imitation of "Western ways," expecting disastrous effects on moral behavior. Because divorce was just a symptom of shallow gender relations, Fukuzawa doubted the desirability of laws against divorce.

A comparison of international statistics inspired Yokoyama Masao, a member of the fledgling Tokyo Statistical Association, to explore the reasons for divorce in a book on marriage produced in 1887 by the publishing company of a women's magazine influenced by Christian beliefs.[12] Yokoyama took a rather detached approach to divorce, although he called it an evil practice (*heigai*), which was more frequent in Japan than in any other society on earth.[13] He identified a plethora of causes for divorce, including the ease of marriage and divorce, parental interference in marriage, lack of consent at marriage, deception by the go-between, cupidity, and simple poverty, echoing the previously advanced reasons.[14]

His survey was less impressionistic than most studies of divorce in the 1880s, and he presented rather detailed evidence in the language of social science, at times resorting to foreign statistics if none were available for Japan. He took the most restrictive stance in terms of legislation, enumerating six specific grounds for divorce to be included in a future Japanese civil code.[15]

The evolutionary theory of divorce advanced in 1885 by the legal professional Hozumi Nobushige deserves particular attention. Divorce systems, Hozumi said, went through a historical cycle: free divorce (*jiyū rikon*), no divorce (*rikon kinshi*), restricted divorce (*seigen rikon*), and, again, free divorce. He linked his four stages in the divorce cycle to the development of a country's culture (*bunka*). At the lowest end, he positioned free divorce in "several East Asian countries"; countries of "low and high culture," such as Belgium and Italy, prohibited divorce; and civilized countries with "above average culture," such as England and Prussia, restricted divorce. No country had yet reached the fourth stage of culture with free divorce. From this view of progressive divorce cycles, Hozumi derived his prescriptions for a Japanese system of divorce. Japan should aim to move gradually from the first to the last stage of divorce. Although both ends had free divorce, in the first stage, men retained the exclusive freedom to divorce, whereas in the last stage, spouses decided together, based on equality (*byōdō*), resulting in genuinely free divorce.[16] By proposing a theory that reinterpreted the free system of divorce, associated with past and present practice in Japan, as the ultimate stage of cultural progress, Hozumi was able to discount the relevance of Western legal systems of divorce as models for Japan. Pushing Japanese lawmakers toward a codification of the last stage of his progressive cycle, he attempted to make free divorce palatable to those supporting a more restricted system. Through the establishment of a civil code in Japan, he implied, it was possible to surpass European countries by jumping to the latest stage in the historical cycle of divorce. The government officials then in charge of civil code preparation were not responsive to Hozumi's position, however, as shown by the draft of 1887, which had the most restrictive divorce provisions in the Meiji period. In the long term, Hozumi's ideas contributed to a transformation of the perception of free divorce from a traditional to a modern practice, partly by his own involvement in the committees revising the family provisions of the civil code in the next decade.

The Napoleonic Code and the Early Codification Process, 1873–1887

On 10 March 1873, just before the government passed Decree No. 162, affirming a wife's right to sue for divorce, the Ministry of Justice completed a provisional draft of a Japanese civil code containing 88 articles. The driving force behind this was the ministry's activist leader, Etō Shinpei, who was also responsible for Decree No. 162.[17] While this draft code made little reference to divorce (*rien*), an expanded version of 140 articles completed in October, entitled "Civil Code, The First Part, Book on Persons," had fairly detailed regulations on the procedure and consequences of divorce.[18]

The divorce provisions distinguished between uncontested and contested divorces. Article 61 suggested a simple procedure for uncontested divorces: "Following mutual deliberations [*sōhō jukudan*] and approval by the go-between and relatives, the registration official [*kochō*] should be notified of the divorce." Contested divorce was more complicated. Either spouse could sue for divorce, invoking any of several grounds, such as excessive sexual desire, cruelty, or grave harm (*kayoku kagyaku mata wa shichō no gai*), murder, theft or assault (*zokutō jinmei nado no tsumi*). Two articles had a gender-specific component. Under "unbearable circumstance," a wife could even sue for divorce on her own in the absence of her husband's consent. Only a husband, though, could sue for divorce on grounds of adultery (*kantsū*). Despite their ambiguity, especially in the case of unbearable circumstances, the grounds for divorce implied that the other spouse was at fault. As a result, depending on the kind of divorce and the grounds for divorce, the regulations varied for arrangements of property division, support payment (*yōryō*), and dowry money return, even affecting child custody and remarriage.[19] This draft of October 1873 already contained what was to remain an integral feature of further divorce codification, namely, a bifurcation between no-fault consensual divorce and contested divorce according to specific "fault" grounds. There were two primary sources of inspiration for this split in divorce procedure.

One important model for Japanese draft codes was the so-called Napoleonic Code, enacted in France in 1804, interest in which in Japan dated back to translation projects begun in the late 1860s.[20] Marriage under the Napoleonic Code was a secular civil contract, and divorce was permitted, which was by no means a standard European practice in the early 1800s. Although familiar to the Japanese, freedom to divorce was an innovation in the European context, where the Church regulated matrimony in many countries, especially those with large Catholic populations. Even in France, the right to divorce was not firmly entrenched. After the return to power of the Bourbon dynasty, divorce was prohibited again in France in 1815 "in the interest of religion, of morality, of the monarchy, of families." It took much acrimonious political debate before the parliament reestablished divorce—and then only by reason of some specific fault—in 1884.[21] Most important, the Napoleonic Code offered both divorce on specific grounds (*le divorce pour cause determinée*) and consensual divorce (*le divorce par consentement mutuel*).[22] Several European countries permitted divorce on specified grounds by a decision of parliament (legislative divorce), royal decree (executive divorce), or court decision (judicial divorce), but consensual divorce had only occasionally been accepted and, when it was, this was often under French influence. The particular regulations for divorce that made the Napoleonic Code appeal to the Japanese in the 1870s were thus far from being standard contemporary European legal practice. In fact, the divorce provisions of the Napoleonic Code, which permitted divorce after rather onerous procedures, were a legacy of previous reforms of the French Revolution, which in September 1792 instituted the most liberal divorce regime then available in Europe. The French Revolution thus indirectly provided Japanese bureaucrats with suggestions on how to regulate divorce.

Because Japanese customary law in the 1870s left the decision to divorce to the spouses and their families, without forcing them to follow specific restricted divorce grounds imposed by the state, the appeal of the French provisions to Japanese officials drafting civil codes is immediately obvious. They enabled them to codify Japanese customary divorce practices through reference to one of the most influential European civil codes, which the French armies had exported to Belgium, the Netherlands, Italy, and parts of Germany, and which later was applied throughout the French empire.[23] The fact that several European countries never accepted or subsequently restricted and eliminated the divorce laws, just as France did, was ignored by Japanese officials. As late as 1891, an important Japanese civil code drafter cited the French civil code in reference to consensual divorce without mentioning that it had long ceased to exist in France itself.[24] The Japanese draft of October 1873 diverged from the Napoleonic Code in one important provision, namely, by permitting divorce by registration without the need for any form of judicial involvement to ascertain "consent." This specification for obtaining a divorce by registration when uncontested and by suit (in court) when contested not only conformed to the recently instituted requirement of registering family events in the family register but also must have been motivated by the simple lack of courts to fulfill such functions. When attempts were made to abolish divorce by registration in civil code drafts of the late 1880s, this was a break with earlier drafts that condoned and reaffirmed popular practices.

Other features of family law, often linked to samurai traditions, received more attention, as was revealed in a newspaper debate on adoption, which incidentally contributed to a renewed interest in Japanese customs.[25] Ōki Takatō, the minister of justice since the autumn of 1873, responded by calling for officials to gather customs throughout the land, the results to be returned by March 1875.[26] In June, Ōki was appointed to head the next compilation committee, but work started in earnest only in March 1876.[27] The small committee included Mitsukuri Rinshō and the French legal advisor Gustave-Emile Boissonade de Fontarabie, who had come to Japan in November 1873. They completed a substantial draft with 1,820 articles by April 1878. This draft, like its predecessor, failed to be promulgated; it lacked full support from Ōki, who was dissatisfied with the provisions on adoptions, and, as usual, it was criticized for insufficient deference to Japanese customs. Even if the government had not already committed itself to compiling a constitution before a civil code, with the Satsuma rebellion just put down in 1877, it probably lacked the financial and administrative resources to put such a code into effect at the time.[28]

Despite years of intermittent drafting, the civil code took a back seat to legal work on the constitution, which in 1881 the emperor promised by the end of the decade. The government made a fresh attempt with a group working again with the French advisor Boissonade, which completed most of the civil code by 1886. In 1887, two Japanese legal experts with degrees from French universities, Isobe Shirō (1851–1923) and Kumano Toshizō (1854–99), drafted the family provisions to forestall criticism that these were at variance with Japanese traditions. Isobe and Kumano nevertheless chose to closely follow the divorce provisions of the Napoleonic Code, which, as noted, had been abrogated in France. With the passage of the so-called Naquet Law in 1884, the French parliament readmitted divorce, but without the consensual clause of the revolutionary and Napoleonic eras.[29]

In addition to the option of divorce by mutual consent (*sōhō kyōgi*) or by one-sided demand based on special reasons (*tokutei gen'yu no tame ippōteki yori*), the draft presented to Japan's Ministry of Justice in 1888 introduced the very cumbersome divorce procedures of the Napoleonic Code.[30] The draft asked spouses to file for divorce every three months for a total of four times (Article 126), required consent to divorce by parents or lineal ascendants (Article 120), and urged a certificate detailing property division and funding for support of the residence, spouse, and children during the divorce preparation period (Article 121). Only after passing through repeated attempts at admonishments and conciliation by the judge (*hanji*) were the spouses able to divorce (Articles 124 and 126).[31] Earlier Japanese drafts based on the Napoleonic Code omitted most details of that code's long divorce procedures. This draft thus differed from previous drafts, Japanese legal tradition, and contemporary practice. Most important of all, it required all divorces to pass through a court of law, a divorce procedure included for the first time in a Japanese civil code draft.

The close adherence to the divorce provisions of the Napoleonic Code by this unusually restrictive draft was driven by the aspiration of committee members to contain divorce as far as possible. The commentary explained:

Marriage is the base of society.... Legislators should not prohibit divorce, but should regulate its usage for the benefit [*rieki*] of society and stop its abuse [*ranyō*]. In view of the actual conditions in our country today, freedom of divorce, because it gradually leads to evil customs [*heifū*], needs to be regulated and evil customs reformed. Freedom of divorce increases careless marriages, and careless marriages become the reason for divorce.... Therefore by restricting marriages, the number of divorces will decrease, and again by restricting divorce, [people] will marry more cautiously.... to change the system of divorce, and to restrict its freedom, is the purpose of court interference [*saibansho no kanshō*].[32]

At the heart of the belief in strict regulation of divorce was the notion that the role of the government was to get involved in divorce to preserve marriages. What compelled this call for state activism was the stress on the conjugal couple as the basis of society, as opposed to lineage or the family. In the face of this redefinition of social priorities, divorce could not be left up to spouses, families, and society, since it threatened the very core of personal relations, instead of being just an incidental byproduct of human behavior. Emphasis on marriage did not mean gender equality, as seen in the grounds for divorce. The draft retained the sexual double standard, albeit in a weakened form, as grounds for divorce. Adultery (*kantsū*) by the wife constituted grounds for divorce, but adultery by the husband was grounds only if he had been legally punished for it.[33]

The Backlash against "French" Divorce, 1887–1892

The Ministry of Justice disagreed with the spirit of the family provisions of the Isobe-Kumano draft, considering it too egalitarian and conjugal-centered. It revised the draft fundamentally, among other things enhancing the position of the household head in relation to household members and insisting on indivisible inheritance of property by a single heir.[34] In terms of matrimony, it rejected the draft's restrictive approach to divorce, eliminating judicial procedures in the case of consensual divorce.[35] The senate (*genrōin*) later abolished even the requirement for court approval of a consensual divorce.[36] Some outspokenly conservative senate members attacked the divorce provisions of the code in a debate on 21 April 1890. Murata Tamotsu considered the provisions permitting a wife to secure a divorce despite her husband's opposition as "sheer individualism" and branded as "nonsense" the expectation that a husband be faithful to his wife.[37] Finally, the government eliminated court involvement in consensual divorce, but reaffirmed an institutional dichotomy between consensual divorce by simple registration and court divorce based on specified grounds.

In May 1889, four months after the promulgation of the constitution, the Society of Legal Scholars (Hōgakushikai) of Tōkyō University graduates started what turned out to be a virulent public controversy over codifications then in progress. Afraid of losing professional influence, since many of its members were trained in English law, it called for amendments aiming at greater legal consistency in the Japanese codes. Instead of a French-influenced civil law and a German-influenced commercial law and law of procedures, it urged delay and the consideration of a wider body of laws. What might have ended as a professional squabble among lawyers gained a large political dimension due to the government's determination to pass important legislation before the newly established Diet convened on 25 November 1890. The government promulgated several laws in 1890, including a civil code to take effect on 1 January 1893. In its very first session, the Diet voted for postponement of the implementation of the commercial code, further encouraging criticism of the civil code. An August 1891 article with the provocative title "Adopting This Civil Code Will Destroy Loyalty and Filial Piety," by the Tōkyō University law professor Hozumi Yatsuka, the younger brother of Nobushige, provided a rallying cry for the opposition. In May 1892, the Diet voted by a large majority to also delay implementation of the civil code. The government established a code review committee (*hōten chōsakai*), including members of both the fast-implementation and postponement factions among professors of law at Tōkyō University, such as Ume Kenjirō, Tomii Masaaki, and Hozumi Nobushige.[38]

Reaffirming the Dual Divorce System, 1892–1898

Between 8 and 13 January 1896, the code review committee examined the divorce provisions paragraph by paragraph, with the head of the committee, the legal scholar Tomii Masaaki, first explaining the reasons for each paragraph before the seventeen members in attendance responded with questions or silent agreement. After looking at all existing regulations, the committee discussed further amendments. Although high divorce rates were the recurrent starting point for most discussions on divorce in public debate, during the meetings, the code drafters seem to have been less eager to deal with the frequency of divorce.

The easiest way to combat divorce, if desired, would have been to require court intervention for all divorces, according to state-sanctioned grounds, as was the widespread legal practice in Europe. If consensual divorce was to be permitted, onerous procedures, such as those in the earlier Isobe-Kumano draft, could have dampened the desire to divorce. Nothing along these lines happened in the committee meetings; consensual divorce by registration was one of the least controversial paragraphs, with only one member, Tomii Masaaki, even speaking on the issue.

Tomii's view on divorce, shared by the majority of the committee through silent approval, was marked by a laissez-faire approach. Using the law to force spouses to remain in a dysfunctional marriage defeated the very purpose of marriage based on a feeling of harmony (*kokoro no wagō*), so Tomii concluded that divorce should be permitted. "When conjugal life in peace" was impossible, "it was preferable to break up the marriage by mutual consent [*sōhō no kyōgi*]." While his marriage philosophy stressed the circumstances under which the dissolution of a marriage was desirable, it did not yet justify a particular method for such consensual divorce. Tomii rejected foreign legislation as a model for codifying divorce in Japan outright, arguing that religious opposition to divorce in foreign countries had made judicial divorce predominant worldwide, with few consensual divorce systems. Having reduced other laws and institutions of divorce to the restrictive influence of Christianity, he then proceeded to elaborate on the logic of including consensual divorce by registration in a Japanese civil code.

Consensual divorce conformed to "established laws" in Japan, Tomii elaborated, and, especially if it were based on the grounds for judicial divorce, had several advantages over an exclusively legal divorce process, notably in that it kept indecencies (*futeisai*) within the family instead of broadcasting them. Moreover, Japanese disliked bringing personal affairs into court, and a strong insistence on judicial divorce would infringe upon the "distinctively beautiful manners and customs of our country."[39]

Although there was a consensus in the committee in favor of consensual divorce, it limited contested divorce to specific grounds. This appears contradictory. If both spouses agreed on divorce, they needed no justification, but if only one spouse wanted the marriage dissolved, a court of law would terminate it exclusively on the basis of grounds approved by the state. A marriage based on the feeling of harmony, to use Tomii's definition, would lose its purpose as soon as one of the spouses wanted to dissolve it. So why did the committee prevent this spouse from leaving? Committee members were aware of the clash between free consent and restrictive court divorce. The legal scholar Hozumi Nobushige proposed an amendment to solve this problem, namely, the inclusion of a no-fault provision for judicial divorce, but the majority rejected this amendment consistent with the permissive philosophy of consensual divorce.

The philosophy behind establishing specific grounds for divorce, now under the rubric of "Court Divorce" (*saiban rikon*), as opposed to the previous title, "Special Reasons," was explained as usual by Tomii, who praised it as "reform of the system of divorce":

In the old days, divorce was accepted for various strange reasons, such as not having a child, jealousy, talkativeness, and sickness.[40] All of these enabled the husband to divorce at his own discretion, which was the system in the Tokugawa period. When we look at documents of this period, we see that divorce of the wife depended on the will of her husband, who also decided whether to return the wife's dowry furniture and money. The husband could divorce at any time, even when the wife was pregnant. This may have been necessary in such a world, but in today's society such licentious [*midara*] behavior is inappropriate. While I do not think that divorce should be difficult, if the grounds are ambiguous, as today's troublesome grounds for divorce certainly are in the extreme, that means that law courts have to judge according to customary law. . . . which must lead to many evil practices [*heigai*].[41]

In contrast to arbitrary divorce decided by the husband, Tomii posited the ideal of a law court judging according to grounds specified by national law. The intent behind codifying the grounds for divorce was to provide protection from divorce unless specific grounds violated the nature of the marriage. The state became arbiter in contested divorces, and the existence of a spouse's right to divorce simply upon breakdown of a marriage was denied.

The no-fault amendment proposed by Hozumi Nobushige,[42] too, left it up to a court to decide whether spouses should remain married: "Article 824 . . . when one of the spouses sues for divorce on the grounds of disharmony when life together is unbearable [*taezaru*], a court may declare a divorce when there is no hope of future harmony [*wajuku*]."[43] Nevertheless, the amendment opened up possibilities for divorce against the wishes of a "faultless" spouse. While a different term was used to describe the necessary conditions for divorce than in the divorce decrees of 1873, the intentions in the amendment are comparable. Attached to the article was a commentary, but since Hozumi suspected that "few had the time to read it," he also justified his no-fault amendment in a long speech in favor of a system of consensual divorce paired with free judicial divorce (*saibansho no jiyū rikonshugi*).

The essential premise of Hozumi's argument in favor of no-fault judicial divorce was that love (*aijō*) and free consent (*jiyū shōdaku*) were the basis for marriage and conjugal life, and these were things that a law could hardly regulate. When love expired and life together became impossible, the marriage de facto ceased to exist, and thus it should be dissolved. He criticized the planned civil code for limiting divorce to grounds defined by legislators, whereas love might expire for all kinds of other reasons. When a law made marriage indissoluble, he said, it ignored the nature of marriage (*kon'in no honshitsu*) and opposed morality (*tokugi*). He invoked the principle of human liberty (*hito no jiyū*) when advocating no-fault divorce, as did the divorce decrees of 1873. He was far more drastic in his elaboration, however, calling restricted divorce a "system of slavery," something otherwise outlawed in Japan.

After polemical remarks on the social side effects of restricted divorce, such as predicting an increase in illicit unions (*yago*), illegitimate children (*shiseiji*), adultery (*kantsū*), and the crumbling of morality among spouses, especially among the lower classes, he concluded his commentary with his theory of progressive liberalization of divorce laws as outlined more than a decade earlier, but this time with more concrete facts. Not only had Prussia and Switzerland already adopted provisions resembling his amendment, but the divorce laws of European countries had loosened generally, and European statistics showed divorce to be broadly on the rise.

Hozumi's fervent support for a no-fault amendment raises the question of why he did not support the even more radical solution of allowing either spouse to decide unilaterally on divorce without judicial barriers. This option he discarded as an extreme liberty (*kyokutan no jiyūshugi*), although permitted by the past and present divorce system in Japan, in which divorce was possible by unilateral registration and through a divorce notice. The role of the court was to prevent such abuse.⁴⁴

Here Hozumi seems inconsistent. If love is the base of marriage, a husband should be permitted to divorce his wife even against her wishes if he does not love her, so why require court intervention? What Hozumi intended, without writing it into his commentary, probably for fear of conservative criticism, was that the role of the court should be to support the wife in her divorce suit when her husband refused to give in. The short inquiries after his speech support this impression. When asked to clarify whether the current Japanese divorce procedures enabled unilateral divorce, he replied invoking a timeless East Asian pattern of divorce: "The custom was [divorce] by the consent of the husband and, as you all know, even the Taihō Code included no provision for a divorce request by the wife. In China also . . . a husband leaves his wife and divorces her, but he has the power to refuse her divorce request. Compared with this custom, consensual divorce is an enormous revolution [*taihen na kakumei*]."⁴⁵ This rather sweeping answer puzzled the inquiring legislator, who felt compelled to repeat his question, asking specifically whether it was possible under the current system to divorce a wife unilaterally in Japan. Hozumi's evasive reply, "I am not really that informed about our country's customs," still had him insisting that it was not a system whereby "both are on the same level, the wife requesting divorce from her husband and the husband leaving his wife."⁴⁶

Since no committee member criticized the amendment before the chair pronounced it dead, there is room for speculation as to why it failed. Hozumi's egalitarian notion of a love-based marriage that was dissoluble by either husband or wife, regardless of the grounds for divorce, could have been resisted both by those wanting to restrict the wife's power and by those afraid of the husband's abuse. In either scenario, approval of Hozumi's proposal meant opening up more possibilities for divorce. Although not voiced in committee, it is likely that opposition to no-fault divorce also derived from an aversion to granting the wife the right to obtain a divorce against her husband's consent, which was an issue touched upon in the debate on mental illness as grounds for divorce. Hasegawa stated, "I have never seen or heard of a case in which the wife asked for divorce on the grounds that the husband was ruined [*reiraku*] or had become ill [*hatsubyō*] or insane [*fūten*]."⁴⁷ Nevertheless, Hozumi Nobushige persisted and again proposed a no-fault amendment during a session of what was then called the code consolidation committee (*hōten seirikai*) in July 1897, the main opponent of which was the legal scholar Ume Kenjirō, who said: "Marriage is not simply based on love . . . divorce greatly harms society . . . the fewer divorces the better." The bad effects Hozumi expected when divorce was restricted, Ume called absurd fears (*kiyū*).[48] Unlike a year and a half earlier, several committee members, including Hozumi's younger brother Yatsuka, spoke in support of the amendment, but when it came to a vote, only a minority stood up for it.

The Civil Code of 1898: Divorce, Family, and Gender

The permanence of Japan's dual system of divorce for more than a hundred years evolved from a drafting process that with interruptions took about thirty years. Establishing a system of divorce in a civil code became entangled in larger issues of the proper role of a modern state vis-à-vis the family, conflicting interpretations of modernity and Japanese traditions, desire for international recognition and a search for national identity, antagonistic views of the desirability of individualism and community, and incongruous expectations regarding patriarchy and gender relations. The debates leading to the civil code left such a deep mark on social discourse that the battles of yesterday are still being fought today, especially when critical scholarship lambastes the code for a betrayed modernity or for picking the wrong tradition. In their most recent guise, old antagonisms reappeared in a leading Japanese feminist scholar's characterization of the code as an invented tradition in the Hobsbawmian sense, repeating claims that samurai patriarchal family ideals shaped the provisions of family law.[49] We should not, however, overlook the fact that the process of codifying divorce provisions in Japan, although intimately linked with the above problems, also had a particular history of its own.

In contrast to twentieth-century scholarship's emphasis on the lack of protection (for the wife) from divorce prior to the 1898 civil code, influential Meiji legal experts and legislators stressed the importance of maintaining the freedom to divorce (or expanding it to include the wife). Efforts by French-trained Japanese lawyers to establish a restrictive system of divorce with mandatory judicial involvement for all divorces, in a draft of 1887, failed to gain wider government support and were quickly reversed in the ensuing revision process. By 1890, consensual divorce by registration was firmly entrenched in the so-called Old Civil Code, which was never enforced. Later arguments focused on the specific grounds for court divorce; a strong majority defeated attempts to ease judicial divorce by rejecting no-fault grounds. To divorce a reluctant spouse, the code provided only the avenue of specific grounds based on the principle of "fault." According to the code's legal theory, a legally innocent spouse opposed to divorce was thus secure in marriage. In contrast to other intellectuals, legal experts in the codification debates construed society according to abstract ideals, mostly ignoring such mundane issues as high divorce rates, although they professed awareness of those issues. There is no evidence of the Japanese government pressuring the various drafting committees to devise ways to reduce divorce rates through civil code legislation. Neither is there any indication that the code review committee as a whole intended to limit divorce "directly as a political program" as some scholars have assumed.[50] When a massive slump in the divorce rate followed the promulgation of the 1898 Civil Code, this happened more by default than by design.

Any legal system of divorce must set priorities, ranging from freedom to divorce even against the wishes of the other spouse to total protection from divorce by its outright banning. The effects of divorce, moreover, such as property and custody settlements and remarriage, often fall under divorce law. As noted, the dual system of divorce in the 1898 Civil Code reflected an ingenious adaptation of the divorce provisions of the Napoleonic Code and of the customary Japanese practice of minimal government arbitration in matrimonial matters. The outcome of codification, it should be noted, not without irony, bore some resemblance to the liberal and egalitarian divorce legislation of the French Revolution in 1792, which also let the family play a large role in divorce arbitration. Just as in Japan, the French law left consensual divorces up to the family, entrusting it to an assembly of relatives; unlike in Japan, however, in revolutionary France even in contested cases of unilateral demand, a family court, composed of relatives, friends, or neighbors, acted as a regular court with the power to dissolve the marriage.[51] Consensual divorces in both legal systems were available to all because of the lack of expense, a characteristic not shared by other pre-twentieth-century systems of royal, legislative, or judicial divorce.

Beyond the codification of consensual divorce, the 1898 Civil Code stands out by virtue of its relative neglect of the consequences of divorce, an influential legacy still seen in the late-twentieth-century philosophy and practice of divorce in Japan. One of the reasons for this neglect was the notion that the end of marriage also terminates mutual obligations, an assumption also found in the popular culture of divorce in the 1870s.

The code accordingly lacked regulations on property division and alimony after divorce, implicitly assuming the heads of the natal households to be responsible for upkeep of the respective spouses. Committee members at times considered the possibility of including provisions for alimony as seen in drafts until the mid 1890s. In 1896, for example, the draft had a paragraph regulating the duty to maintain a divorced spouse during litigation and after a court decision, until death or remarriage, depending on the grounds for divorce and whether the spouse was self-supporting. The presentation of this paragraph was followed by critical remarks by those afraid of divorced wives demanding lifelong support from their ex-husbands, along the lines of "Japan's customs should not be restricted," "excessively selfish," "excessively free," and sheer "liberalism."[52] Eventually, this paragraph was discarded. By contrast, committee members never proposed alimony in cases of consensual divorce.

Spouses were permitted to settle child custody any way they wanted in consensual divorce, but in case of disagreement, the father received custody of his children, unless he was an in-marrying husband. In this way, the law thus granted the father a right to veto any custody arrangement he disliked. Judicial divorce did not, however, follow exactly the same principle. The court was to decide custody for the benefit of the child.[53] Nevertheless, paternal custody was still presumed. As explained during deliberations, established laws and practice granted the father custody, and child custody for the mother would be inconvenient (*fuben*) and impractical (*futsugō*) in Japan. In cases where the father was guilty of cruelty, or when the child had not yet been weaned, though, the child was judged better off with the mother.[54] The committee members, all men, agreed unanimously on the principles of custody arrangements. None mentioned divergent foreign laws with custodial preference for the mother, or even the other Japanese customary principles as recorded in 1875, which granted custody of girls to mothers and boys to fathers. The regulations of the code were, however, flexible enough not to obstruct alternative arrangements.

Unlike her ex-husband, the ex-wife had one obligation resulting from marriage after divorce, namely, to wait six months before remarriage (Article 767). This waiting period, still on the books today, also applied to widows. The period also ended "from the day of her delivery," showing that its intent was to assure the paternity of children born after the end of a marriage. This provision, which was contrary to practice as recorded in the 1875 survey, was a borrowing from similar regulations in Europe and had been included since the first civil code drafts.

Divorce codes have often contained provisions limited to a particular time or ideology—such as, for example, making political emigration (revolutionary France), alcoholism (nineteenth-century Anglo-Saxon codes), or racial mismatch (Nazi Germany) grounds for divorce. What sets Japan's 1898 Civil Code apart is its privileging of lineage. The requirement that parents or lineal ascendants approve the consensual divorce of a spouse under twenty-five years old involved senior family members in divorce, just as they had a say in the marriage of sons under thirty and girls under twenty-five, ages far above the average age at first marriage. More eye-catching are two particular grounds for divorce not found elsewhere: divorce due to insult by or of the spouse's lineal ascendants, and divorce consequent to dissolution of the adoption of a *muko yōshi* (Article 813: 7, 8, 10).

A double standard for husbands and wives in terms of sexuality is visible in the Japanese code and still existed in some contemporary European laws such as in England, France, and Germany.[55] As grounds for judicial divorce, the Japanese code recognized simple adultery (*kantsū*) of the wife, whereas in the case of the husband, adultery was recognized only if he had first been sentenced for illicit sexual intercourse. Already when it was included in the code, the double standard was not beyond reproach. The legal scholar Tomii Masaaki regretted practical obstacles during deliberations, saying "On this point, today's Japanese customs are very difficult to change."[56] Only the adultery of the wife was mentioned as legitimate grounds for divorce in the 1875 survey, so here the code followed the divorce customs of a previous generation. During the first half of the twentieth century, this double standard was repeatedly attacked as epitomizing the legal inequality between men and women, and it became one of the most contested issues of Japanese divorce law, but it remained on the books until the New Code of 1948.

The choice of providing the option of consensual divorce enabled families to decide on their own what they considered to be just grounds for terminating a marriage. As popular attitudes toward marriage changed, divorce could accordingly adapt without the government initiating legislation each time a political consensus formed for new divorce grounds. This highly practical and flexible approach kept most divorce decisions in the family and prevented the state from intervening in divorces. What was mainly meant as the legal institution of tradition appears progressive in retrospect, for the Western world moved away from adherence to the strict fault principle to adopt no-fault court divorce in a process called "the divorce revolution."[57] With just cause, scholars of gender have denounced Japan's 1898 Civil Code as reaffirming patriarchy in the family, but in terms of the divorce provisions, the real gender problem may lie elsewhere. When the issue was raised during deliberations of how really to prevent a husband from forcing a divorce on his wife, in what Tomii called "our country where men have such strong powers," the response was an uncomfortable silence.[58] Finally, the chair moved on, remarking, "This is an important question deserving careful consideration." Nevertheless, the broader problem still lingers on unresolved in Japan and in other countries: What happens when the law institutes formal equality in divorce between men and women while they are still unequal in the society at large?

6

When Marriage Was on the Rise

*Declining Divorce Rates,
1898–1940*

THE MOST SPECULATIVE writings on the history of divorce in Japan and elsewhere are the interpretations of divorce rate changes. Why masses of spouses (and/or their families) chose to divorce (or not to divorce) during a certain period is the basic question in need of resolution. A reform in the system of institutional divorce arbitration is always a natural first target for inquiry, but while new laws often visibly led to short-term shifts in divorce rates, it is less evident to what extent these actually had a long-term impact on setting divorce trends. Gradual movements of divorce rates, unless there was a continuous new direction in legislation, were rarely caused by legal change. In the case of gradual shifts, scholarship has often advanced socioeconomic and attitudinal explanations, such as the employment of women, the ages of spouses at marriage, changing expectations of marriage, the life experience of the divorcing couple, and the feedback effects of changing divorce rates. The standard work on the history of divorce in the West, however, concludes sadly that "despite the wealth of plausible explanations and causes that have been offered to us for consideration, we seem almost as poor in our understanding of divorce as earlier generations were."[1]

Moreover, scholarship on divorce has been preoccupied with a search for explanations for rising divorce rates, reflecting the divorce trajectory in the United States and Europe, with the exception of divorce rate declines after major wars. Since historical scholarship on divorce still barely notices the experiences of the non-Western world, one of the main contributions of writings in English on divorce in Japan so far has simply been to point out that divorce rates do not automatically increase with industrialization, urbanization, and modernization.² Since divorce rates in prewar Japan declined in two stages, abruptly and gradually, this inquiry into the possible reasons for the decline falls into two sections.

Legislation and the Precipitous Drop in Divorce, 1897–1899

Cautious scholars prefer to limit their analyses of divorce to the twentieth century. The 50 percent drop in the number of divorces between 1897 and 1899 is one important reason for this restriction, for it is still unclear whether it reflects an actual change in divorce behavior or is a statistical quirk. If the latter, divorce data for the late nineteenth century must indeed be taken with a grain of salt. This inquiry looks at the problem from a new angle, scanning the official annual Meiji divorce statistics before proposing that both redefinitions of marriage and divorce and new requirements for registration contributed to this steep divorce rate slump.

Meiji Divorce Rates: An Alternative Approach

As previous chapters have shown, divorce rates were high for selected localities in the Edo period, but on average they still appear lower than the extreme ratio of one divorce per three marriages recorded for the two last decades of the nineteenth century. There are three explanations for this disjuncture: (1) insufficient and unrepresentative sampling of Edo-period localities; (2) increase in divorce after the 1870s; and (3) statistical exaggeration of divorce rates since the 1880s.

There are still few data available on Edo divorce rates, since marriage in itself has not usually been one of the main lines of inquiry by demographers, who tend to be preoccupied with the link between economic production and biological reproduction. Nevertheless, as noted, several village studies provide data on divorce.³ Analysts of Edo statistics sometimes face the problem of not clearly knowing when a divorce occurred, since officials registered the departure of a person from a family, but not always whether this was by reason of divorce or death.⁴ In recent years, research on Edo villages has expanded into northeastern Japan, discovering villages with high divorce rates. Although the average frequency of divorce appears somewhat lower during the Edo period than in the last two decades of the nineteenth century, in terms of regional distribution, a correlation is visible between Edo divorce data and later national data. Future research may reveal more diversity and also more places with high divorce rates, probably closing the perception gap between the high-divorce Edo period and the very-high-divorce early Meiji period.

Another possibility is that divorce increased in the turbulent years leading to the Meiji Restoration of 1868 but only became visible in national statistics published in the 1880s. The breakdown of the old political, economic, and cultural order must have put additional stress on dissolution-prone marriages. Once people were used to high marriage rates, correspondingly high rates of divorce persisted until criticism of it mounted and the trend reversed. Although difficult to prove empirically due to the discontinuity in statistics, this hypothesis should not be ignored, for we are still fairly ignorant of the impact of the Restoration on the social fabric of everyday family life.

Much twentieth-century scholarship discounts national statistics for the last two decades of the nineteenth century as exaggerating divorce. That is a reasonable, commonsense stance, considering the incredible abruptness with which they plummeted around the turn of the century, but it raises a question that calls for an explanation. Why did Meiji commentators believe in the general validity of their statistics? This general observation, however, does not prove a particular level of the divorce rate. Even when they pointed to some hypothetical other reason for high divorce rates, such as lower-class behavior, they seem to have had no difficulty accepting that divorce was frequent. Contemporaries did not question this fundamental assertion, and it is hard to imagine that divorce statistics that ran counter to actual social practice led to a national delusion on the issue of divorce.

Japan's first modern census, the enumerative census of 1879 for Kai Province (now Yamanashi Prefecture), provides a statistical alternative to the national Meiji divorce figures, enabling us to compare the results of 1879 with those of the national censuses after 1920. The divorce status of each individual in the 1879 census can be directly compared with the data from the modern enumerative censuses of 1920 and 1935, as shown in table 4. The difference is immediate and striking—divorce was much more common in 1879 than in 1920. Although the population of Yamanashi Prefecture had grown by almost 50 percent, the number of divorced people had nearly halved. This change is reflected in all the indicators. There were three times as many divorced individuals in the population and two and a half times the ratio of divorced to married people in 1879 compared with 1920.[5] The crude divorce rate for Yamanashi shows an even sharper drop. The rate fell from 4.11 in the 1880s to 1.2 in 1905, roughly a quarter of its former height. Although the rate had

TABLE 4
Divorce Indicators in Yamanashi Prefecture, 1879, 1920, and 1935

Indicator	1879	1920	1935
Population	397,416	583,453	646,727
Divorced people	12,141	6,590	4,616
Divorced people aged 23	543	136	68
Married people	165,075	221,756	235,257
Married people as a percentage of population	41.54%	38.01%	36.38%
Divorced people as a percentage of population	3.05%	1.13%	0.71%
Divorced people as a percentage of married population	7.35%	2.97%	1.96%
Divorced age 23 per 1,000 population	1.37	0.23	0.11
	1883–87	1908–12	1932–36
Official divorce rate (divorces per 1,000 population)	4.11	1.08	0.53

SOURCES: Tōkeiin, *Kai kuni genzai ninbetsuchō* (Tōkeiin, 1882), 43; Naikaku Tōkeikyoku, *Kokusei chōsa hōkoku. Fuken no bu. Taishō 9nen* (Tōkyō tōkei kyōkai, 1924), 17: 52–54; Naikaku Tōkeikyoku, *Kokusei chōsa hōkoku. Fukenhen. Shōwa 10 nen* (Tōkyō tōkei kyōkai, 1937), 2: 24–26.

been far above the national average in the 1880s, it was below average in 1935, suggesting that divorce declined faster in Yamanashi Prefecture than in the rest of Japan.

The divorce rate dropped faster between 1879 and 1920 than between 1920 and 1935. The average annual decline in the number of divorced people in Yamanashi Prefecture was 0.1 percent in the earlier period, but it was only 0.028 percent in the latter. The change in Yamanashi Prefecture looks most dramatic when shown by age group, as in figure 8. This graph shows the greatest decline in the percentage of divorced people in the younger age groups. The 1879 pattern, with a peak for divorcés and divorcées in the young age group and a gradual decline with age, was replaced by a much more gradual and even distribution of divorced people of all marriageable ages.

The 1879 Yamanashi census registered the marital status of the population, such as "divorced," so it is impossible to calculate either a crude divorce rate (number of divorces/population) or the ratio of number of divorces/number of marriages in a particular year. Through comparison, a crude divorce rate may nonetheless be estimated. The crude divorce rate, or number of divorces per 1,000 people, was about 0.7 for both 1920 and 1935. Assuming the ratio was the same in 1879, which means that remarriage, death, and migration rates of divorced people remained constant, the crude divorce rate should have been around two divorces

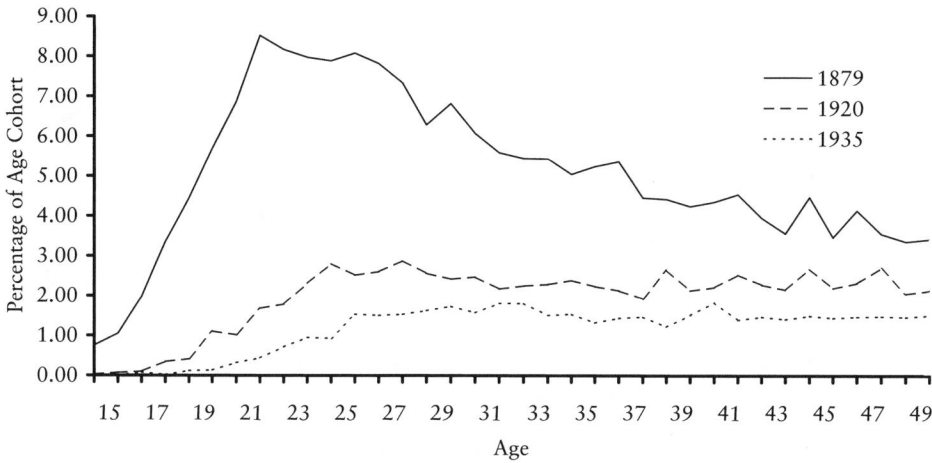

FIG. 8. Divorced Persons in the Population by Age in Yamanashi Prefecture, 1879, 1920, and 1935. (Sources: Tōkeiin, *Kai kuni genzai ninbetsuchō* [Tōkeiin, 1882], 43; Naikaku Tōkeikyoku, *Kokusei chōsa hōkoku: Fuken no bu. Taishō 9nen* [Tōkyō tōkei kyōkai 1924], 17: 52–54; Naikaku Tōkeikyoku, *Kokusei chōsa hōkoku: Fukenhen. Shōwa 10nen* [Tōkyō tōkei kyōkai, 1937], 2:24–26.)

per 1,000 people. This would be double the official rate in Yamanashi Prefecture in 1905, for example, which was 1.2. By contrast, this estimate is only half of the official crude divorce rate for Yamanashi Prefecture between 1883 and 1887, which was 4.11. This comparison both suggests that the official crude divorce rate exaggerated divorce and supports the argument that divorce rates were higher during the last decades of the nineteenth century than in the subsequent decades of the early twentieth century, probably twice as high. The reasons for the precipitous drop in official divorce rates around the turn of the twentieth century should thus be sought both in a redefinition of statistical categories and in changing social practices.

The Great Decline in Divorce, 1897–1899

Japanese contemporaries praised the 1898 Civil Code for significantly transforming the family, marriage, and divorce. The liberal thinker Fukuzawa Yukichi saw in it "an unprecedented revolution in Japanese society." The Socialist Sakai Toshihiko explained that the code protected the position of women and brought "modernity" to the family.[6] Yamakawa Kikue, a socialist and feminist activist, argued that the divorce rate had dropped because the code "greatly strengthened the wife's legal status." In broader terms, a decline in divorce meant "progress for women and society alike."[7]

Foreigners, too, felt that the code had changed marriage for the better. The wife of a British diplomat assigned to Japan commented that the "position of married women has been greatly improved" by the code.[8] The code obstructed divorce by interfering with the loose marriage customs of a large part of the population, the German geographer Johann Rein argued.[9] The English legal scholar J. E. de Becker was convinced that the code embodied a new set of values. In his preface on the articles on divorce, he wrote:

> In former days the Japanese wife was not regarded so seriously as at present by the husband, and she could be divorced and turned out of the house . . . when she was unfortunate enough to incur the displeasure of her lord and his relatives. . . . But now that marriage is regarded as perhaps the most solemn event in human life, and the status of women has been raised by the spread of modern education, repeated divorce is condemned as an act of which a civilised person ought to be ashamed. It was for this consideration that . . . more rigorous provisions were enacted in regard to marriage in the present code, [and] the law does not easily permit divorce unless it is effected by an agreement between the parties concerned.[10]

Like many Japanese legal experts, de Becker interprets early modern divorce customs as detrimental to the wife, assuming that it was usually the husband who initiated divorce. With a change in the perception of marriage and the role of wives, he said, divorce became as shunned as it ought to be. The Meiji Civil Code was both an expression and a facilitator of the movement to enhance marriage and reduce divorce. As noted in another chapter, code drafters in the 1890s had already discussed the issue of whether there was a level playing field in families for reaching such an agreement and were aware of the problems of fraud and coercion still permitted by the proposed system of divorce registration. The result was an emphasis in the law on documented "mutual consent," through affixing the seal of each spouse.

Despite contemporary praise for the civil code, it is not immediately obvious that it alone caused the fall in divorces between 1897 and 1899. On 16 July 1898, the national government enacted both a civil code and a new family registration law. A consensus soon formed on the important impact of these laws on divorce rates, but confusion remained on the issue of whether the drop was the consequence of new statistical methods, a change in actual divorce practices, or a combination thereof.[11] A redefinition of marriage and divorce seems to have been accompanied by changes in divorce practices. Although each explanation is insufficient in itself, taken together, they help us understand the reasons for the sharp decline in the divorce rate.

The 1898 Civil Code ruled that a marriage took effect upon the act of registration (Article 775). The government, which had been inconsistent in its legal definition of marriage since the institution of family registers in the early Meiji era, had now established a clear criterion, beyond which it did not return. Since the law on family registration followed the regulations of the code, unregistered unions of cohabitation, now branded common-law marriages (*naien*), should have been excluded from the marriage statistics after 1898. Similarly, dissolutions of common-law marriages should not have been counted as divorce. So both the formation and the dissolution of common-law marriages should have disappeared from the statistics.[12]

The crucial problem in the redefinition-of-marriage hypothesis is whether common-law marriages (and their dissolutions) had been included in statistics prior to 1898. The very definition of a common-law marriage after 1898 was that of an unregistered union, but how could local government officials have incorporated such unions into their statistical reports to the central government previously? Did local officials, intimately familiar with their locality, register cohabitative unions as marriages on their own initiative? According to the 1875 survey, a couple, or their representatives, had to report their marriage to the local office, and since there is no evidence that officials recorded marriages without such information, it seems rather unlikely that common-law marriages made it into marriage statistics on a large scale prior to 1898.

The marriage statistics themselves, however, show some support for the hypothesis that common-law marriages were excluded. If common-law marriages had been included in the statistics prior to 1898, we would expect a drop in the marriage rate registered annually and in the percentage of married couples in the population. Figure 9 reveals the turbulence in marriage statistics during the implementation phase of the 1898 Civil Code.[13] There is a significant drop in the marriage rate from 1898 to 1899 due to the exclusion of common-law marriages from the marriage statistics. In the following three years, however, the rate bounced back to a level that was about average before World War II. It seems likely that the code induced some couples living in common-law marriages to formalize their unions by registration. In the subsequent three years, fewer marriages were recorded, because some of the registration had already taken place in 1898. The crude marriage rate is not only high in 1898 but

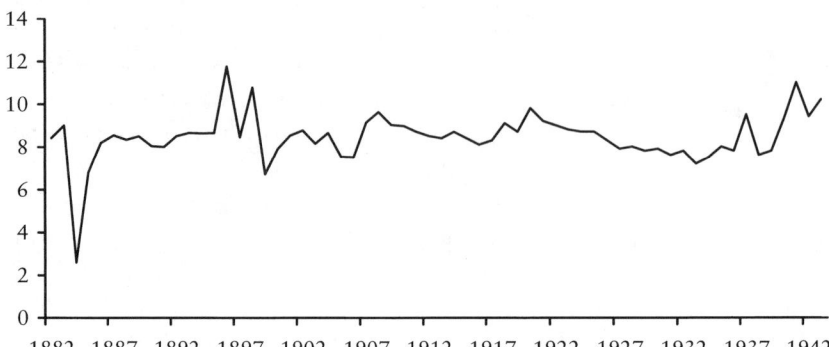

FIG. 9. The Marriage Rate in Japan, 1882–1943 (per 1,000 population). (Source: Kōseishō, *Rikon tōkei* [Kōsei tōkei kyōkai, 1984], 34–36.)

also in 1896, in what looks like a double peak. The scholar Tamaki Hajime interprets the high 1896 rate as a response to the termination of the Sino-Japanese War, during which many couples delayed their marriages.[14]

By contrast, the percentage of married couples in the so-called population of legal residence (*honseki jinkō*) is rather stable.[15] The slight long-term decline seems to have nothing to do with the exclusion of common-law marriages, but rather relates to how the population grew. The sociologist Toda Teizō estimated that about 16 percent of all marriages counted in the 1920 census were common-law marriages.[16] If the percentage of common-law marriage was the same around the turn of the century, and if common-law marriages were excluded in 1898, the percentage of married couples in the population should have declined to a level of about 30 percent from its previous level of about 35 percent. Instead, no long-term change appears in this percentage, but crucial data for the years 1899–1902 are missing.

Another reason for the sharp drop was a redefinition of divorce. As already discussed, divorce in the nineteenth century was more than just the separation of husband and wife. Some of the common terms for divorce in popular perceptions and legal writing, such as *rien*, simply meant separation from a house—for example, in the dissolution of an adoption. Another separation from a house was the parting of a widow from her parents-in-law. In early drafts of the Japanese Civil Code, a marriage ended not with the death of one spouse but with the remarriage of the bereaved spouse.[17] Article 808 of the 1898 Civil Code uses the term *rikon* (literally, "separation of a marriage"), which is also used in previous divorce statistics. Nevertheless, it is possible that, in practice, other forms of "divorce" were included in the pre-1898 statistics, and that their subsequent exclusion contributed to the sharp fall in the divorce rate. It is interesting to note that the percentage of women with "unclear" status at remarriage in the first years of the early twentieth century far exceeded that of men. This could have been a way to hide the fact that a widow was remarrying, which had previously been camouflaged by use of the term "divorced." Moreover, among newlyweds, the percentage of widowers exceeded that of widows by far.[18]

The third reason is that the Meiji Civil Code and Meiji Family Registration Law obstructed divorce.[19] Many scholars simply point to the decline in the number of divorces as evidence, but an unresolved question lingers as to which part of the legislation hampered divorce.[20] Since 99 percent of the divorces recorded between 1898 and 1940 were consensual and became effective simply by registration, without court intervention, an explanation focusing on changes in registration methods seems promising.

The Meiji Civil Code regulated divorce in Articles 808 to 812. Divorce became effective with the act of registration (Article 810). The consent of both spouses was necessary for registration (Article 808). In addition, the parents, legal guardians, or relatives whose permission was necessary for marriage also had to approve divorce if one of the spouses was under twenty-five years old (Article 809). The formalities for divorce registration were the same as those for marriage (Article 810). The second part of Article 775 on marriage registration stated: "The notification . . . must be given either orally or in a document signed by both the parties concerned and at least two witnesses of full age."[21] Submitting a sheet of paper with seals was sufficient proof of both marriage and divorce. There was no required registration ceremony by which the spouses expressed their consent in front of an official and two or more witnesses, as in many European marriage registration ceremonies. In contrast to the Japanese Family Registration Law of 1886, which only asked for registration by the head of the household, the law in 1898 made the certified consent of both spouses mandatory.[22] According to the code, unilateral divorce by registration through the family head against the wishes of one or both of the spouses should have become impossible.

We shall never know how many divorces these new regulations requiring the formal agreement of a larger group of people prevented. The example of Ishimoto Shidzue shows that such a regulation could at least delay divorce. Ishimoto Shidzue had agreed with her husband to apply for a divorce, but her husband's family refused to sign the application.

Her case was especially complicated because as a member of the high nobility, she needed the signatures of two other aristocrats to obtain a divorce. In 1944, many years after the original decision, her brother and brother-in-law finally signed the divorce petition.[23]

The fact that multiple interpretations of the sharp fall in the Meiji divorce rate have continued to coexist for a century suggests that no single factor caused it. Because the decline is so sudden and unusual, some scholars maintain that it is just a statistical quirk. This study, using statistical and literary evidence, argues that the change was partly real, but that official statistics probably exaggerate the occurrence of divorce prior to 1898.

The Gradual Decline, 1900–1940

Much ethnographic evidence shows unequivocally that the subsequent gradual decline in divorce rates reflected changing practices. While it is beyond doubt that divorce decreased, the reasons are not immediately obvious. Reversing the factors contributing to higher divorce rates in Europe, the United States, and postwar Japan seems a useful starting point for an inquiry into the gradual decline in prewar Japan, but this approach reaches its limits when it begins explaining phenomena outside their particular historical context. Rising expectations of marriage, for example, are plausibly held responsible for increasing the rate at which marriages have been dissolved in many countries in recent decades, but did a lowering of expectations of marriage, if it ever occurred, decrease divorce? For Japan, previous scholarship has, on the contrary, suggested that declining divorce rates were accompanied by a weakening of ties to the wider group of kin and a strengthening of marriage.[24] So it seems conceivable that increased emphasis on marriage, depending on social context, may result in either more or less divorce. After a brief look at why court divorce proceedings were not typical of divorce in general, the following section considers changes in marriage and the family as the area most likely to have had an impact on divorce.

The Predominance of Female Plaintiffs in Judicial Divorce

As already mentioned, throughout Japanese history, state institutions rarely settled divorce disputes. Between 1900 and 1940, court divorces comprised less than 1 percent of all divorces, ranging from a low of 0.3 percent in 1902 to a high of 0.9 percent in 1931. Despite their statistical insignificance, they seem to have served particular functions within the overall system of divorce, but not necessarily the one anticipated. Contrary to the expectation of Meiji legal experts, it was wives who initiated most divorce suits under the Meiji Civil Code. Female plaintiffs received a judicial divorce in 85 percent of the cases in the first four decades of the twentieth century.[25] The fact that even in the second half of the twentieth century, it was mainly wives who obtained court divorces in Japan and elsewhere does not fully explain the specific reasons for the incentives or need for Japanese wives to resort to the courts in such disproportionate numbers. Still, the most widely accepted view is that the courts supported the desire of wives for divorce, since it was almost impossible for a woman to force a divorce by "mutual consent" on a reluctant husband, whereas a man had multiple social, economic, and psychological means of doing so.[26] While there is sufficient evidence of strong-willed women dissolving marriages by themselves, we shall never know how many less demanding wives simply remained in marriages they found dissatisfying.

A less sweeping but certainly not less true explanation of the gender gap in judicial divorce emerges when looking more closely at the distribution of the suits according to the grounds for divorce. The majority of women applied for judicial divorces for the same reason men did, namely, that their spouses had disappeared from their lives. For female plaintiffs, the primary reasons were the husband's desertion (37%), unknown whereabouts (28%), or imprisonment for three years or more (16%), totaling 81 percent of cases.[27] Excluding divorce for adultery, these three reasons would also apply to 90 percent of all male-initiated divorces. For both men and women, most court decisions in fact legitimized previous separations after the breakdown of the marriage.[28]

Once a spouse had deserted, disappeared, or been jailed, it became impossible to follow the normal procedure of recording a divorce in the family register based on verification of mutual consent by either oral testimony or a sealed written statement by the spouses. When either spouse had been physically removed, the remaining spouse had to receive a judicial divorce before being able to register a divorce. Women probably went to court more frequently than men because husbands were more mobile, absconded, and were jailed more often than their wives. Men might have deserted for reasons unrelated to their marriage. A man might have wanted to escape his creditors or the military, or might simply have died in an accident while working away from home. If a young woman were to remarry, and thus regain economic security, a certified divorce was essential. Wives' numerous suits for judicial divorce must have been motivated by a desire to remarry and get on with life.

One crucial difference in the grounds for divorce in the Meiji Civil Code was its treatment of infidelity. Only husbands could sue based on adultery, which made up 30 percent of all successful male divorce suits. Despite a landmark Supreme Court decision in 1927 permitting a wife to divorce her husband for adultery, wives did not usually divorce their husbands in court for adultery in the prewar period.[29] Wives, however, were permitted to divorce husbands who had been punished for sexual crimes. Sixty wives actually did so. Besides this difference, the rules for judicial divorce were the same. The comparable proportional importance of mistreatment as grounds for divorce is somewhat surprising, despite the huge discrepancy between 1,650 female plaintiffs compared to 186 male. Whether forms of mistreatment were gender-specific only a detailed analysis of cases can tell.

Grounds for divorce based on wider family strife were rarely invoked in divorce, in contrast to the relative weight these cases have in the Edo historical record. Mistreatment of one's parents by one's spouse, grounds reflecting the ideal of filial piety, made up a mere 2 percent of the cases. Similarly, abuse by in-laws amounted to a bare 1 percent. Dissolution of a relationship with an adopted husband was grounds for divorce for only 1 percent of men and 2 percent of women. Divorce suits involved in-marrying husbands less frequently than might have been expected from the overall proportion of divorces with in-marrying husbands.

The relative unimportance of the courts as a means of conflict resolution is explained by the fact that the Meiji Civil Code's ten legal grounds were too restrictive to apply to the entire spectrum of divorce. Conflicts between parents and in-laws were dealt with in three clauses, and criminal punishment and disappearances in four, and the only other reasons for the dissolution of a marriage were adultery on the part of the wife, bigamy, and mistreatment by the other spouse. As no other form of incompatibility was permitted, it was natural that divorce-seekers preferred to obtain divorces by simple registration, which the lawmakers had provided as an alternative to court divorce. The rigid rules for court divorce contrasted with the flexibility of simply registering a divorce without having to conform to narrow legal norms. Moreover, popular aversion to the use of courts appeared ingrained to contemporary observers. When the government set up a deliberative committee in 1919 to revise the civil code to combat the dissolution of families, arguments voiced in the original drafting process were repeated.[30] Okano Keijirō, a member of the commission, justified the creation of a new court institution, the family court, by saying that Japan was in need of an institution for the mediation of family affairs beyond the courts of law, where one had to make a cold claim for one's right. The family court was to provide privacy and warmth (*onjō*) instead of the strict legality of the ordinary public court.³¹ Few made such a claim in court, whereas the vast majority divorced outside of it. Changes in the divorce behavior of this vast majority accordingly have to be sought outside the legal system.

The Conjugal Family as an Impediment to Divorce?

Prewar social discourse highlights the difficult transition a woman faced before being fully accepted into her husband's household. While a bride adapted to her new environment, her husband and his family, but especially the mother-in-law, were meant to train her in the duties of the wife of the (future) household head. This process had the potential for friction, and it is against this background that the concept of not fitting into the "ways of the house," a frequently repeated reason for divorce, has to be understood.³² If this transition failed, and, as noted, most divorces occurred early in marriage, popular perceptions often presumed the mother-in-law to be responsible for an ensuing divorce, and the bride is often portrayed as meekly consenting to an unwanted divorce.³³ This generic explanation was so common that even in cases where the two had never met, it was said that the mother-in-law had caused the divorce. Considering this rather widespread view, diary accounts of a smooth relationship between bride and mother-in-law come almost as a surprise.³⁴ Such personal documents of individual cases reflect the marital life and divorce experience of individuals without explaining how significant the "family factor" in divorce was in general. Research on the population register of an Edo village, for example, revealed that divorce was not more likely when the mother-in-law was present during the first five years of marriage, suggesting that she may in fact have facilitated the transition of the bride into her new family.³⁵

Although, as we have seen, magistrates in the Edo period upheld the prerogative of senior household members, whether male or female, to divorce a bride or an in-marrying husband, it is impossible to estimate the frequency of such divorces. One should never forget that the "standard scenario" described above, of a young bride marrying into a complex household with parents-in-law still alive, was most likely in wealthier commercial and peasant households, which on average had more complex family structures.

The problem of co-residence figures prominently in explaining why, unlike in most other societies and also in postwar Japan, the prewar Japanese divorce rate was higher in the countryside than in urban areas. The Japanese sociologist Toda Teizō attributes this mainly to friction between in-laws and a young bride, pointing to the larger percentage of extended families in the rural population than in cities.[36] After 1900, books on marriage-centered families and an extensive public debate over the dissolution of the "traditional Japanese family" implied the end of extended families and postulated that the "small family" had arrived. Population statistics, however, show strong continuities. Average household size, serving as a crude indicator of household complexity, was fairly stable at around five members per household in selected localities during the Edo period and remained so until the drop in the birthrate induced by the liberalization of abortion after World War II, declining from 4.97 (1955) to 2.71 (2000) members per household. But at the height of concern over the dissolution of the extended family, the average household size in Japan was the largest during the previous three centuries.

The attention in the emerging mass media to the urban middle classes stemmed from the social phenomenon of younger sons migrating to cities to find employment and starting families there, a pattern that increased in magnitude just before the turn of the twentieth century. Ever since 1920, the year of the first national census, the nuclear family has been the predominant household type, accounting for about 60 percent of all households, and despite a startling rise in single-person-households during the 1990s, it remained so throughout the twentieth century. The proportion of extended families started declining after the 1950s, however, just as average household size had.[37] Household size, like the percentage of nuclear families, is a rough correlate of how many brides (or in-marrying husbands) cohabited with extended families in the early stages of their marriages. The statistical category of nuclear families includes those families where the parents or in-laws have already died, as well as those couples that have never ever lived with any relatives except their own children. Nevertheless, when taken together, the constancy of household size over the centuries and household composition after 1920 suggest that it was only in the postwar period that the size and complexity of households decreased markedly. Since the divorce rate decreased before that time, it seems unlikely that changing patterns of co-residence were a significant factor in the gradual decline during the first decades of the twentieth century.

This does not mean that co-residence had no impact on divorce. A correlation at the level of prefectures implies that mothers-in-law deserved some of their bad reputation, as figure 10 illustrates. The in-law ratio for

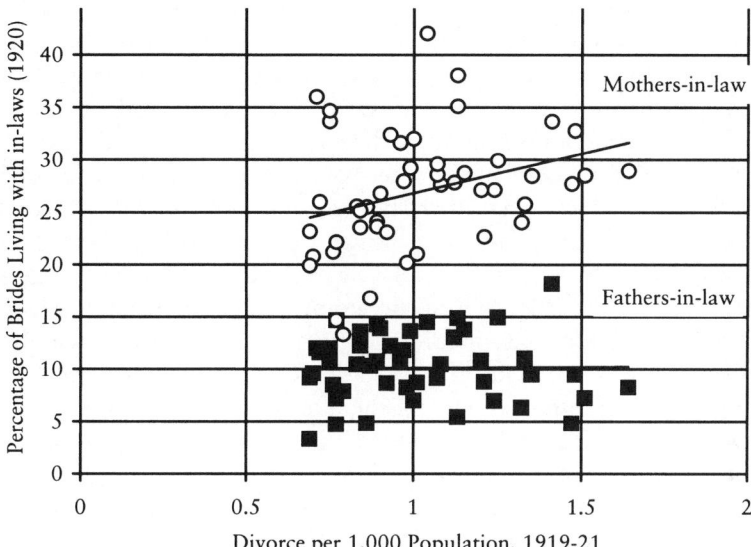

FIG. 10. Correlation of the Divorce Rate with Patterns of Cohabitation at the Prefecture Level Around 1920. (Sources: Toda Teizō, *Kazoku kōsei* [Kōbundō, 1937], 330–46, for cohabitation figures; Hayami Akira, ed., *Kokusei chōsa izen Nihon jinkō tōkei shūsei* [Hara shobō, 1993], and Takahashi Shin'ichi, ed., *Kokusei chōsa ikō Nihon jinkō tōkei shūsei* [Hara shobō, 1994], for divorce rates.)

families in each prefecture was computed according to estimates based on the 1920 census. When these ratios are correlated with the divorce rate, the presence of fathers-in-law seems to have had no effect on divorce, whereas the ratio of mothers-in-law accompanied higher divorce rates. Even if mothers-in-law contributed somewhat to divorce, whether they repudiated the bride or whether the bride left of her own volition is an issue on which the statistics remain silent. Ethnographic research in villages has revealed instances both of brides who fled and of brides who were sent back home after trouble adjusting to their new environments.[38]

Numerous Japanese commentators have connected the frequency of divorce to the way spouses were selected and interacted, arguing that so-called love marriages were essentially more enduring. A proponent of this view was the scholar of English literature Honma Hisao (1886–1981), who in 1916 criticized arranged marriages and spoke of the prevalence of "divorce by disillusioned women."[39] As the leading role of the family in choosing spouses waned, increased familiarity with a future spouse and more individual "choice" might have enhanced the personal component in marriage, heightened emotional affection, and downplayed the functional work roles. A change in this direction did occur during the first decades of the twentieth century, but at a glacial pace, and practices continued to differ according to social status, occupation, and wealth.

The early twentieth century saw the spread of "love marriages" in media discourse and marriage advice books. Women's mass magazines, themselves a product of the emerging mass consumer society, debated the pros and cons of various types of spouses and how to find them at length in articles and letters to the editor. Marriage advice books by the publishers of the most popular prewar women's mass magazine, *Shufu no tomo* (A Housewife's Companion), began to discuss the possibility of choosing a spouse without family mediation, even in respectable families.[40] Despite the public debate on the alternatives of arranged marriage or love marriage, the matter remained a theoretical issue for most young people, however. The percentage of so-called love marriages gradually rose from 3 percent (1912–26) to 11 percent (1936–45) to over 20 percent (1950s), but it was not until the 1960s that so-called love marriage became dominant.[41]

Prospective spouses also had more opportunity to see each other before marriage, as is reflected in the increase of so-called see-meeting (*miai*) marriages, from 38 (1912–26) to 51 percent (1936–45). During the Taishō period, newspapers reported that the Imperial Theater and the Mitsukoshi and Shiroki department stores were the locations of such conspicuously innocuous meetings for more than half a dozen couples each day.[42] Konosuke Matsushita, who in later life became the highly successful founder of an electrical company, described a planned encounter with his future wife in the street on a May day in 1915:

My brother-in-law called out, "They've come, they've come." The people in the crowd gave us knowing looks and began whispering; apparently this was the scene of frequent such staged meetings. I became jittery and blushed with embarrassment. Not until my brother-in-law shook me, saying, "Konosuke, look, look!" did I recover my senses. He pointed out the girl, standing not far away, but with her back to us. . . . I thought, she must not have been able to see me well either. I could hardly decide whether she was the right girl or not, but it seemed my sister and brother-in-law, who had been in control of the situation, had observed her well enough. My brother-in-law urged me to marry her, assuring me, "She's not bad looking," so I consented, and it was agreed I would wed Mumeno Iue.[43]

Highly superficial as these meetings appear today, some contemporaries perceived them as an improvement over previous practices. Suye Mura villagers in the 1930s believed that the opportunities for young people to meet before marriage had increased. An old village woman joked that in her youth, a bride might wake up the day after the marriage ceremony, see her husband's face for the first time in broad daylight, and think to herself, "I hate it. I hate it."[44]

Freedom of choice does not in itself, however, guarantee a longer-lasting marriage. People in Western societies today are by and large free to choose their spouses, but this is accompanied by the highest divorce rates in historical memory. Moreover, surveys among Japanese rice farmers in the 1960s continued to record strong popular rejection of love marriages as fickle and unstable, especially when lacking family support. The possibility that increased initial personal compatibility led to fewer frictions in marriage thereafter is difficult to refute, of course, but in light of the strong evidence of family control in the process of selecting spouses until World War II, it appears unlikely that the divorce rate declined because of increased spousal social interaction before marriage.

As divorce rates declined, marriage age rose. In the late nineteenth century, following the introduction of compulsory elementary education, people started marrying later. The average age at marriage stabilized after 1910 at around twenty-three for women and twenty-seven for men in the case of first-time marriages, until the dearth of prospective husbands due to the Second Sino-Japanese war in the 1930s led to an increase of about two years by 1940. Taishō social reformers, just like their Meiji predecessors, encouraged later marriages, "since there is much unhappiness in early marriage," where the will of the parents often took precedence over that of the immature spouses.[45] Although at first glance, marriage age and divorce rate trends appear unrelated, they deserve to be examined together, since younger spouses, then as now, were especially likely to divorce.[46] On the assumption that age-specific divorce rates remained constant, a decrease in the proportion of marriages of younger spouses, more prone to divorce, helped to contain the divorce rate.

Concurrent with a rise in marriage age, the age-specific divorce rate changed. In relative terms, younger spouses still remained most likely to divorce, but less so, as table 5 illustrates. Age at divorce rose faster than age at marriage because more mature spouses had a more realistic worldview and stronger standing in their new households, or so contemporaries believed. The effect of this change was a dramatic decline in the number of younger divorced spouses. For example, 23 percent of all divorcées were twenty and younger in 1899, but only 5 percent were that young in 1933.[47] An index based on the rate of divorce per unit of population confirms that divorce declined especially among younger spouses.[48]

TABLE 5
Divorce and Marriage by Age Group in Japan, 1900–1940
(percent)

Year	Men			Women		
	Under 20	Under 25	Under 30	Under 20	Under 25	Under 30
	Divorce by age group as a percentage of all divorces					
1900	4.9	31.6	59.6	19.3	55.4	76.3
1910	2.1	20.0	48.1	11.7	42.5	66.2
1920	1.9	18.5	45.9	11.3	43.2	65.5
1930	0.7	12.4	39.5	6.5	35.2	60.2
1940	0.3	7.3	34.9	3.7	28.3	57.7
	Marriage by age group as a percentage of all marriages					
1900	7.8	44.7	73.9	33.3	75.1	89.8
1910	4.8	35.6	66.7	26.8	68.9	86.3
1920	3.9	33.5	67.8	25.7	70.0	85.4
1930	2.0	30.7	72.0	20.8	72.9	88.3
1940	0.9	15.9	63.6	10.6	61.8	85.2

SOURCES: Hayami Akira, ed., *Kokusei chōsa izen Nihon jinkō tōkei shūsei* (Hara shobō, 1992–93); Takahashi Shin'ichi, ed., *Kokusei chōsa ikō Nihon jinkō tōkei shūsei* (Hara shobō, 1994).

The most telling example is that in 1939–40, the rate of divorce per 1,000 population was 17 percent of what it had been only in 1919–21 for women aged between fifteen and nineteen. By contrast, for women between forty-five and forty-nine, the percentage change over twenty years was 92 percent. Like the previously discussed changes in marriage arrangement, a higher average marriage age is in itself no guarantee of lower divorce rates, for in Japan both have risen together since the mid 1970s.

A clear, but tiny, contribution to the divorce rate decline was the slow decrease of marriages with in-marrying husbands. Already around 1905, only a minority of men chose *muko yōshi* and *nyūfu* marriages (9.7 percent), and by 1935, such marriages had declined to 7.7 percent. Several local studies showed a higher incidence of divorce in marriages with in-marrying husbands than in regular marriages, while others found no difference. Social critics suggested that the divorce rate increased for such marriages among samurai after the Edo period, after the government abolished the stipend system and the requirement of male succession.[49]

A higher dissolution rate for such marriages can be deduced from national population statistics for the early twentieth century, which are based on three post-divorce scenarios: the wife left the husband's house; the husband left the wife's house; or they continued to live together. The concept of spouses separating and leaving each other is absent in these categories informed by lineage-based marriage ideology. Despite different terms, departing husbands most likely meant dissolution of marriages with in-marrying husbands. During the interwar years, the annual percentage of departing husbands exceeded the percentage of in-marrying husbands among newlyweds in a parallel way in almost every prefecture.[50] In 1935, 90 percent of divorces dissolved marriages that had lasted less than fifteen years. The percentage of in-marrying divorces in 1935 should have ranged somewhere between that for in-marrying marriages between 1920 and 1935, but the percentage was even higher than around 1900. The decline in divorce-prone in-marrying marriages thus helped lessen the national divorce rate in the early twentieth century.[51]

The Strengthening of Marriage as a Social Institution

The most decisive change in marriage that contributed to a decrease in divorce came from the realm of values and attitudes stressing marriage and the maintenance of its continuity. One result of this shift was, of course, a decrease in divorce and a lengthening of marriage before divorce. This new emphasis on marriage, however, occurred within the prevailing family system. Two indicators of the rising importance families attached to marriage were the acceptance of new wedding rituals and increases in the value of the dowry.

Since the Meiji period, reformers had called for improvement of Japanese marriage rituals to instill the importance of marital commitment into the population at large and to combat divorce. They called the Japanese ceremony deficient in religious sanction. Missionaries, not surprisingly, wanted to add religious sanction to the Japanese marriage ceremony. William Erskine, a missionary and long-term resident of Japan, explained that in the West, the Church had institutionalized marriage, but in Japan there was neither a religious nor a legal ceremony. In Japan, "a wedding is merely a family affair until it is properly registered. Then it becomes legal," he remarked.[52] Reforming the old wedding style, he believed, was essential for imbuing the population with beliefs in the seriousness of marriage. Erskine wrote: "Japan needs a social and religious sanction to marriage to overcome the many trial marriages which if numbered with her divorces would make her stand out more than ever."[53] Erskine believed that changing the symbolism of the wedding would lead to a new attitude toward marriage, decreasing trial marriages and divorces. To Erskine, the religious wedding was a vehicle to infiltrate Japanese marriages with the Christian ideal of lifetime commitment. In "a country in which the anniversary of everything except weddings" was celebrated, he interpreted "the reasons for the one exception [as] being that marriage and the establishment of a new home has never had a pure or deep religious significance."[54] Another foreign missionary, Walter Weston, even argued that the lack of religious sanction for Japanese marriage facilitated divorce, which was "rampant."[55]

An amusing anecdote shows the different legal standing of the religious marriage ceremony in Britain and Japan in the early twentieth century. In 1908, when a divorce suit came before the court in England, it was discovered that in Japan, "thirty English couples were living in sin," although they had been married by the Anglican bishop of Tokyo. The explanation was that up to July 1899, religious marriages performed in churches within the foreign concessions in Japan were valid under English law, but when extraterritoriality ceased, the laws of England also stopped applying to church marriages. That meant that marriages without an additional civil ceremony at a consulate were consequently legally invalid. The British Parliament needed to pass a special act to recognize those marriages retrospectively. This shows that the prior registration that Erskine required of Japanese couples was not usually asked of foreigners.[56]

The Christian wedding inspired Japanese reformers of the Japanese marriage ceremony. Ueki Emori, who rose to fame with his radical proposition that spouses should live separately from their in-laws, also supported a new wedding style in several issues of the *Tōyō shinbun* in 1887 to emphasize the importance of marriage. In Ueki's view, the Japanese marriage ritual lacked the sanction of publicity and religion. In Europe and the United States, he said, the intention to marry was first announced in a church in front of a priest, who performed the ceremony with at least two or three witnesses present. Witnesses served to scrutinize obstacles to marriage, to ascertain the free will of the spouses, and to provide an audience. Marriage celebrated in this Western way would eradicate "evil practices" in Japan. First, the proclamation of an intention to marry before the ceremony prevented polygamy. Second, an enhanced wedding imbued husband and wife with a sense of the importance of marriage. This new awareness prevented easy, fast divorce, he said.[57]

Emori was not alone in proposing changes in the wedding procedure to combat divorce. Japanese commentators later took up the issue of wedding reform, but dropping references to foreign models. An 1898 editorial in the *Tōkyō asahi shinbun* criticized Japanese weddings for being much too simple, lacking in solemnity, and, most important, failing to stress the importance of marriage and the disgrace of divorce.[58] Shorn of overt symbols of Christianity, these ideas were influential in transforming Japanese marriage ceremonies. The pivotal event starting to spread religious wedding styles to the population was the marriage of the Crown Prince Yoshihito, who later became Emperor Taishō, which was celebrated in a newly designed Shinto-style marriage ritual in 1900.[59]

In subsequent years, newspapers reported repeatedly on the spread of weddings in a religious style. In 1913, the main localities for a Shinto ceremony were the Hibiya Grand Shrine "for scholars, nobility and gentlemen" and the Shimodani Shrine for "common people." Only built the previous year, the Izumo Grand Shrine also became a site of ceremonies. Christian weddings were celebrated in the Tenshū church in Tsukiji.[60] In the next year, the *Yomiuri* newspaper recorded an increase from 513 to 718 in the number of Shinto weddings celebrated at the Hibiya Grand Shrine up to September; this was reported in relation to 450 marriages registered in the city of Tokyo in an average month.[61] The success of the new-style wedding continued unabated and even attracted couples from out of town. Compared with 400 to 500 couples in 1908, in 1915, 1,550 couples married at the Hibiya Grand Shrine. Most were from Tokyo, but one-fifth came from such places as Yokosuka, Takasaki, and Sakura.[62] By 1931, advice books on the marriage ceremony enumerated places for a Shinto-style wedding in Tokyo, Osaka, and Kyoto, and presented the alternatives of Christian and Buddhist weddings. Descriptions of these religious weddings were still, however, preceded by accounts of a traditional marriage ceremony at home.[63]

Even without the religious trappings, weddings came to carry more symbolic, economic, and social weight in the countryside. A man named Kubo in the remote village of Suye Mura in Kyūshū's Kumamoto Prefecture opined in the 1930s:

The present elaborate wedding ceremony is more or less an innovation. Formerly they were very simple, and one could get married for five yen. That is why divorce was so frequent; for five yen you could go to a restaurant, visit a whorehouse, or get married. As a result, one broke up marriages without much thought. Now, however, so much money goes into them that one thinks a long time before getting a divorce.[64]

The increased cost of a wedding made a marriage more valuable and worth keeping in Kubo's view, but he did not explain why people spent more money on weddings in the first place. The anthropologist Ella Wiswell's observations confirm the preceding view of changes in marriage and the marriage ceremony:

> There were many divorces and remarriages in the old days, but now things have changed. Formerly the marriage ceremony was extremely simple and did not mean much in itself, so if a girl disliked something or other in her new home, she would go back to her family and start over again. Virginity in a bride did not seem important. That is why you find so many old women who have been married so many times.... But now weddings have become elaborate affairs, and so girls take them less lightly and do not seek divorce so readily."[65]

Neither more publicity nor the influence of religion was the crucial wedding transformation in this village. Economic outlay made these people sense the "sanctity" of the institution.

The heightened status of the ceremony was accompanied by stronger "investment" in the marriage in the form of a dowry. Domain authorities during the Edo period repeatedly issued regulations against sumptuous dowries, showing that the population was not averse to this practice. Nevertheless, dowries appeared more common and more valuable afterward. In 1892, a Japanese diplomat, Daigoro Goh, discerned a spread of once-forbidden dowry practices and explained the new popularity of the dowry as being "in imitation of Western customs."[66] Twentieth-century ethnographic research in rural Japan discovered a continuation of the same trend. The anthropologist Thomas Elsa Jones contended that there had been a stunning tenfold increase in the dowry over the preceding twenty years in two villages of the Maki District in Shimane Prefecture, which he visited between 1917 and 1924.[67] Suye Mura villagers in Kumamoto Prefecture also declared that the value of a dowry had risen greatly before 1935.[68]

Disappearance of domain prohibitions, imitation of Western customs, and the spread of the market economy are all explanations for a rise in dowries. The Japanese anthropologist Ariga Kizaemon, an expert on prewar financial arrangements at marriage, believed that it was especially in cities that brides brought dowries, since city women wed later and incomes were generally higher than in most villages.[69] Other scholars also point to economic factors, such as the spread of the market economy, as increasing the importance of a wife's dowry.[70] Memoirs tell of the fate of women unable to marry due to the lack of an adequate dowry. An increase in dowry may have contributed to a decline in divorce, since the investment in a marriage increased. More likely, though, the increase in dowry and the decrease in divorce both reflected the new importance of marriage, also evident in the ready acceptance of new wedding styles.

The crucial change in Japanese marriage practices in the early twentieth century was not a shift from a marriage arranged by others to a marriage arranged by the spouses themselves, commonly referred to as a transition from arranged (*miai*) to love marriages (*ren'ai*). Instead, the important transformation was the aggregate decrease in the frequency of separations and divorces among the population as a whole, resulting in an increase in the average length of marriage. Japanese, then, valued economic and social stability in marriage above romance and affection.

New Sexual Morality: Divorce as a National Disgrace

Divorce was never entirely above reproach in the late nineteenth century. Memoirs and the 1875 customs survey explain that divorce could be seen as shameful. Contemporaries interpreted the samurai ritual of lighting a fire in front of the house of the bride's family on the wedding day as symbolizing the bride's complete separation from her family and her family's wish that the marriage be permanent. Ethnographic writing shows examples of divorced women remarrying below their socioeconomic position. Still, what is striking is the lack of intensive censure of divorce practices. The handful of Meiji newspaper articles on divorce are not as reproachful in tone as those a few decades later.

From the late nineteenth century onward, American and European visitors and residents, especially missionaries, reprimanded Japanese for their casual attitude toward divorce. They believed that Japanese behavior was based on a disregard for the seriousness of marriage and on the low position of women in Japan. Not surprisingly, they proposed Christianity as a means to sanctify marriage and make wives and mothers secure. Japanese intellectuals, politicians, scholars, lawyers, teachers, and women of the emerging professional class started to criticize divorce as a national disgrace, often with reference to Western marriage ideals in the early twentieth century. They interpreted the decline in divorce as a sign of increased happiness in marriage and of the strengthened position of wives, as well as a proof of modernity.

Despite social and geographical variation, the most striking feature of the decline in prewar divorce is its universality. In all Japanese prefectures and social classes, divorce declined in the first four decades of the twentieth century. This suggests a common force behind the divorce decline, such as new values and attitudes to divorce. The print media, which disseminated a new concern with, and criticism of, divorce during the first four decades of the century, played an important part in the decline in the divorce rate.

As has been noted, divorce rates came to be perceived as a national disgrace precisely when they were on the decline. A 1916 article titled "Japan Leads the World in Divorce," while recognizing that fewer divorces occurred in Japan every year, regretted that compared with other civilized countries, Japan was "peerless" in the world in this respect. It was also concerned with marriage and sexuality. The bright spring wedding was often related to the gloom (*an'ei*) of divorce and the related chastity problem. A detestable inclination was reflected in the "sad broken mirror" of divorce in the statistics. Statistics, though, only reflected official marriages and divorces. High divorce rates, it said, showed that women's rights were probably inadequate in Japan, as further proven by the alleged "fact" that 375 husbands, but only 34 wives, had initiated court divorce before 1912. Nevertheless, there was reason for hope, since recently a "true understanding" of marriage had emerged, illegitimate children had become fewer, and divorce had declined. Women's rising confidence and better education made them demand continued cohabitation and reject their husbands' divorce requests.[71]

The link between Japan's world leadership in divorce and the position of Japanese women in society was also a central concern in other newspapers of the period. "Let's Liberate [*kaihō*] Women" was the subtitle of a 1917 article in *Yomiuri* titled "The Most Divorces in the World," which argued against the perception that the liberation of women was the only reason for frequent divorce. Liberated wives went out to work without properly managing the affairs of their households and facilitated strife (*funsō*) in society, it was alleged, whereas an intelligent (*rikō*) and liberated woman could build a strong home life and live peacefully in marriage, the writer asserted.[72]

Reporting on court divorce cases was also often done from the perspective of women's rights. The mainstream publication *Chūō* praised the Supreme Court for attacking the customary glorification of men and contempt for women (*danson johi*), saying that usually "there is no right for the person called 'wife'" in Japan. For example, in a decision on 27 February 1915, the court had ruled in favor of the wife. On 13 April 1911, through the offices of the go-between Tanaka, a bride named Hideko had entered a family in Ibaragi Prefecture. The family continued to refuse to have the marriage registered even after the couple had lived together for two weeks, and although she was blameless, Hideko was suddenly sent home as "divorced" (*ribetsu*) on 4 May 1911, on the grounds that she "did not fit into the way of the house" (*kafu ni awanu*). Hideko's natal family thereupon demanded compensation (*baishō*) for the injury (*songai*) to her honor. The court in Shimotsuma decided that the marriage had never been legally effective, however, and the plaintiff lost. Hideko's family then appealed to the Mito district court, which found for the plaintiff and ordered the defendant to pay compensation. The husband's side, with the help of a lawyer, appealed to the Supreme Court, but there it lost again. The court ruled that failure to register a marriage and withdrawal of a marriage promise entitled the injured party to compensation. The article mentions other legal precedents in which compensation ranging from 1,110 to 8,390 yen had been granted in divorces because the wife "did not fit into the way of the house."[73] Payment of damages became a sign of a wife's guiltlessness rather than a matter of economic relevance. If their honor, or loss of their virginity, needed to be compensated for after separation or divorce, it meant that for some women at least, divorce had become a shameful event during the first decades of the twentieth century.

7

Forward to the Past
A Historical Perspective on Japanese Divorce After World War II

"THE DIVORCE RATE Has Reached European Levels," a headline in Japan's foremost economic daily, the *Nihon keizai shinbun*, proclaimed on New Year's Day, 1999. In reference to new estimates of population trends by the Ministry of Health and Welfare, the newspaper emphasized that Japan had caught up with France in frequency of divorce.[1] On the same day, all major Japanese newspapers reported that the Japanese divorce rate in 1998 was the "highest in history" (*kako saikō*). "More than 243,000 couples were divorced last year," it was noted; "the number of divorces has risen for the eighth consecutive year." Several articles even specified that "one couple split every two minutes and ten seconds."[2] By making the comparison with continental Europe, however, the *Nihon keizai shinbun* distinguished itself from its less original competitors, which, as usual, stressed how low Japanese divorce rates were in contrast to those of the United States and the United Kingdom.[3] By shifting the context, the *Nihon keizai shinbun* openly challenged the still-prevalent belief that for an industrialized society, Japan had an exceptionally low divorce rate.

From the 1960s on, the general movement of divorce in Japan began resembling that of most western European societies, and by the end of the twentieth century, the Japanese divorce rate no longer stood out internationally. In 1995, the rate of divorce in Japan was higher than in Spain, Italy, Yugoslavia, and Greece and only slightly lower than in France, Germany, and the Netherlands. Compared with the United States and Russia, which currently top the world's divorce rate table, Japan can be called a low-divorce-rate society, but so can most other societies on this planet.[4] On the other hand, Japan stopped being what critics of divorce

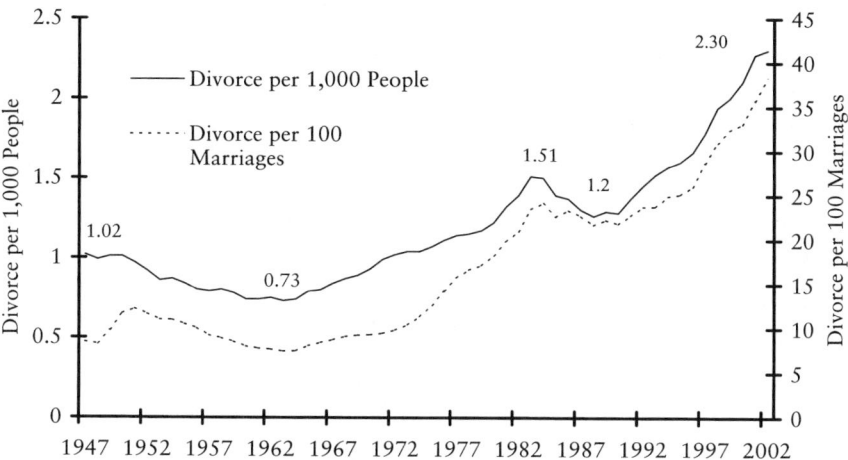

FIG. 11. Divorce Rates in Japan, 1947–2002. (Sources: Kōseishō, *Rikon ni kan suru tōkei* [Kōsei tōkei kyōkai, 2000], 42–43, for annual data from 1947 to 1998; Kōseirōdōshō, *Jinkō dōtai tōkei Heisei 12nen* [Kōsei tōkei kyōkai, 2002], 1: 441, for 1999–2000; Kōseirōdōshō, *Jinko dōtai tōkei Heisei 14nen* listed at http://www.mhlw.go.jp/toukei/, 29 July 2003, for 2001–2.)

saw well into the 1930s as "number one in the world" with respect to divorce.

In Japan, the most important postwar reversal in the divorce rate occurred during the 1960s, but the divorce rate changed direction three times after 1945. As shown in figure 11, it declined gradually from 1947 (1.02) to 1963 (0.73), rose steadily for twenty years until 1983 (1.51), then decreased and leveled off for five years (1988: 1.26) before beginning its current explosion, reaching 2.30 divorces per 1,000 people in 2002.[5] For most of the postwar period, the Japanese divorce rate remained lower than those of major European countries, but this gap was closing fast in the 1990s, a decade also marked by record lows in the birth and marriage rates. At the dawn of the twenty-first century, Japanese divorce rates had come full circle, reverting to the high levels noted at the dawn of the twentieth century, although not yet as high as those recorded in the last two decades of the nineteenth century. What was uncommon then, however, has now become a widespread pattern among industrialized nations. By returning to the divorce rates of its past, Japan has become a normal country in the present.

Changes in divorce rates in Japan and elsewhere often result in research and speculation on the social, economic, legal, political, and ideological causes and consequences of such transformations. Since sufficient Japanese, and even Western, scholarship in the fields of law, sociology, and legal sociology has been published on the subject of postwar divorce,[6] this chapter will restrict itself to examining divorce after World War II from a historical perspective, outlining broad trends in the areas covered in this book: the institutional framework for divorce, aggregate divorce practices, and public perceptions of divorce. Particular focus is on the three most important periods of postwar divorce change: reform of the law during the American Occupation, the 1960s revolution in behavior, and the return of the divorcing society in the 1990s.

Legislative Reform During the American Occupation

The only change in the legal framework of divorce in Japan during the entire twentieth century took place under the American Occupation (1945–52). Although efforts at reform were made before and after, only the authority of the Occupation provided sufficient strength for those advocating change in the laws and institutions of divorce to overcome the numerous political obstacles. Ever since Japan's civil code had been enacted in 1898, legal experts, politicians, and journalists had called for its revision. The most significant prewar attempt at reforming the family provisions of the code occurred during the Taishō period. To protect Japan's "good manners and beautiful customs" (*junpū bizoku*) and the "family system" (*kazoku seido*) in consideration of the "trend of the times," the Hara government in 1919 instituted a special expert committee, which submitted drafts in 1925 and 1927. The issues discussed ranged from a new definition of the grounds for divorce, especially focusing on whether to eliminate the sexual double standard, to the need for establishment of family courts following an American model.[7] Politicians nevertheless blocked these civil code changes in the Diet. The same issues related to divorce resurfaced during the Occupation period.

The constitution of May 1947 established some fundamental legal principles reordering relations in the family. It called in particular for the eradication of the house (*ie*) as defined by the special prerogatives of its head, anchoring the family instead around the married couple. "Marriage shall be based only on the mutual consent of both sexes," Article 24 stated, specifying that "laws shall be enacted considering choice of spouse, . . . divorce and other matters pertaining to marriage and the family from the standpoint of individual dignity and the essential equality of the sexes."[8] The civil code, the most important compendium of family law, was revised mainly in line with this philosophy. Within six months, a government committee completed a code that became effective on 1 January 1948, known as the New Civil Code, which replaced the Meiji Civil Code of July 1898.

As the code now defined marriage exclusively as a union formed by the will of two individuals, the previous requirements for consent of parents as a precondition for marriage registration of men under the age of thirty and women under the age of twenty-five became obsolete.[9] Legislators, however, retained the requirement of one parent's consent to the marriage if the couple were minors, a status ending at twenty.[10] Since the minimum ages for marriage, now augmented by a year, were eighteen for men and sixteen for women, parents could only delay the marriage of their children until they had reached maturity by withholding consent.[11] In contrast to this change for marriages, the code eradicated any need for parental consent in divorce, because at marriage, an individual also obtained legal maturity.[12] The shift in legal ideology away from the house was also influential in eliminating some grounds for judicial divorce, such as divorce due to mistreatment of or by the lineal ascendants of the other spouse and divorce due to the dissolution of adoption. The new law left no role for the extended family—divorce was now considered the concern exclusively of the married couple. This legal philosophy of limiting the divorce decision to the husband and wife marked a drastic break from the past, representing the last step in the slow legal emancipation of spouses from their families that had begun after the Edo period.

The New Civil Code's interpretation of equal rights for both spouses led to the abolishment of the sexual double standard in law, since adultery by either spouse became grounds for judicial divorce.[13] In contrast to the silence of the Meiji Civil Code on the issue of post-divorce property arrangements, the New Civil Code gave either spouse the right to ask for a division of matrimonial assets (*zaisan bunyo*) without specifying any principles for such a division.[14] In the draft stage of this provision, the Occupation legal expert Thomas L. Blakemore urged the adoption of a clear criterion, such as that property acquired by either party belonged to both in equal shares, but the Japanese drafters rejected the idea as too radical.[15] Despite the fact that the new code freed marriage from the family and postulated equality between husband and wife, Japanese legislators adhered to the nineteenth-century legacy of two routes to divorce: consensual divorce and judicial divorce. The resulting strong continuity in the legal framework of divorce is thus not adequately conveyed in the common belief today that during the American Occupation, "Japanese family law was radically revised."[16]

The decision to retain consensual divorce (*kyōgi rikon*) in the New

Civil Code was of the greatest practical importance. The Meiji Civil Code included consensual divorce as a codification of Japanese divorce practices of the Edo period, legitimized anew in the Meiji era by the French legal principles the Japanese discovered in the Napoleonic Code. Under both the Meiji Civil Code and the New Civil Code, the formalities for consensual divorce were simple, following those for marriage registration. The New Civil Code prescribes that spouses only have to inform officials at the local government office orally or in writing that they are divorcing. When they have underage children, spouses also have to designate a custodial parent, without needing to make any further arrangements for financial support of the children. After acceptance of the divorce document by the local official in charge of registration, who checks on the formalities, the marriage is dissolved.[17] Neither for marriage nor for divorce is there a need for attendance in person. It is common for spouses simply to send the registration documents by mail, with their seals impressed on them. Spouses continue to be free to set their own criteria for dissolving their marriages and settle all related issues.

Critics alleged that this simple system of registration failed to guarantee consent. An early draft of the New Civil Code suggested that to prevent fraud and coercion, all consensual divorces should require court permission, but just as similar proposals had failed during the 1880s, this idea was not included in the final code. An amendment to that end passed the upper house of the Diet but was defeated in the lower house. In 1952, in response to concern over the possibility of unilateral divorce, the Ministry of Justice started permitting the rejection of a registration by officials when one of the spouses changed his or her mind after sealing the divorce papers. A decade later, the ministry developed this into a petition system for nonacceptance of divorce documents, which was systematized in 1976. Ever since then, spouses afraid of fraudulent divorce have had the opportunity to inform the local office of their desire to remain married, so that no divorce registration will be accepted. Since 1964, this request expires every six months, so it needs continual renewal. The number of anxious spouses who filed for nonacceptance doubled from about 13,000 petitioners in 1969 to around 26,000 in 1985. The fear of divorce was generally stronger among wives; for example, 78 percent of the petitioners were wives and only 22 percent were husbands in 1969.[18] A government subcommittee examining civil code revisions in 1955 rejected the need for a system confirming mutual consent due to the small number of suits seeking invalidation of divorce and argued that the state should not unnecessarily intrude in such private affairs as divorce.[19]

Despite its shortcomings, widespread acceptance throughout the twentieth century supports the view that consensual divorce satisfies a popular need, even if only for lack of a better alternative. On average, 99 percent of divorces were consensual in the prewar years, and this remains by far the most common form of divorce, averaging about 90 percent of divorces throughout the second half of the twentieth century.[20]

In addition to drafting a new civil code, the Japanese government created family courts to mediate in family conflicts.[21] According to the law of domestic judgment of 1947, all family dispute cases first had to be submitted for conciliation by a committee consisting of a judge and two lay commissioners, with at least one female member.[22] All contested divorce cases, too, first had to be submitted to a family court for mediation before one of the spouses could sue in a district court. Family courts offered divorce either by conciliation (*chōtei rikon*) or by adjustment (*shinpan rikon*). In divorce by conciliation, a mediator tried to get the spouses to agree on divorce. In divorce by adjustment, a mediator settled the case, but this decision became invalid if either party objected within two weeks of the decision.[23] The two kinds of divorce by family courts together have never exceeded 10 percent of all divorces during the postwar period. The percentage of divorces by conciliation rose after the introduction of this form of divorce from 1.5 percent (1948) to 9.3 percent (1970) but has leveled off since (7.7 percent in 2000). Divorces by adjustment remained statistically minute, constituting a mere 0.03 percent of all divorces in 2000.[24]

The workings of the family court deter its more widespread use, argue scholars. Judges are so overworked that mediators are entrusted with the bulk of the proceedings. Sometimes a judge only appears to sign the agreement reached by the two parties. Several weeks or months may elapse between mediation sessions. As caseloads increased, the ratio of successful to unsuccessful mediations declined from 7:1 in 1950 to 3:1 in 1980.[25] An American legal scholar who observed sessions in the early 1980s believed that conservative mediators, usually from the upper social and economic echelon of society, and sixty years old on average, were putting pressure on the parties to reconcile. She attributed the fact that only 40 percent of divorce petitions in family court resulted in dissolution of marriages to the unrealistic expectations and unresolved emotions of the petitioning parties, in addition to the fact that family courts were part of a legal regime that did not support divorce.[26]

Only after failing to reach an agreement in family court can spouses finally sue for a judicial divorce. Legislators reduced the ten grounds for divorce in the Meiji Civil Code to five in the New Civil Code.[27] The classic grounds of adultery, malicious desertion, and unknown whereabouts for three years were already part of the Meiji Civil Code. Instead of the sexual double standard, the doctrine of gender equality shaped the provisions on adultery. Under the Meiji Civil Code, a wife could judicially divorce her husband for adultery only if he had previously been sentenced for sexual misconduct with a married woman. By contrast, the other two grounds, severe irrecoverable mental illness and grave reasons preventing the continuation of marriage, were new. In the 1890s, the majority of legal experts had rejected these two grounds in heated committee debates. Revision committees considered them again in the Taishō period before both were incorporated in the 1948 Civil Code. Despite this new set of divorce grounds, the ratio of judicial divorces among all divorces barely budged throughout the twentieth century, lingering at around 1 percent.[28]

Grave reasons preventing the continuation of marriage was an omnibus clause that had the potential to become a venue for divorcing a reluctant spouse. The courts, however, took a rather restrictive stance. In a 1952 landmark case, the Supreme Court ruled that a spouse at fault could not obtain a divorce over the objections of the other spouse.[29] This decision marked the beginning of the most restrictive divorce regime in Japan since the seventeenth century. Two years before the inception of the conservative Liberal Democratic Party dominance, often called the 1955 system, the Supreme Court created a divorce system that essentially guaranteed lifetime marriage to any legally innocent spouse. This form of marriage guarantee probably reinforced the pronounced sexual division of labor among Japan's new salaried urban middle class,[30] which was accompanied by the guarantee of lifetime employment to male workers at large corporations,[31] in the context of an ideology of "GNP nationalism."[32] Wives were thus enabled to devote themselves entirely to household chores and child rearing.[33]

Unlike most other industrialized nations, Japan has never experienced a "divorce law revolution"; its institutional framework for divorce has remained surprisingly stable.[34] During the last decades of the nineteenth century, Western visitors to Japan portrayed Japan as exotic, backward, and not yet civilized, in part because it practiced a form of divorce that required no judicial intervention and lacked clearly defined grounds for divorce. While the Japanese civil code of 1898 opened up the possibility of suing in court for divorce based on specific grounds, it also permitted spouses to divorce by simply notifying the official keeping family registers. Both avenues for obtaining divorce were retained in the civil code of

1948 formulated under the auspices of the American Occupation. This single reform amended the grounds for judicial divorce and established the family court as an institution of divorce mediation, but the previous system of divorce by mutual consent was retained, and it continued to be the most popular form of divorce. The flexibility and privacy of consensual divorce deflected much popular pressure to reform divorce laws.

In terms of the legal framework of divorce, one could argue that it was the United States and Europe that moved inadvertently closer to the Japanese model by abolishing fault-based grounds for divorce from the early 1960s onward. In a massive legal transformation sweeping across several countries and closely watched by Japanese legal experts, Western laws began permitting divorce when a marriage had broken down in such a way that it was "irremediable," "irreconcilable," or "irretrievable." The laws asked not for the reasons for the breakdown but simply for proof of it. The evidence most laws required was that couples had lived apart for a specified time, which could be as short as one year (Canada 1986) or as long as ten years (Belgium 1974). Several laws also had different qualifying periods if the divorce was contested. The English law of 1969 required two years of actual separation if both spouses wanted a divorce, but five years if one spouse objected. An unusually permissive country, Sweden, in 1973 recognized the right to divorce at the request of either or both spouses without any qualifying period of separation.[35] In permitting no-fault divorce, the Western divorce codes adopted the nonmoralistic approach to divorce found in Japanese legislation since the nineteenth century.

In many countries the abolishment of fault as grounds for divorce went hand in hand with concern (or hopes) for a shift in the consequences of divorce, especially in regard to the socially and economically weaker spouse, who then had to be supported by public funds. Some scholars argue that since the majority of divorce petitioners were women, they tended to obtain most of the property after divorce under the old fault regime. In several instances, such as in California in 1970, the introduction of no-fault and equal-division-of-property rules worked to the relative disadvantage of women, inasmuch as their share of property fell dramatically.[36] To prevent such outcomes, other legislatures devised elaborate rules to regulate the consequences of divorce and provide mechanisms for enforcement. For example, with the introduction of no-fault divorce in 1976, courts in West Germany could no longer determine child custody and financial arrangements on the basis of fault but had to adhere to a new set of principles, such as the best interests of the child, length of marriage, age of each spouse, previous work experience, and, most important, which spouse took care of any underage children.[37] By contrast, the fundamental legal rules governing the consequences of divorce in Japan, despite comparable public debates on the socioeconomic consequences of divorce, have not yet been altered.

The 1960s Revolution in Japanese Divorce Behavior

The "divorce law revolution" in industrialized societies was accompanied by a "divorce rate revolution," usually jointly subsumed under the term "divorce revolution."[38] In Japan, changes in the rate of divorce were not induced by divorce law reform, but the 1960s were nonetheless a watershed period in divorce. After more than six decades of decline, interrupted by the disruptive effects on marital life of World War II, the divorce rate began an upward creep for twenty years after 1963, before shooting upward quickly from 1988 to 2002. Many of the likely reasons for the increase in divorce commonly advanced for Japan resemble those presented for the same phenomenon elsewhere.

Before the divorce rate finally reversed direction in Japan, a period of high economic growth had begun in 1955 and lasted about twenty years, until the oil shock. Not surprisingly, the demand for female labor accelerated. The number of female employees in industry rose from 693,000 in 1960 to 1,109,000 in 1971, and the proportion of married women in the female industrial labor force increased from 24.4 percent to 43.2 percent.[39] Even after the oil shock, the number of female workers continued to grow until the end of the century, while the share of married women in the labor force, after peaking at 59.2 percent in 1985, began to stagnate in the following years.[40] Despite persistent huge gaps in income between men and women, even when discounting the fact that about a third of the women worked only part-time in Japanese terms,[41] there is no doubt that access to wage labor by married women rose, making them financially more independent of their families and husbands.[42]

There is some evidence that with the rise in Japanese divorce rates, the social stigma of divorce weakened. A large majority, 70 percent, of respondents opposed divorce in the first divorce survey of the Prime Minister's Office in 1972, whereas a majority of 60 percent approved of it in 1987.[43] Ten years later, though, despite a renewed increase in divorce, the level of approval had not substantially changed; a majority of 62 percent still believed that divorce disadvantaged women more than men in today's society.[44] Since more couples divorced, the share of remarriages of the divorced among all marriages rose. The number of divorced grooms as a percentage of all newlywed males, for example, doubled from 6.3 percent in 1968 to 12.5 in 1990.[45] This must have further accelerated the increase in the divorce rate, since such remarriages seem more likely to end in divorce than do first marriages.

Despite the similarity in the direction of divorce rate change between Japan and other countries, differences in the accompanying socioeconomic context of the family, marriage, and parenthood should not be overlooked. One of the most significant changes in Japan was the decrease in family and community control over marriage arrangements. The ideal of spousal selection according to individual choice had already been spread by some elements of the emerging Taishō mass media, such as women's magazines, but only a mostly urban minority had accepted it. Following endorsement by the New Civil Code, the idea of individual choice became more popular in a period that was in the middle of a significant rural-urban dislocation, when the part of the population employed in agriculture, forestry, and fisheries declined from 47.9 percent (1950) to 19.3 percent (1970).[46] By the late 1960s, the majority of newlyweds called their marriage a "love marriage" rather than an "arranged marriage."[47] Although the differences between the two forms of marriage in length and contentment are unclear, this indicates a rising emphasis on and hope of emotional fulfillment on the part of spouses.

After marriage, from the 1960s on, fewer couples lived with their in-laws. The main reason for this was less a rejection of older ideals of cohabitation, mutual assistance, and obligation than the result of a sheer surplus of children reaching adulthood who had been born in the demographic transition decades of high fertility and low mortality. Contrary to popular perception, the absolute number of three-generation households remained stable until the end of the century; it was the number of nuclear families—households consisting only of parents and children—that increased. Nevertheless, because of the rising number of one-person households, nuclear families continued to make up about two-thirds of all households. Overall, it is to be expected that help or interference in marital life by family members, whether in-laws or siblings, declined with the relative increase in the proportion of nuclear families among all families.

Together with the decrease in family control over marriage, there was a shift in the occurrence of divorce toward the later stages of marriage, which is the reverse of the pattern in some European countries.[48] In Japan, the long-term trend throughout the twentieth century was a lengthening of the mean duration of marriage before divorce, rising from about

3 years in 1899 to 5.3 years in 1950, before almost doubling to a constant level of about 10 years since the mid 1980s. The most conspicuous changes were at either end of the duration spectrum. Divorces after less than two years of marriage declined from 46.3 percent of all divorces (1899) to 35.7 percent (1950), then to 15.5 percent (2000), whereas divorces after twenty years of marriage rose from 2.6 percent (1899) to 3.5 percent (1950), then to 16.6 percent (2000). Even the decline in the ratio of divorces after less than five years of marriage from 75.1 (1899) to its postwar low of 34.0 (1985) is striking evidence of a new function for divorce in the Japanese life cycle.[49] Although at the end of the twentieth century, divorce rates in Japan had reverted to their old heights, the couples affected are now on average older and have a far greater time investment in the dissolved marriage than divorced spouses in previous periods.

Indeed, the current high divorce rates have not been accompanied by resurrection of other aspects of the older matrimonial system, as is seen in the gradual lengthening of the duration of marriage before divorce. Dating by prospective spouses has replaced cohabitation as the most common means of mate testing in Japan. This is not as obvious as it sounds. In many contemporary European societies, high rates of divorce go together with high rates of common-law marriages and out-of-wedlock childbirth. That is more than a spurious correlation; some scholars believe there is a strong causality involved, since few societies with frequent divorce have strict systems of marriage. As noted, the Japanese divorce rate today is within the same range as divorce rates in Europe, but in terms of common-law marriages and out-of-wedlock birth, Japan stands apart. The average rate of out-of-wedlock births was about 20 percent for the nations of the European Union, ranging from as high as 50 percent in Denmark to as low as 6 percent in Greece, in contrast to Japan's minuscule rate of 1.6 percent in 2000.[50]

Social scientists have been interested in the relationship between cohabitation and divorce for some time. The economist Gary Becker argues that cohabitation is an effective means of testing mutual compatibility so that a more-informed decision to marry is possible. As a result, divorces due to insufficient knowledge about the other spouse should become less likely.[51] Recent empirical studies have shown, however, that couples who live together before marriage are also more prone to divorce.[52] The sociologist Anthony Giddens explains this phenomenon with his theory of "plastic relationships," whereby those people who have more casual attitudes toward marriage as an institution are both more likely to live in a common-law union and more likely to dissolve their marriages.[53]

Neither theory, however, depicts the system of matrimony found in Japan, past or present. In the early twentieth century, regions with fewer common-law unions indeed had higher divorce rates, hinting at the existence of the kind of causation Becker expects to find at the individual level. Both common-law marriages and divorces, though, began declining after around 1900, and both reached their lows after the first postwar decade. In the historical trend until the 1960s, a positive connection between the two rates appears, just as Giddens points out for modern societies, but his explanation in terms of casual attitudes applies only with a twist. According to Giddens, "plastic relationships" are marked by high expectations of conjugal emotional fulfillment, but there is scant evidence to that effect in prewar Japan. It is striking that although divorce rates in Japan rose after the 1960s, there was no similar increase in common-law marriages as in many other countries. Marriage as an institution, ambiguous until the end of the nineteenth century, became firmly entrenched during the twentieth century, as is reflected in part in the continuous spread of public wedding ceremonies, which include elements of Shinto, Buddhism, and Christianity. In contrast to prewar weddings, the majority of which were at home, more than 99 percent of the weddings in the 1980s were in public places, such as wedding halls, hotels, public meeting halls, and churches. Only 0.2 percent of married couples had no wedding at all. The costs of marriage often exceeded two years of the average groom's income. In 1983, weddings were religious, public, expensive, and essential for starting married life. An American anthropologist summarized the marital ideals then projected: "Marriage in Japan . . . is celebrated in a big way, and is expected to last."[54] Japanese attitudes to marriage ceremonies had changed significantly since the first Shinto wedding ceremony was created for the marriage of the crown prince in 1900.

While the first phase of strengthening the institution of marriage led to less divorce, the second phase of strengthening it caused a rise in divorce rates, because it enhanced expectations of one's marriage partner. A reversal of stock divorce depictions reflects this change. Whereas popular images of divorce until the early twentieth century included the mother-in-law forcing out the young bride who failed to fit into the ways of the house, today popular advice books on divorce describe wives throwing out surprised husbands for, among other reasons, excessive emotional attachment to their mothers.[55] To add insult to the injury of the ex-husbands, the title of one of these books uses a euphemism for layoffs: *Restructuring Through Divorce: When Wives Dispose of Husbands.*[56] Even those prewar wives who left their husbands of their own volition did not dare to resort to such strong language when writing about their divorce experiences.

Because of the lengthening of marriage before divorce and the increase in the divorce rate, since the 1960s, more children have experienced their parents' divorce than ever before. This increased exposure to divorce occurred despite a fast drop in the birthrate following the legalization of abortion in 1949 and a gradual decline in the birthrate beginning in the 1970s, usually attributed to a rise in the average age at marriage. The number of children affected by divorce climbed from a postwar low of 40,452 in 1960 to a postwar high of 157,299 in 2000.[57] There is a strong link between the divorce rate and the number of children affected by divorce, since the proportion of divorcing couples with children remained roughly constant, fluctuating at around two-thirds of all divorces for most of the postwar period.[58] Although no comparable national data exist for the prewar period, it seems likely that fewer children were affected by divorce then, even at comparable or higher divorce rates, because marriages commonly lasted for a shorter time before a divorce. An early-twentieth-century study of several Tokyo wards estimated that only about one-fifth of divorcing couples had children.[59] After the war, though more children lost a parent through divorce, fewer experienced the premature death of a parent, thanks to the long-term postwar decline in mortality. Just as in other societies, divorce replaced death as the most important reason for single parenthood.[60]

Child custody practices, on the other hand, saw a conspicuous reversal after World War II. As we have seen, customary law in the Edo period recognized two main ideals of post-divorce child custody: whole custody based on lineage, whereby all children remained in the house of the father (or of the mother if she had taken an in-marrying husband), and split custody according to sex, whereby each parent took custody of the same-sex children. The 1898 Civil Code left it up to the spouses to decide on custody arrangements in consensual divorces, but in cases of spousal disagreement, it showed a preference for custody based on the lineage principle. In judicial divorces, however, the court was able to make arrangements for "the benefit of the child."[61] The 1948 Civil Code also gave the parents the option of deciding by themselves on the issue of post-divorce parental rights, but expressed no preference in the event of disagreement.[62] The second part of the twentieth century saw a rise in the

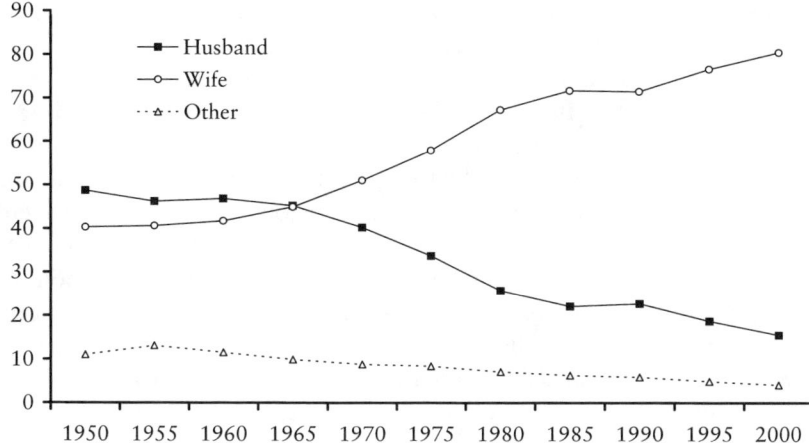

FIG. 12. Child Custody Arrangements in Japan, 1950–2000 (percentage of children). (Source: Kōseirōdōshō, *Jinkō dōtei tōkei Heisei 12nen* [Kōsei tōkei kyōkai, 2002], 1: 450.)

unprecedented practice of mothers chiefly taking custody of their children.

As figure 12 shows, until the 1960s, rather more fathers than mothers took custody, but by 2000, maternal custody (80.3%) had largely eclipsed paternal custody (15.5%) and other arrangements, such as split custody (4.1%).[63] The best interests of the child, already invoked in custody disputes in the late nineteenth century, had never before been linked so strongly to belief in the importance of a maternal presence for child development. The spread of second-wave feminism in Japan during the 1970s, arguing as elsewhere for a strengthening of women's legal, economic, and social positions, was accompanied by the greatest inequality in post-divorce parenting arrangements visible in the statistical record.

A shift favoring mothers in post-divorce custody also occurred in other societies, but at earlier times. In the United States, for example, from 1790 to 1890 there was a swing from paternal custody and control over children to an emphasis on the best interests of the child, with the mother presumed to be more suitable because the more nurturing parent. This trend toward maternal custody in the United States only began to be challenged in the 1970s, when custody law reversed its well-entrenched preference for mothers.[64] By contrast, in Japan, a similar reversal in preferences has not yet occurred, although child experts and legal scholars have discussed the possibility of incorporating the principle of joint custody into the law. As long as motherhood continues to play such an important role in defining female role identity, no change in custody practice should be expected.

With the lengthening of marriage before a divorce and the shift in child custody toward mothers, the issue of financial consequences of divorce for women, especially when they had spent their married lives as homemakers, took on completely new dimensions. Japanese divorce culture in the 1870s encouraged the return of property that a spouse, whether a wife or an in-marrying husband, had brought into the marriage. This was reflected in the principle of dowry return, which a spouse could expect unless she or he was divorced for a grave fault. Only in rare cases of exceptional hardship were there claims for further material support. The custodial parent was usually supposed to cover all child-rearing and education expenses, but in rare cases payments toward the upbringing of children of which the other spouse had custody could occur. Unlike the earlier Meiji Code, the New Civil Code of 1948 recognized the possibility of a division of property at divorce. In consensual divorces, an appeal to the family court was permitted within two years of divorce to divide marital property according to "the circumstances."[65]

In practice, the form of divorce has an impact on the amount of the financial settlement. Settlements are lowest in consensual divorce, higher for divorces in a family court, and highest in judicial divorce.[66] This distribution supports the argument that the financially less-well-endowed spouse, usually the wife, has a weaker bargaining position in consensual divorce. Besides support by the judges in judicial divorce, another reason for higher awards in court cases is that spouses with marriages of long duration are those most likely to seek divorce in court.

Spouses tend to avoid mutual financial obligations beyond divorce. Only in a minority of divorces were there any financial settlements.[67] Among those spouses agreeing on a financial settlement, the majority (1992: 61%) chose a lump sum as a means of payment at divorce, even though the total amount was higher when paid in installments.[68] Moreover, only few parents who did not have custody paid child support. A study of divorced mothers with small children receiving public funding in Osaka found that only 10 to 20 percent of fathers had contributed to the support of their children. The reasons given by the divorced mothers for the lack of support by their former husbands are instructive concerning post-divorce socioeconomic realities. About a third were unaware of the whereabouts of their former spouses; in another third of the cases, the fathers could not pay; and only in the remaining cases was there any hope of obtaining some form of paternal payment for children. One explanation for the low financial settlements at divorce is linked to the issue of social class. Just as in the prewar period, most divorcing couples belonged to the poorer sections of the population in terms of household assets and income.[69] They often had no property to divide, and husbands could not pay alimony or child support even if they had wanted to.

Moreover, the institutional mechanism of enforcing compliance was rather weak. A divorced spouse who wanted to receive back payments had to enter the slow process of family court mediation, and even then there was little court enforcement. It is no surprise that family court mediators encouraged spouses to settle for a lump sum in exchange for agreeing to divorce as the most certain method for receiving payments.[70] Neither is it surprising that survey after survey shows a low level of annual household income in divorced single-parent households, usually about one-third that of ordinary households. This level is substantially lower even than that of widowed single-parent households, which averages about half the amount of ordinary households.[71]

The historical legacy of how post-divorce financial support is arranged is visible in contemporary institutional mechanisms and payment practices. The crucial government decision on divorce in the Meiji era was to leave it up to the population to define the reasons for divorce in customary divorce practices. This policy became codified as consensual divorce in the Meiji Civil Code. As a result, there was no court that needed to, or could, identify a "guilty party." Guilt, however, often in combination with entitlement and need, was at the very heart of moral and legal claims to maintenance in the case of separation of bed and board from which the modern European and American divorce systems evolved.[72] Variations in laws and practices of maintenance and child support in and among those countries today reflect, in part, their degree of abandonment of the fault paradigm and their acceptance of the idea that a divorce marks a new start in life. In the traditional pattern of Japanese divorce, in contrast, divorced spouses knew that they had to rely on themselves, their natal families, or a new spouse for material subsistence. With increased duration of marriage before divorce and the shift in child custody, the consequences of divorce changed dramatically in the later decades of the twentieth century, but policy on divorce still ignored these new realities.

Agency in Japanese divorce, often written about but rarely documented historically in first-person accounts, remains an area of great speculation. This study argues that older research relying exclusively on legal documents exaggerated the lack of possibilities for wives to initiate and push through divorces in the past, while exaggeratedly portraying them as victims of their husbands and in-laws. Such images, however, which are to be found in literature, plays, and legal precedents since the Edo period, became recycled in Meiji popular and legal debates on gender issues, and in the next era, the Taishō era, divorce and the women's question were important themes in the popular press. Legal, economic, and social inequalities between husbands and wives, whether real or imagined, remain at the heart of much debate on divorce. Over the very long term, from the seventeenth century to the twentieth, a decrease is visible in the degree of legally and socially accepted family interference in married life and intervention in divorce. A husband is less likely today to physically attack his parents for divorcing his wife against his (and presumably her) wishes. Though the Meiji Civil Code divorce clauses still required documentation of family consent in addition to that of spouses who were under twenty-five years of age, the New Civil Code clearly ruled that only the wishes of the spouses mattered in divorce. Surveys further show how marginal the influence of the family in initiating divorce has now become.

Previous scholarship emphasized ad nauseam the power of the husband or mother-in-law to expel a young bride at will, but recent scholarship, including this book, shows that there is mounting evidence that wives, too, have in practice been able to leave their husbands since the Edo period. Household status (whether one had married into or been born into the family) was often crucial in divorce negotiations and contributed to the ambiguous position of in-marrying husbands (*muko yōshi*). The question of the extent to which divorce was detrimental to women, one of the most common present questions posed about divorce in the past, may never be satisfactorily answered, because of the scarcity of historical records in Japan, if research is limited to the act of divorce itself. In Edo-period popular plays, divorce was often reduced to the image of an innocent bride victimized by her husband and mother-in-law. If, instead of focusing on a single tragic moment, divorce is considered in the broader framework of the life course, a different picture emerges. Remarriage rates were higher and the sexual gap was smaller in certain localities in the Edo period; in 1879, Yamanashi Prefecture showed more equality than the national average in the low-divorce-rate decades in the middle of the twentieth century. Though more detailed research into remarriage patterns after divorce is needed, high divorce rates after short marriages, accompanied by frequent remarriages, appear to have functioned as a corrective to original mate selection—and either party was able to leave, even if at different socioeconomic costs.

Female plaintiffs have in fact outnumbered men in judicial divorces since the turn of the twentieth century. They won 85 percent of judicial divorces between 1900 and 1940 and still constitute the majority of divorce petitioners today in court or family court. In that sense, Japanese wives show as much initiative as wives in other industrialized countries, where most divorce suits are also female-initiated. Since the vast majority of divorces are in consensual divorce form, there is no empirical evidence to prove whether this is indeed a predominantly male domain, as so often alleged by scholars and the media, past and present.[73] My own guess is that there is little reason to assume that Japan should be an exception here. If indeed in Japan, too, the initiative for consensual divorce mostly came from wives, this would be despite the obvious economic drawbacks of divorce for many women.

The Return of the Divorcing Society in the 1990s

Several years before the political hegemony of Japan's Liberal Democratic Party ended, the system of guaranteed lifetime marriage came under attack. On 2 September 1987, the Supreme Court reversed its stance on divorce, which had been upheld since 1952, that no guilty party should obtain a court divorce over the objections of a legally innocent spouse. In a case widely reported by the press, the Supreme Court granted a divorce to a husband who had deserted his wife. The petitioner, a company president, left his wife after twelve years of marriage to live with another woman. During this cohabitation, two children were born to him and his new partner. After the petitioner stopped paying support, the wife sold a house purchased by her husband, but eventually she had to live with her brother's family. Despite the termination of emotional and financial ties, she persistently rejected divorce demands because the stigma of divorce would tarnish their mutual daughter. Her husband, however, claimed that her reasons were greed and spite. Unlike its 1952 decision, in this case the court believed a justifiable dependency relationship existed between the second woman and the husband. More broadly, it declared: "When one or both of the spouses no longer desire to live together in pursuit of a permanent spiritual and physical union, the marriage has lost the reality of communal life. . . . To continue such a marriage simply on paper in the family registry is unnatural."[74] The Supreme Court justified its new approach to divorce as being in line with current social norms and values.[75]

Shrinking away from advocating a right to divorce against the opposition of the other spouse, regardless of circumstances, the Supreme Court defined several preconditions in a series of seven decisions before the fall of 1990: a long period of separation relative to the marriage period; no severe financial, social, or psychological consequences for dependent children or spouses; and a court decision that divorce is preferable to continuation of the marriage.[76] Besides extending the opportunity for spouses to obtain a judicial divorce, it gave courts greater leeway to decide whether spouses deserved to be divorced. Although this marks a substantial departure from the Supreme Court's previous interpretation, the concept of a judicial divorce not restricted to a particular legal ground was not an entirely novel idea. As described earlier, eminent legal experts unsuccessfully supported this form of divorce based on the breakdown of marriage in the committees drafting the Meiji Civil Code in the 1890s, and the discretion of judges was also rather wide until 1898.

Politically active groups of attorneys, such as in the Tokyo Bar Association (Tōkyō bengoshikai), used the Supreme Court's divorce precedent to call for a large-scale examination of family regulations in the civil code.[77] Later this also became the official position of the influential Japanese Federation of Bar Associations. Armed with new public opinion surveys on changing perceptions of gender roles, the media responded favorably and generally supported such a general reconsideration.[78]

In 1991, the Ministry of Justice announced the establishment of a review committee to examine the family provisions of the civil code in relation to "the trends of the world" and the principle of "equality of men and women." Keeping intact the Japanese system of multiple forms of divorce, the committee focused on two basic issues in its final draft on 26 February 1996: redefining the grounds for judicial divorce and specifying some rules for the divorce settlement.

Retaining adultery, malicious desertion, and unknown whereabouts, the draft also included the no-fault provision of marital breakdown as grounds for divorce. To assess the existence of a situation "when the marriage relation broke down and no recovery is expected," the draft specified as proof a continuous separation of the spouses for more than five years that denied the purpose of marriage. Even the fulfillment of that condition did not automatically constitute a right to unilateral divorce, however. A court might reject a divorce petition when the divorce would lead to undue hardship in livelihood (*ichijirushii seikatsu no konnan*) or unbearable pain (*taenikui kutsū*) for the other spouse or the children. The same applied when the petitioner had violated the principle of loyalty (*shingi*) by substantially failing to cooperate with or support the other spouse.[79] This provision became widely referred to as divorce by marital breakdown (*hatanshugi rikon*), although this is what the existing system of consensual divorce had been providing all along. Now, though, this philosophy was also meant to guide judicial decisions in what is known elsewhere as no-fault divorce.

The review committee, which unlike its Meiji predecessor included female members, also discussed issues of child visitation and support and the basis of property division.[80] To balance possible side effects of the introduction of marital breakdown as grounds for divorce, it suggested criteria for the division of marital assets where the New Civil Code had specified none. The court was to consider degree of contribution, length of marriage, lifestyle during marriage, conditions of cooperation and support during marriage, and the age, health, work, and income of each spouse. For arrangements with respect to children, parents were to give the highest priority to the interests of the child (*ko no rieki*), a principle already meant to guide the court in child custody arrangements. Now that it was to apply also to consensual divorce, it became leverage for breaking with the long tradition of legal and social practice that assumed that divorce also ended the relationship between children and the noncustodial parent. The proposal stated explicitly: "When parents divorce by mutual consent, they should determine together who is to care for the child, visitation [*menkai*] and exchange [*kōryū*] of father or mother and child, the respective share of expenses for bringing up the child, and other items important for child rearing."[81] When parents reached no agreement on the above issues, the family court decided them.

The suggested changes in divorce law were less controversial than was the planned simultaneous introduction of optional separate spousal surnames, but the pros and cons were exhaustively debated both in the popular press and in specialized journals, especially after 1994, when a detailed interim report outlined possible alternatives.[82] The arguments echoed those in debates at the end of the nineteenth century. Supporters insisted on the nature of marriage tied together by love, whereas opponents pointed to the ample possibilities of divorce provided by the existing system of consensual divorce. Objections to no-fault court divorce were raised mainly on practical, rather than philosophical, grounds. Such a divorce reform, resisters feared, would be detrimental to housewives, who were in a disadvantaged economic position. The existing system at least forced a husband to bribe a reluctant wife into consent, they often argued. In the future, with a system of no-fault court divorce, they alleged, this became unnecessary.

One small symbolic issue in marriage and divorce indicates the committee's less-than-radical feminist interpretation of its mandate from the Ministry of Justice to reconsider the civil code with regard to gender equality. The compromise solution reached for the waiting period for divorced women before remarriage is a case in point. Set by the Meiji Civil Code at 300 days, in order to ascertain the paternity of children born after divorce, it still is on the books today. Although the committee proposed to shorten it, it failed to abolish the waiting period altogether. The new period was the result of arithmetic by legal minds; subtracting the paternity presumption of 200 days after marriage from the paternity presumption after divorce of 300 days, it came up with a new period for which remarriage was prohibited of 100 days. That medical science had developed new methods for ascertaining paternity in the past century did not persuade the committee to do away with the waiting period altogether. The Supreme Court upheld the constitutionality of the clause in 1992, claiming that it reflected the physical differences between men and women and thus did not constitute an undue form of sex discrimination. But contentions that the regulation is superfluous and discriminatory, and should thus be entirely abolished, have not subsided.[83]

By themselves, the proposals for divorce law reforms would probably not have met such long and continued political resistance on the part of shifting conservative cross-party alliances in the Diet, since only a small minority of the population opposed judicial divorce based on marital breakdown.[84] As a package deal connected with the introduction of optional separate spousal surnames and eradication of the difference in inheritance rights between marital and extramarital children, however, civil code reform appeared to many Diet members to emphasize individual rights and gender equality excessively. As the population remained evenly divided on what has become the crucial issue in family law reform, namely, whether a unified family surname is necessary to foster a feeling of family unity,[85] the majority of politicians had few benefits to expect from a reform stance. In this context, a successful legal reform would mark the official end to a postwar consensus tightly linking family, marriage, and parenthood. At a time when Japan is not only enduring a prolonged economic recession and increasingly obsessed with what it calls the aging society problem, politicians are unwilling to be viewed as dismantling such "traditional" social institutions. The question of how the legislators will react to changes in divorce is still unresolved, but it appears that, as in the past, they remain the driven, and not the driving, force in Japan's divorce system.

One continuity concerning divorce in Japan since the Meiji era is a firm common belief in progress toward greater gender equality. When a reporter finds out that in the past, too, divorce rates were high, the same phenomenon is presented in a different light. In today's case, high divorce rates are seen as a sign of "progress," since wives are increasingly taking the initiative to liberate themselves from the fetters of marriage. For the past, however, this is attributed to the prevalence of divorces in which wives were thrown out of their families.[86] Why this depiction is interesting is that it resonates with a way of describing the past that was already common in the Meiji era. An eminent legal scholar argued in committee debates for the enhanced position of the wife to be gained by the consensual divorce regulation in the planned civil code. When asked to clarify what he thought of current Japanese divorce procedures, he called consensual divorce an "enormous revolution" when contrasted with divorce in the distant past.[87]

Nevertheless, what is striking about the late 1990s is the repetition in the popular press of the image of unsuspecting men as the surprised victims of divorce. The last example in the twentieth century of this genre is probably the December 1999 issue of the Japanese version of the business magazine *Forbes,* in a special section with several articles under the title: "One Day, Suddenly, a Three-and-a-Half-Line Divorce Notice [*mikudarihan*] from the Wife." By using the image of the divorce notice, which in contemporary views is associated with the arbitrary male divorces of the past, the magazine thus created the impression of a world turned upside down, since it is now wives who divorce unilaterally. After claiming that more husbands are being "restructured" (*risutora*) out of marriage by their wives, one of the articles directed a rhetorical question at businessmen: "Are you safe?"[88] The language of business is applied to family matters; not only lifetime employment but lifetime marriage is increasingly uncertain.

Usually based on anecdotal evidence, this perception has been especially promoted in the 1990s by *Aera,* a general interest weekly magazine with a large female readership. Headlines in *Aera* stress female expectations of emotional satisfaction in title stories such as "Women in Their Thirties Divorcing Without Grounds."[89] In a rare concern for the health of divorced men, a headline says divorce hurts men, too.[90] "The Divorce Was Because of My Selfishness," a wife confesses in another article.[91] The theme of husbands as victims of divorce is widespread in the press. "'Husbands' Disposed of by Their 'Wives' Are Rapidly on the Rise," one title says bluntly.[92] A frequent subtheme is the negative impact on men of divorce in old age.[93] The story of a divorced Shizuoka man attempting suicide—although this reaction is highly unusual—conveys the new message that husbands are being discarded against their will.[94] Whether this image is more than a press fad is difficult to tell at this stage. Certainly husbands, except those marrying into a family as adopted sons (*muko yōshi*), have never before been popularly portrayed as so feeble and helpless.

This current weak husband theme coincides with another popular concept: the happy divorce. In the 1970s, to combat the stigma of divorce, an advice service for wives called "Divorce with a Smile" (Nikoniko rikon) was founded by feminists associated with Madoka Yoriko, a female Diet member prominent in the media. In the late 1990s, the image of divorce as a positive step of liberation for women was especially promoted by some women's magazines. *Fujin no kōron* has in recent years run special features with a positive outlook on divorce under titles such as "Divorce with a Smiling Face" and "Divorce and Become Happy."[95] Besides a historical reversal of images of pitiable divorce victims, from young bride to old husband, the act of divorce is praised more than probably ever before, as captured by the book title *Pojitibu rikon* (Positive Divorce).[96] What this suggests is that the divorcing society (*rikonka shakai*), as some scholars have begun to call Japan, is going to be with us for a good part of the twenty-first century.

REFERENCE MATTER

APPENDIX

Tables

TABLE A.1

Japanese Divorce Rate by City Size, 1910–1935

(per 1,000 population)

Percent	City	Town	Small Town	Japan
1910	0.99			1.18
1915	1.02			1.10
1920	0.88	0.93		0.94
1925	0.79	0.87	0.86	0.87
1930	0.77	0.81	0.79	0.80
1935	0.67	0.72	0.72	0.70

SOURCES: Hayami Akira, ed., *Kokusei chōsa izen Nihon jinkō tōkei shūsei* (Hara shobō, 1992–93); Takahashi Shin'ichi, ed., *Kokusei chōsa ikō Nihon jinkō tōkei shūsei* (Hara shobō, 1994).

NOTE: In 1910: city over 50,000 inhabitants, town under 50,000 inhabitants. Since 1925: city over 100,000 inhabitants, town 50,000–100,000, small town 10,000–50,000.

TABLE A.2
Prior Status of Newlywed Brides by Age in Japan, 1919

Age	Unmarried	Widowed	Divorced	Total Brides
15–19	122,135	151	1,020	123,306
20–24	200,542	1,677	6,962	209,181
25–29	63,322	2,973	8,370	74,665
30–34	23,335	2,824	6,368	32,527
35–39	11,529	2,214	4,849	18,592
40–44	5,770	1,649	3,229	10,648
45–49	2,605	1,098	1,795	5,498
50–54	1,208	785	1,158	3,151
55–59	493	404	488	1,385
60–64	221	195	257	673
65–69	67	69	91	227
Over 70	28	40	33	101

SOURCE: Kokuseiin, *Nihon teikoku jinkō dōtai tōkei* (Kokuseiin, 1922), 36.

TABLE A.3
Index of Divorce by Age Group in Japan, 1919–1940
(per 1,000 people)

Age	1919–1921	1924–1926	1929–1931	1934–1936	1939–1940
15–19	100	65	43	26	17
20–24	100	84	70	55	48
25–29	100	88	82	77	74
30–34	100	91	88	81	79
35–39	100	93	96	89	79
40–44	100	94	106	94	89
45–49	100	100	108	92	92
50–54	100	100	114	100	100
55–59	100	100	125	100	100
60–64	100	100	150	100	100

SOURCE: Index based on Irene B. Taeuber, *Population of Japan* (Princeton N.J., Princeton University Press, 1958), 229.

TABLE A.4
In-Marrying Husbands Among Newlyweds and Spouses Departing After Divorce, 1905–1935

	Whereabouts after divorce (%)			In-marrying among new grooms (%)
	Wife leaves	Husband leaves	Stay together	
1905	85.2	12.1	2.7	9.7
1910	85.2	12.0	2.8	9.4
1915	86.1	11.2	2.8	8.8
1920	86.3	11.2	2.5	8.7
1925	85.9	11.4	2.7	8.2
1930	86.2	10.8	2.9	7.9
1935	86.9	10.5	2.7	7.7

SOURCES: Hayami Akira, ed., *Kokusei chōsa izen Nihon jinkō tōkei shūsei* (Hara shobō, 1992–93); Takahashi Shin'ichi, ed., *Kokusei chōsa ikō Nihon jinkō tōkei shūsei* (Hara shobō, 1994).

TABLE A.5
Court Divorces, 1900–1940

			Reasons for divorces filed by husbands								
	Total	Husbands	I	II	III	IV	V	VI	VII	VIII	IX	X
1900	196	29	1	8	0	3	1	5	0	2	9	0
1901	194	28	0	6	0	6	3	5	0	0	8	0
1902	175	23	0	4	1	3	2	8	0	1	3	1
1903	194	26	0	7	0	6	4	6	0	0	3	0
1904	267	26	0	7	0	3	2	5	0	3	5	1
1905	237	19	0	6	0	1	0	8	0	1	3	0
1906	275	32	0	5	0	4	3	9	1	1	9	0
1907	295	32	0	8	0	4	3	6	0	1	10	0
1908	311	34	0	10	0	4	2	7	0	0	11	0
1909	368	39	0	11	0	3	1	9	0	1	14	0
1910	413	42	0	10	0	6	5	11	0	0	10	0
1911	425	49	0	11	0	10	4	10	0	0	14	0
1912	419	44	0	6	0	3	2	14	0	0	19	0
1913	364	37	0	6	0	2	7	9	0	0	13	0
1914	375	29	0	9	0	2	5	8	0	1	4	0
1915	325	32	0	6	0	7	0	8	1	0	10	0
1916	375	38	1	8	0	3	2	8	0	0	16	0
1917	396	32	1	9	0	4	1	9	0	1	6	1
1918	451	44	1	8	0	2	4	17	0	0	12	0
1919	478	47	1	9	0	6	2	14	0	1	13	1
1920	450	52	0	7	0	2	4	16	0	2	21	0
1921	430	47	0	10	0	1	3	17	0	0	16	0
1922	375	54	0	9	0	3	3	16	1	0	21	1
1923	344	44	0	11	0	1	3	15	1	1	11	1
1924	386	49	1	12	0	1	4	21	0	3	7	0
1925	372	59	1	30	0	0	4	14	1	1	8	0
1926	402	62	0	18	0	4	4	20	2	0	14	0
1927	377	72	0	20	0	2	6	30	1	0	13	0
1928	373	59	1	20	0	2	7	22	0	0	7	0
1929	439	81	2	27	0	3	7	29	3	2	8	0
1930	378	81	3	32	0	0	7	29	0	2	8	0
1931	329	69	1	24	0	2	7	24	0	1	8	2
1932	341	69	0	29	0	1	7	22	0	1	9	0
1933	373	78	1	37	0	1	8	24	0	2	5	0
1934	419	79	1	29	0	1	6	29	1	3	8	1
1935	394	89	0	38	0	3	4	33	0	0	11	0
1936	373	77	1	35	0	1	8	18	0	0	14	0
1937	383	86	1	26	0	3	11	27	1	0	16	1
1938	344	81	3	19	0	2	10	35	0	2	10	0
1939	325	85	1	28	0	3	9	28	2	0	13	1
1940	369	122	2	36	0	2	11	44	1	2	23	1
1900–40	14,509	2,177	24	651	1	120	186	689	16	35	443	12
Percent			1%	30%	0%	6%	9%	32%	1%	2%	20%	1%

SOURCE: Ōta Takeo, *Rikon gen'in no kenkyū* (Yūhikaku 1956), 585–86.

KEY: Meiji Civil Code, court divorce according to Article 813: I, bigamy of the spouse; II, adultery by the wife; III, punishment of the husband for a sexual crime; IV, spouse jailed for three years or punished for crimes; V, mistreatment by the spouse; VI, desertion by the spouse; VII, mistreatment by

TABLE A.5 —*continued*

	Wives	\multicolumn{10}{c	}{Reasons for divorces filed by wives}	Male	Female
		I	II	III	IV	V	VI	VII	VIII	IX	X		
1900	167	1	0	1	68	23	47	1	6	16	4	15%	85%
1901	166	1	1	1	52	15	64	0	5	17	10	14%	86%
1902	152	0	1	0	53	20	51	1	2	20	4	13%	87%
1903	168	2	0	4	60	27	49	0	4	16	6	13%	87%
1904	241	1	0	0	60	20	53	0	6	91	10	10%	90%
1905	218	0	0	0	59	20	60	0	2	70	7	8%	92%
1906	243	0	0	1	58	17	59	0	3	100	5	12%	88%
1907	263	1	0	2	60	20	81	1	7	89	2	11%	89%
1908	277	2	0	0	44	30	85	2	4	105	5	11%	89%
1909	329	0	0	1	55	31	121	2	2	112	5	11%	89%
1910	371	1	0	2	83	36	106	2	5	129	7	10%	90%
1911	376	3	0	0	94	40	106	2	3	121	7	12%	88%
1912	375	3	0	2	86	40	98	1	8	126	11	11%	89%
1913	327	0	0	0	53	42	106	2	4	110	10	10%	90%
1914	346	2	0	4	63	36	104	2	7	123	5	8%	92%
1915	293	3	0	0	45	33	104	1	7	92	8	10%	90%
1916	337	1	0	4	65	27	127	2	5	98	8	10%	90%
1917	364	2	0	0	71	24	128	0	5	128	6	8%	92%
1918	407	1	0	0	84	30	137	0	6	140	9	10%	90%
1919	431	3	0	2	67	50	153	1	13	136	6	10%	90%
1920	398	1	0	2	66	35	141	1	5	141	6	12%	88%
1921	383	6	0	0	38	46	138	0	8	145	2	11%	89%
1922	321	3	0	2	33	54	115	2	4	102	6	14%	86%
1923	300	1	0	0	33	42	121	2	5	92	4	13%	87%
1924	337	3	0	1	29	45	161	0	3	88	7	13%	87%
1925	313	2	0	1	40	45	136	1	2	84	2	16%	84%
1926	340	3	0	1	35	55	141	3	3	92	7	15%	85%
1927	305	4	0	3	45	41	132	1	5	70	4	19%	81%
1928	314	0	0	4	39	53	131	2	4	76	5	16%	84%
1929	358	1	0	3	19	66	171	2	9	79	8	18%	82%
1930	297	0	0	2	26	59	127	2	7	72	2	21%	79%
1931	260	1	0	2	25	55	102	3	3	65	4	21%	79%
1932	272	5	0	2	19	50	117	4	2	69	4	20%	80%
1933	295	2	0	5	24	52	127	6	6	70	3	21%	79%
1934	340	3	0	3	44	62	153	2	5	61	7	19%	81%
1935	305	0	0	0	41	66	123	5	4	58	8	23%	77%
1936	296	2	0	0	34	70	131	2	2	53	2	21%	79%
1937	297	2	0	2	36	61	127	2	4	61	2	22%	78%
1938	263	0	0	1	36	46	126	1	5	46	2	24%	76%
1939	240	4	0	1	22	33	113	1	3	58	5	26%	74%
1940	247	0	0	1	27	33	101	1	5	76	3	33%	67%
1900–40	1,2332	70	2	60	1991	1650	4573	63	198	3497	228	15%	85%
Percent		1%	0%	0%	16%	13%	37%	1%	2%	28%	2%		

(KEY—*cont.*:)
spouse's ascendants; VIII, spouse's mistreatment of one's own ascendants; IX, unknown whereabouts of the spouse for three years; X, wife's separation from an in-marrying husband.

Notes

NOTE: Tokyo is omitted if it is the place of publication of a Japanese-language book.

Chapter 1: The Forgotten History of Japanese Divorce

1. See William J. Goode, *World Changes in Divorce Patterns* (New Haven: Yale University Press, 1993), 214–43.
2. Alessandro Valignano quoted in Michael Cooper, ed., *They Came to Japan: An Anthology of European Reports on Japan, 1543–1640* (Berkeley: University of California Press, 1981), 62.
3. A. B. Mitford cited in Felix Baumann, *Japaner Mädel* (Berlin: Langenscheidt, 1908), 57.
4. E. Lamairesse, *Le Japon: Histoire, religion, civilisation* (Paris: Augustin Challamel, Librairie coloniale, 1892), 12.
5. Basil H. Chamberlain, *Things Japanese* (1890; 5th ed. rev., 1905), reprinted as *Japanese Things: Being Notes on Various Subjects Connected with Japan, for the Use of Travelers and Others* (Rutland, Vt.: Charles E. Tuttle, 1971), 313.
6. William Hugh Erskine, *Japanese Customs: Their Origin and Value* (Tokyo: Kyo Bun Kwan, 1925), 8.
7. Daigoro Goh, "The Family Relations in Japan," *Transactions and Proceedings of the Japan Society, London* 2 (1892–93): 150.
8. See, e.g., "Katei no kakumei jinrin no hanji" (editorial), *Kokumin no tomo*, no. 160 (1892): 2.
9. Go Bunsō, "Bankoku ichi no rikon koku," *Chūō kōron*, February 1902, 45–46; *Jiji*, 29 November 1916; *Yomiuri shimbun*, 27 February 1917; "Nihon no rikon wa sekai ichi: Hozumi Shigetō hakushi ga 'mikudarihan' no kenkyū," *Tōnichi*, 9 January 1921.
10. Okamatsu Michi, "Honpō rikon tōkei ippan (1)," *Tōkei shūshi* 383 (1913): 3–8.
11. Toyoda Tamotsu and Yokoe Katsumi, "Fūfu kankei keizoku kikanbetsu rikon no kenkyū (ka)," *Tōkei shūshi* 659 (1936): 33.

12. Rutherford Alcock, *The Capital of the Tycoon: A Narrative of a Three Years' Residence in Japan* (1863), reprint (New York: Greenwood Press, 1969), 1: 194.

13. Erskine, *Japanese Customs*, 8.

14. Alice M. Bacon, *Japanese Girls and Women* (Boston: Houghton, Mifflin, 1891), 66.

15. L. W. Küchler, "Marriage in Japan. Including a Few Remarks on the Marriage Ceremony, the Position of Married Women, and Divorce," *Transactions of the Asiatic Society of Japan* 13 (1885): 117.

16. Yasu Iwasaki, "Divorce in Japan," *American Journal of Sociology* 36, no. 3 (November 1930): 435.

17. "Nihon no rikon wa sekai ichi."

18. Teizo Toda, "Divorce—A Comparative Study," *Contemporary Japan*, September 1933: 302.

19. Murakami Kazuhiro, *Meiji rikon saibanshiron* (Kyoto: Hōritsu bunkasha, 1994), 187, 191.

20. Yuzawa Yasuhiko, *NHK bukkusu*, vol. 531, *Zusetsu: Gendai Nihon no kazoku mondai* (Nihon hōsō shuppan kyōkai, 1987), 169.

21. *Yomiuri shinbun*, 30 June 1997.

22. Ishii Ryōsuke, *Nihon kon'in hōshi* (Sōbundō, 1977), 431.

23. Kawashima Takeyoshi and Kurt Steiner, "Modernization and Divorce Rate Trends in Japan," *Economic Development and Cultural Change* 9, no. 1, pt. 2 (October 1960): 216–17.

24. Laurel L. Cornell, "Peasant Women and Divorce in Preindustrial Japan," *Signs: Journal of Women in Culture and Society* 15, no. 4 (1990): 710–32.

25. Diana E. Wright, "Severing the Karmic Ties That Bind: The 'Divorce Temple' Mantokuji," *Monumenta Nipponica* 52, no. 3 (Autumn 1997): 376.

26. Robert J. Smith, "Making Village Women into 'Good Wives and Wise Mothers' in Prewar Japan," *Journal of Family History* 8, no. 1 (Spring 1983): 79–80.

27. Publications in Western languages relevant to the history of Japanese divorce law before 1945 include, in English: Zennosuke Nakagawa, "A Century of Marriage Law," *Japan Quarterly* 10, no. 2 (April–June 1963): 182–92, and Nobushige Hozumi, *Lectures on the New Japanese Civil Code: As Material for the Study of Comparative Jurisprudence* (Tokyo: Maruzen, 1912); in German: Margret Neuss-Kaneko, "Scheidung auf Japanisch," in *Japanologentag*, ed. Ernst Lokowandt (Munich: Iudicium, 1990), Wolfgang Humbert-Droz, *Das Ehescheidungsrecht in Japan* (Cologne: Carl Heymanns KG, 1985), Torataro Araki, *Japanisches Eheschließungsrecht* (Göttingen: Univ.-Buchdruckerei von W. Fr. Kästner, 1893), Saburō Sakamoto, *Das Ehescheidungsrecht Japans* (Berlin: Georg Pintus, 1903), and Kojiro Iwasaki, *Das japanische Eherecht* (Leipzig: Roßberg'sche Verlagsbuchhandlung, 1904); in French: Dominique Wang, "Le Divorce en Chine et au Japon," *Zeitschrift für Schweizerisches Recht* 93 (1974): 609–39, and Tadaki Matsukawa, *La Famille et le droit au Japon* (Paris: Economica, 1991).

28. Isabella Bird, *Unbeaten Tracks in Japan* (1880), reprint (Rutland, Vt.: Charles E. Tuttle, 1973), 74.

29. Takei Masaomi, *Naienkon no genjō to kadai* (Kyoto: Hōritsu bunkasha, 1991), 8, 10–11. In a survey of 172 common-law marriages in Kyoto, other reasons for nonregistration were, on the one hand, the absence of parental consent as legally required, and restrictions by the house, and, on the other hand, the low social significance attached to registration.

30. Kōseishō, *Jinkō dōtai tōkei* (Kōsei Tōkei Kyōkai, 1997), 1: 115. Today, marriage in Japan, more than elsewhere, is connected to bearing and rearing children, as is seen in the low rate of out-of-wedlock childbirth of around 1 percent. Among the twelve EU countries, the average for out-of-wedlock childbirth in 1992 was 20 percent. Commission européenne, *Les Femmes et les hommes dans l'union européenne* (Luxembourg: Office des publications officielles des Communautés européennes, 1995), 102.

31. Statistics from Edo period registers of religious affiliation *(shūmon aratame chō)* mentioned in this book have been previously collected and analyzed by other researchers. Scholars have already discussed the merits and demerits of the registers elsewhere, and the discussion here can thus be extremely brief. The registers certified that all registered Japanese were members of Buddhist temples. Once a year, the headman was supposed to walk through his village and compile household lists with each person's name, age, relationship to the household head, and, of course, religious affiliation. For a more detailed discussion, see Laurel L. Cornell and Hayami Akira, "The Shūmon Aratame Chō: Japan's Population Registers," *Journal of Family History* 11, no. 4 (1986): 311–28; Kitō Hiroshi, *Nihon nisennen no jinkōshi* (Kyoto: PHP kenkyūjo, 1983), 91–101.

32. Marius B. Jansen, "The Ruling Class," in *Japan in Transition: From Tokugawa to Meiji*, ed. id. and Gilbert Rozman (Princeton, N.J.: Princeton University Press, 1986), 90.

33. Annual income in terms of rice; one *koku* equals 180 liters.

34. Jansen, "Ruling Class," 113.

35. Article 49 of October 1873 civil code draft. Tetsuka Yutaka, *Meiji shonen no minpō hensan: Etō Shinpei no hensan jigyō to sono sōan* (Shihō daijin kanbō hishoka, 1944), 51.

36. Meiji Civil Code, Article 772.

37. See details in chapter 3.

38. A contrarian view is espoused by an important school of anthropologists and sociologists who assert that individual choice enforced against the family by the community was a prevalent pattern in the countryside before the arrival of modernity. According to the written historical evidence I have seen so far, this seems rather an exceptional and not a common occurrence. For an influential proponent of this opinion, see Chizuko Ueno, "The Position of Japanese Women Reconsidered," with comment by D. P. Martinez, *Current Anthropology* 28, no. 4 (August–October 1987): S75–S85.

39. By the 1936–45 period, these proportions had shifted, reflecting a lessening of family control over the process of marriage arrangement: love mar-

riage (11%), *miai* marriages (51%), and arranged marriages without the future spouses seeing each other (24%). Sepp Linhart, "Familie," in *Japan-Handbuch*, ed. Horst Hammitzsch (Wiesbaden: Franz Steiner, 1981), 552.

40. Laurel L. Cornell, "Why Are There No Spinsters in Japan?" *Journal of Family History* 9, no. 4 (Winter 1984): 326–39.

41. In Yamanashi Prefecture, only 3.36 percent of 46- to 50-year-old men had never been married in an 1879 survey. The census recorded 1.11 percent in 1930.

42. Sōmuchō tōkeikyoku, *Heisei 2nen kokusei chōsa hōkoku*, vol. 2 (Nihon Tōkei Kyōkai, 1992), 46.

43. This can lead to very minute distinctions. For example, Segawa Kiyoko distinguishes among eight forms of marriages with various subkinds: Uematsu Akashi, "Kon'inshi no shomondai," *Kōza Nihon no minzoku*, vol. 3, *Jinsei girei*, ed. Inoguchi Shōji (Yūseidō, 1978), 32.

44. Meiji Civil Code, Articles 732, 788.

45. Ochiai Emiko, "Familie und Geschlechterbeziehung in Japan seit Ende des Zweiten Weltkrieges bis zur Gegenwart," in *Monographien*, vol. 22, *Das Bild der Familie in den japanischen Medien*, ed. Hilaria Gössmann (Munich: Iudicium, 1998), 53.

46. Harald Fuess, "Die japanische BGB-Reformkontroverse (1996): Japanische Identität und die Rolle der Frau," *Japanstudien: Jahrbuch des Deutschen Instituts für Japanstudien* 9 (1997): 258.

47. Decrees number 162 (May 1873) and 247 (July 1873). Other terms for divorce found in Meiji state decrees and directives were *riin* (terminating a marriage) and *kaikon* (opening a marriage). The current term for remarriage, *saikon*, first appeared in 1877; *saien* (retaking a relationship) and *saika* (retaking a bride) were common before. Analysis of the material in Horiuchi Misao, ed., *Meiji zenki mibunhō daizen*, vol. 2, *Kon'inhen* 2 (Chūō daigaku shuppankai, 1974), 237–373. Japan's first civil code drafts in 1873 used the term *rien* for divorce.

48. Ulrike Wöhr, *Frauen zwischen Rollenerwartung und Selbstdeutung: Ehe, Mutterschaft und Liebe im Spiegel der japanischen Frauenzeitschrift Shin shin fujin von 1913 bis 1916* (Wiesbaden: Harrassowitz, 1997), 270–71.

49. Edo period examples are mentioned by Nakada Kaoru, "Rikon," in *Tokugawa jidai no bungaku ni mietaru shihō* (Meijidō shoten, 1925), 136–67, and Tamaki Hajime, *Nihon kazoku seidoron* (Hōritsu bunkasha, 1971), 193–95.

50. Horiuchi, *Kon'inhen* 2, 352.

51. Tetsuka, *Meiji shonen no minpō hensan*, 52.

52. John H. Wigmore, ed., *Law and Justice in Tokugawa Japan: Materials for the History of Japanese Law and Justice Under the Tokugawa Shogunate 1603–1867*, pt. 1, *Introduction* (Tokyo: University of Tokyo Press, 1969), 151.

53. The results of the 1875 survey are reprinted in Shihōshō, "Zenkoku minji kanrei ruishū," in *Meiji bunka zenshū*, vol. 9, *Hōritsu*, ed. Meiji Bunka Kenkyūkai (1929; reprint, Nihon hyōronsha, 1992), 161–374, translated into English in John H. Wigmore, ed., *Law and Justice in Tokugawa Japan: Materi-*

als for the *History of Japanese Law and Justice Under the Tokugawa Shogunate 1603–1867*, pt. 7, *Persons: Civil Customary Law* (Tokyo: University of Tokyo Press, 1972). The English translation is useful as a guide to particular practices, but there is no adequate glossary and Japanese terms are often translated ambiguously or inconsistently. Sometimes several Japanese words are ignored in the English translation, and any statistics of practices based on the English version would be faulty. This book relies on the Japanese version unless otherwise indicated. The 1875 survey is at its most convincing in showing the extent of regional variation, because it recorded differences at the district level. Regional diversities in marriage and divorce customs thus come fully to light. It is a good balance to narrower and deeper local studies, since it indicates the relative frequency of certain practices. Although entries for many districts are missing, the existing records sometimes suggest patterns of regional variation that could not be seen through other contemporary sources.

The greatest weakness of the 1875 survey is the few and inadequate references to social differences. The survey paid insufficient attention to variations in laws and customs of samurai, peasants, artisans, merchants, and townsmen. It is difficult for a reader to deduce how families of a particular social status and profession lived. There are also some inconsistencies in the descriptions of status-based customs. Entries that in the 1877 version only applied to samurai are meant to show general practice in the 1880 version. General references to "lower class" are also not specific enough for us to understand whether marginal elements of society are meant or just ordinary non-samurai commoners.

There is a tendency in the 1875 survey to blur the distinction between present and past. Although one would expect local officials, even when they had served under the former government, to be eager to show their compliance with the regulations of the new Meiji state to the commissioners as representatives of the central government, local officials frequently discussed banned former practices as if they were still current. Closer attention to the distinction between past and present might have elucidated the political and social transition in the early Meiji period, but the Ministry of Justice itself encouraged a tendency to emphasize the past: "The recorded items are meant for reference in the draft of the civil code . . . so that they have been recorded, whether still in use or not. Unless contrary to specific laws promulgated since the [Meiji] Restoration, they can be regarded as being still practiced" (Shihōshō, "Zenkoku minji kanrei ruishū"; see also Wigmore, *Law and Justice*, 7: 158). Sometimes regulations that were clearly opposed to new laws made it into the survey without qualification, such as registration according to an annual religious survey, while in other cases they were designated as belonging to the "old law."

54. Tōkeiin, ed., *Kai kuni genzai ninbetsu chō* (Tōkeiin, 1882).
55. For a discussion on the methods of the trial census, see Saitō Osamu, "Meiji shonen nōka setai no shūgyō kōzō," *Mita gakkai zasshi* 78, no. 1 (1985): 15–17.
56. Tōkeiin, *Kai kuni*, 13.
57. Shihōshō, "Zenkoku minji kanrei ruishū," Yamanashi: Kai.
58. Prewar population statistics have been reprinted by Hara shobō.

Hayami Akira, ed., *Kokusei chōsa izen Nihon jinkō tōkei shūsei*, 22 vols. (Hara shobō, 1992–93); Takahashi Shin'ichi, ed., *Kokusei chōsa ikō Nihon jinkō tōkei shūsei*, 7 vols. (Hara shobō, 1994).

59. Carl Mosk, *Patriarchy and Fertility: Japan and Sweden, 1880–1960* (New York: Academic Press, 1983), 144–45.

60. Hayami Akira, "Jinkō tōkei no kindaika katei: koseki hensei kara kokusei chōsa e," in id., ed., *Kokusei chōsa izen Nihon jinkō tōkei shūsei*, vol. 1 (Hara shobō, 1992), 1–16.

61. Masato Takase, "1890 nen–1920 nen no wagakuni no jinkō dōtai to jinkō seitai," *Jinkōgaku kenkyū* 14 (May 1991): 32.

62. Ōta Takeo, *Naien no kenkyū* (Yūhikaku, 1965), 37.

63. If a man already had a legal wife, this policy became complicated: "A mistress is registered as wife, but if wife and mistress live together, the mistress is not attributed a marital relationship. But if they live apart, the mistress is registered as married . . . rather than according to the family register, spousal relations should be recorded according to the actual state of affairs [*jijitsu*]. . . . In cases where the spouse has left the house for several years, it is up to the remaining spouse to decide whether the marriage still continues, the other spouse has died, or the whereabouts are unknown" (*Hōchi*, 31 August 1920, reprinted in *Shinbun shūroku Taishōshi*, 8: 322).

Chapter 2: For the Sake of the House

1. Wolfgang Humbert-Droz, *Das Ehescheidungsrecht in Japan* (Cologne: Carl Heymanns KG, 1985), 68–73.

2. Basil Hall Chamberlain, *Japanese Things* (Charles E. Tuttle, 1971), 503–4.

3. Yamakawa Kikue, *Women of the Mito Domain*, trans. Kate Wildman Nakai (Tokyo: University of Tokyo Press, 1992), 24–31.

4. Michiko Aoki and Margret Dardess, "The Popularization of Samurai Values—A Sermon by Hosoi Heishū," *Monumenta Nipponica* 31, no. 4 (Winter 1976): 393–413.

5. Ishii, *Nihon kon'in hōshi*, 232.

6. Fukuzawa Yukichi, *The Autobiography of Yukichi Fukuzawa*, trans. Eiichi Kiyooka (New York: Columbia University Press, 1966), 18.

7. Fukuzawa Yukichi, *Kyūhanjō*, trans. Carmen Blacker, *Monumenta Nipponica* 9 (1953): 328.

8. Wakita Osamu, "Bakuhan taisei to josei," in *Nihon joseishi* (Tōkyō daigaku shuppankai, 1982).

9. Based on a Kansei era (1789–1801) genealogical compilation by Asakura Yūko, "Buke josei no kon'in ni kansuru tōkeiteki kenkyū, shiron," in *Edo jidai no joseitachi*, ed. Kinsei joseishi kenkyūkai (Yoshikawa: 1990), 49.

10. No breakdown into kinds of "divorce" is provided for bannermen, but according to my calculations, based on the material in ibid., 60, table 7, of the 186 daimyo "divorces," 50 percent were dissolutions of marriages; 35 percent

were terminations of betrothal engagements; and 15 percent were widows remarrying after their husbands' deaths.

11. Ibid., 56.
12. Ibid., 59.
13. Ibid., 65.
14. Kitō Hiroshi, *Nihon nisennen no jinkōshi* (Kyoto: PHP kenkyūjo, 1983), 105.
15. Ibid., 105.
16. Dana Morris and Thomas C. Smith, "Fertility and Mortality in an Outcaste Village in Japan, 1750–1869," in *Family and Population in East Asian History*, ed. Susan B. Hanley and Arthur P. Wolf (Stanford: Stanford University Press, 1985), 231.
17. Assumption of about 20 percent through divorce in Japan: Ochiai, "Familie und Geschlechterbeziehung in Japan," 48–49.
18. Donald H. Shively, "Bakufu Versus Kabuki," in *Studies in the Institutional History of Early Modern Japan*, ed. John W. Hall and Marius B. Jansen (Princeton, N.J.: Princeton University Press, 1968), 260.
19. Shively, "Bakufu Versus Kabuki," 256–61.
20. Donald Keene, *Chūshingura: The Treasury of Loyal Retainers* (New York: Columbia University Press, 1971), 1–26.
21. Ibid., 150–70.
22. Ibid., 156.
23. Ibid., 165, 167.
24. Ibid., 169.
25. Ibid., 158.
26. Chikamatsu Monzaemon, "Love Suicides at Amijima," in *Major Plays of Chikamatsu Monzaemon*, trans. Donald Keene (New York: Columbia University Press, 1961), 403–14.
27. Keene, *Chūshingura*, 133–36.
28. Ibid., 136.
29. Ibid., 137–49.
30. Chikamatsu Monzaemon, "Shinjū yoigōshin," narrated in *Kabuki kanshō jiten*, ed. Mizuochi Kiyoshi (Tōkyōdō shuppan, 1993), 122.
31. Depictions in popular plays are in line with other Edo-period fiction, which valued the needs of the house more than those of marriage. In *Zenaku mimochi no ōgi*, co-authored by Jishō and Kiseki in 1730, a father divorces a *muko yōshi* against his daughter's will. He justifies his action by saying that even if his daughter dies of longing for her husband, his house is more important than his daughter's life. Cited in Nakada Kaoru, *Tokugawa jidai no bungaku ni mietaru shihō* (Meijidō shoten, 1925), 177.
32. For a detailed discussion on the procedure for arbitration before civil suits reached the magistrates, see Dan F. Henderson, *Conciliation and Japanese Law* (Seattle: University of Washington Press, 1965), 1: 127–81.
33. John H. Wigmore, ed., *Law and Justice in Tokugawa Japan: Materials for the History of Japanese Law and Justice Under the Tokugawa Shogunate*

1603–1867, pt. 8A, *Persons: Legal Precedents* (Tokyo: University of Tokyo Press, 1982), 55.

34. The correct translation is "temple and shrine magistrate," but since shrines are irrelevant in divorce cases, for simplicity's sake *jisha bugyō* is translated as temple magistrate.

35. The *Jikata kikigaki*, cited in Shihōshō, *Jinji no bu*, 2.

36. Nakayama Tarō, *Nihon kon'inshi* (Shunyōdō, 1928), 951.

37. Nakada Kaoru, *Tokugawa jidai no bungaku ni mietaru shihō*, 142.

38. Sayo case from the *Shoji tome* reprinted in Shihōshō, *Jinji no bu*, 7–27. Translated in Wigmore, ed., *Law and Justice*, pt. 8A: 13–34. The Sayo case also discussed in Hozumi Shigetō, *Rienjō to enkiridera* (Nihon hyōronsha, 1942), 243–49, and Igarashi Tomio, *Kakekomidera* (Hanawa shinsho, 1989), 148–52.

39. Shihōshō, *Jinji no bu*, 21. The names, relationships, and ages of the defendants were registered before their testimony. The ages of Sayo's father, Tsunejirō, forty-one, and her mother, Yoshi, fifty-one, suggest that Tsunejirō was not Sayo's biological father.

40. Shihōshō, *Jinji no bu*, 16.

41. The legal scholar Igarashi also assumed a marriage of three months in his discussion of the case: Igarashi, *Kakekomidera*, 148.

42. Shihōshō, *Jinji no bu*, 21.

43. Ibid., 9.

44. Defendants' testimony: ibid., 21–24.

45. Copy of the letter: ibid., 17.

46. Ibid., 24–25.

47. Ibid., 9, 22.

48. From *Sanpi shū*, which contains rulings by the Chamber of Decisions or the three magistrates in response to inquiries filed by daimyo and *hatamoto* between 1772 and 1802. Shihōshō, *Jinji no bu*, 39–40. Most divorce cases came from shogunate territory, especially from Musashi Province, localities for which the divorce notice practice was especially strong.

49. From *Kajō ruiten* in Shihōshō, *Jinji no bu*, 32.

50. From *Kakitome*, which was a collection of rulings made by the Chamber of Decisions in response to legal inquiries. The shogunate collected volumes of that name between the Kanbun (1661–73) and Keiō (1865–68) eras. All of these were destroyed in the earthquake and fire of 1923. Jūrōbei case: Shihōshō, *Jinji no bu*, 44–51. Translated in Wigmore, ed., *Law and Justice*, pt. 8A: 57–68.

51. Wigmore, ed., *Law and Justice*, pt. 8A: 64.

52. Heihachi case from *Kakitome*: Shihōshō, *Jinji no bu*, 51–55.

53. The *Bunden sōsho* is the third series of the *Jikata ochibo shū* containing laws, customs, and legal decisions. The main part was written in 1763. Shihōshō, *Jinji no bu*, 41.

54. Wigmore, ed., *Law and Justice*, pt. 8A: 97.

55. Shihōshō, *Jinji no bu*, 40–41.

56. Ibid., 42.

57. Wigmore, ed., *Law and Justice*, pt. 8A: 88–92.

58. Shihōshō, *Jinji no bu*, 51.
59. From *Shoji Tome*; Shihōshō, *Jinji no bu*, 27–28.
60. Jūrōbei case: Shihōshō, *Jinji no bu*, 44–51.
61. Handcuffing was a punishment reserved for commoners. The usual length for handcuffing was 30, 50, or 100 days. *Nihon kokushi daijiten*, vol. 9, 884. In seventeenth-century North America, the typical penalties for the guilty party in divorce were fines, whippings, and incarceration in the stocks: Glenda Riley, *Divorce: An American Tradition* (Oxford: Oxford University Press, 1991), 15.
62. Shihōshō, *Jinji no bu*, 26–27.
63. By contrast, Henderson, *Conciliation and Japanese Law*, 1: 150, believes that magistrates often intimidated people with harsh punishments, up to the death penalty, but rarely implemented their threats.
64. Diane E. Wright, "Severing the Karmic Ties That Bind: The 'Divorce Temple' Mantokuji," *Monumenta Nipponica* vol. 52, no. 3 (Autumn 1997): 357.
65. Humbert-Droz, *Ehescheidungsrecht in Japan*, 96–97.
66. Some husbands, *muko yōshi* and others, took refuge with officials in the Obata Domain, Kōzuke Province, to initiate divorce and, more important, to enhance their positions in divorce negotiations; Takagi Tadashi, *Enkiridera Mantokuji no kenkyū* (Seibundō, 1990), 474–78.
67. Takagi Tadashi, *Mikudarihan to enkiridera* (Kōdansha, 1992), 124–25. Nakayama Tarō mentions other divorce temples, such as Osaka's Jimeiin and Kyōmizudera in Kyoto. Nakayama, *Nihon kon'inshi*, 961. For the suggestion that basically any women's temple could potentially be a divorce temple based on the articles of the *ritsuryō yōryaku* and *chōseidan*, see Ishii Ryōsuke, *Nihon kon'inhōshi* (Sōbundō, 1977), 381–92.
68. Takagi, *Mikudarihan to enkiridera*, 165–67. For older estimates with fewer cases but showing the same pattern of regional distribution, see Igarashi, *Kakekomidera*, 153–60; Ishii Ryōsuke, *Edo no rikon: mikudari-han to enkiridera* (Nihon keizai shinbunsha, 1965), 131.
69. Inoue's estimate is based on *Kakeiridera—Matsugaoka Tōkeiji no jishi to jihō* (Koyama shoten, 1955) cited in Takagi, *Mikudarihan to enkiridera*, 166, and Ishii, *Edo no rikon*, 134.
70. From *Ko harigami*, which included precedents between 1744 and 1816, in Shihōshō, *Jinji no bu*, 3.
71. Igarashi, *Kakekomidera*, 136–38; Igarashi mentions that there was no divorce notice attached to the records of the temple retainer, and he doubts that the compromise was ever enacted.
72. Since at least the head priestess Tenshū, daughter of Toyotomi Hideyori, in the early seventeenth century, until at least 1805.
73. Shihōshō, *Jinji no bu*, 4–5; Igarashi argues that the ideal and symbolic period of three years was de facto twenty-four to twenty-five months for the divorce temples: Igarashi, *Kakekomidera*, 247.
74. Eleven months: Shihōshō, *Jinji no bu*, 64; three years: Shihōshō, *Jinji no bu*, 2. For legal policy on remarriage after absconding in the Meiji period, see

Hozumi Shigetō, *"Kazoku kon'in" kenkyū bunken senshū*, vol. 4, *Rikon seido no kenkyū*, ed. Yuzawa Yasuhiko (1924; reprint, Kuresu shuppan, 1989), 706–28.

75. Takagi and Ishii explain that especially in the latter part of the Edo period, a large number of temple divorces were by private settlement (*naisai*), because of the increased public recognition of the temples' rights: Takagi, *Mikudarihan to enkiridera*, 201. Of the forty-seven women registered in an 1866 Tōkeiji diary, twenty-five had private settlements (*naisai*) and none had a divorce according to temple law: Ishii, *Edo no rikon*, 133.

76. Shihōshō, *Jinji no bu*, 4–5.
77. Ibid., 6–7.
78. Ibid., 5.
79. From *Ko harigami* in Shihōshō, *Jinji no bu*, 3.
80. Shihōshō, *Jinji no bu*, 12.
81. From *Shoji tome*; Shihōshō, *Jinji no bu*, 7–27.
82. On joint jurisdiction, see Shihōshō, *Jinji no bu*, 11–12.
83. Ibid., 8, 10–11, 12–13.
84. Ibid., 9–10, 11–12, 13.
85. Ibid., 10.
86. Igarashi, *Kakekomidera*, 150–51.
87. Concern with the proper jurisdiction is also central to the Sawamura inheritance case. Town Magistrate Tōyama Saemonnojō only took up the inheritance dispute after clarifying his jurisdiction. Sawamura Gisaburō had died unexpectedly after falling from the scaffolding of his own storehouse in Edo on the sixteenth day of the sixth month of 1848. Relatives quarreled over the authenticity of a testament Gisaburō had made just prior to his death. A certain Kohei appealed to the town magistrate, Tōyama, for help in enforcing the will. Tōyama then decided to consult with the engineering magistrates (*sakuji bugyō*), because Gisaburō had worked as a master carpenter in service of the engineering department of the shogunate (*ōsakuji daiku tōryō*). Since his judgment might set a precedent, Tōyama was reluctant to become involved. He justified his repeated inquiries to the engineering magistrates explicitly with his ability to set precedents: "My disposition of such a suit would affect not only this particular case but the manner of the disposition of all the cases concerning written wills that may be brought to you by those under your superintendence." Tōyama expected the various offices to be consistent in their decisions. Shihōshō, *Jinji no bu*, 152–77.
88. Ibid., 12.
89. Takagi, *Mikudarihan to enkiridera*, 182–83; Takagi Tadashi, *Mikudarihan Edo no rikon to joseitachi* (Heibonsha, 1987), 297.
90. National population statistics show that less than 10 percent of households had a female head during the first three decades of the Meiji period; for the high nobility *(kazoku)*, the proportion of female heads declined drastically, while it rose slightly for the commoner population *(heimin)*.

Chapter 3: Testing a Spouse

1. Hasegawa Akihiko, "'Tsumadoikon' to 'yomeiri,'" in *Mura no kazoku*, ed. Himeoka Tsutomu, Tsuchida Hideo, and Hasegawa Akihiko (Mineruba shobō, 1973). In the Shima District of Mie Prefecture, a husband initially stayed at his wife's home without living there permanently, in a custom called *tsumadoikon*, found especially in fishing villages. Under the designation *ashiire*, a bride moved between her groom's place and her natal home. See also Tokuzō Ōmachi, "Ashiire-Kon, Putting-One's-Feet-in-Marriage," in *Studies in Japanese Folklore*, ed. Richard Dorson (Bloomington: Indiana University Press, 1973), 251–66. For a discussion of trial marriage forms in different localities, see Uematsu Akashi, "Kon'inshi no shomondai," in *Kōza nihon no minzoku*, vol. 3, *Jinsei girei*, ed. Inoguchi Shōji (Yūseidō, 1978); Emori Itsuo, *Nihon kisō bunka no minzoku gakuteki kenkyū*, vol. 2, *Nihon no kon'in—sono rekishi to minzoku* (Kōbundō, 1986).

2. In a landmark decision in 1915, the Supreme Court decided to grant cohabiting couples the status of "engaged to marry" *(kon'in yoyaku)*, which subsequently was interpreted as "preparing for marriage" *(junkon)*, granting the bereaved or divorced party a claim to property. Tamura Gorō, *Katei no saiban (fūfu)* (Nihon hyōronsha, 1985), 388–90.

3. Susan B. Hanley, "Family and Fertility in Four Tokugawa Villages," in *Family and Population in East Asian History*, ed. Susan B. Hanley and Arthur P. Wolf (Stanford: Stanford University Press, 1985), 216.

4. Only three brides already had children, and only three among sixty-four brides gave birth within the first year of marriage: Thomas C. Smith, *Nakahara: Family Farming and Population in a Japanese Village, 1717–1830* (Stanford: Stanford University Press, 1977), 88–89.

5. None of the 190 brides had a child at marriage registration, and the average duration from marriage to first birth was 2.8 years, too long to suggest a pattern by which marriage and birth were registered simultaneously. Laurel L. Cornell, "Peasant Women and Divorce in Preindustrial Japan," *Signs: Journal of Women in Culture and Society* 15, no. 4 (1990): 714.

6. In the early nineteenth century, at least, the domains that experienced population decline or stagnation had the strictest rules on birth registration and inspections of stillbirth. Anti-abortion policy was phrased as a humanitarian act in Rikuzen Province, Ōu District: "Uesugi Yōzan, the daimyo of Yonezawa, grieved by the evil, made a law by which the company men were to inspect every case of stillbirth, and the domain was to give one man's ration to a family bringing up five children under fifteen years of age."

7. Shihōshō, "Zenkoku minji kanrei ruishū," in *Meiji bunka zenshū*, vol. 9, *Hōritsu*, ed. Meiji Bunka Kenkyūkai (1929; reprint, Nihon hyōronsha, 1992), 3: 191.

8. Kōzuke: Ōraki.

9. Ugo: Akita; or after the ceremony in Settsu: Nishinari and Kawachi: Sara.

10. Hyūga: Usuki.

11. Buzen: Kiku.

12. Mino: Atsumi, Kagami, and Kagata.

13. Shinano: Saku.

14. Anthropologists have recognized trial marriages called *ashiire*. They believe this to be a mixed form in the transition from matrilocal to patrilocal systems of marriage. See, e.g., Yanagita Kunio, *Japanese Manners and Customs in the Meiji Era*, trans. Charles S. Terry (Tokyo: Ōbunsha, 1957), 162; Uematsu Akashi, "Kon'inshi no shomondai," *Kōza nihon no minzoku*, vol. 3, *Jinsei girei*, ed. Inoguchi Shōji (Yūseidō, 1978), 46–49; Hasegawa, "'Tsumadoikon' to 'yomeiri,'" 153; Ōmachi, "Ashiire-Kon, Putting-One's-Feet-in-Marriage," 251–66. Walter Edwards explains that the evolutionary framework of the shift from matri- to patrilocal marriages was borrowed in the early twentieth century from Lewis Henry Morgan (*Ancient Society: or, Researches in the Line of Human Progress from Savagery Through Barbarism to Civilization*, 1877). Although now discredited in the West, his views still enjoy a surprising degree of influence in Japan: Walter Edwards, *Modern Japan Through Its Weddings: Gender, Person, and Society in Ritual Portrayal* (Stanford: Stanford University Press, 1989), 152.

15. Yamashiro: Otagi and Kadono.

16. Kaga: Ishikawa, Higo: Akita, and Chikugo: Mitsuma. Omitted in the 1880 version. In other places registration was delayed without giving specific reasons. In Kaga Province, village officials were notified of a marriage only half a year, or even an entire year, after the wedding: Kaga: Kahoku. The usual practice in Echigo Province was to delay registration for about the same period: Echigo: Kubiki.

17. Iwami: Nima; Mimasaka: Saihokujō; Aki: Numata and Aki; Izu: Tagata.

18. Suō: Tsuno.

19. Mikawa: Atsumi, Mikawa: Nukada, Izumo: Nogi.

20. Etchū: Nei.

21. Uzen: Oitama. This location also has references to child-marriages that were registered long before an actual wedding celebration.

22. Shinano: Takai.

23. Rikuchū: Izawa. Examples for registration at childbirth from the western Japanese provinces are Tanba: Kuwata, and Higo, Amakusa.

24. Chikugo: Mii.

25. Awa: Awa and Hei. In Myōtō District, a marriage did not need to be reported.

26. Bitchū: Kuboya.

27. Bingo: Mitsugi.

28. Buzen: Kiku.

29. Oshima: Kameda.

30. Ugo: Akita and Tosa: Kōchi.

31. Shinano: Saranashi; Kai: Yatsushiro; Higo: Aso; Higo: Kuma; Kaga: Ishikawa.

32. Higo: Aso.

33. Yamato: Sōnokami.

34. Kawachi: Kawachi; Izumi: Ōtori; Noto: Fugeshi. The mother took custody of the girl in Sagami Province, Ashigara District: "an illegitimate child, if male, belongs to the father, and if female, to the mother, and is registered as the offspring of some married relative."

35. Kai: Yatsushiro; Shinano: Saranashi; Shima: Tōshi; Tōtōmi: Fuchi; Kaga: Ishikawa; Etchū: Imizu; Sado: Sawata.

36. Kawachi: Kawachi.

37. Laurel L. Cornell and Hayami Akira, "The Shūmon Aratame Chō: Japan's Population Registers," *Journal of Family History* 11, no. 4 (1986): 322. For example, the ratio of children born with either parent absent in Edo registers is higher than in the statistic on illegitimacy compiled by the government in the 1880s.

38. Jichikan, ed., *"Kazoku kon'in" kenkyū bunken senshū*, additional vol., *Jinji kanrei zenshū*, ed. Yuzawa Yasuhiko (1911; reprint, Kuresu, 1990), 490.

39. Meiji Civil Code Articles 827, 829, 836.

40. Hayami Akira, "Illegitimacy in Japan," in *Bastardy and its Comparative History*, ed. Peter Laslett, Karla Oosterveen, and Richard M. Smith (Cambridge, Mass.: Harvard University Press, 1980), 397–402.

41. Kōseishō, *Jinkō dōtai tōkei*, vol. 1 (1997), 115.

42. Hayami argues that the rate of illegitimate childbirth already reached its peak in several localities between 1890 and 1900: Hayami Akira, "Illegitimacy in Japan," 402.

43. Takei Masaomi, *Naienkon no genjō to kadai* (Kyoto: Hōritsu bunkasha, 1991), 8.

44. Takei, *Naienkon*, 9; Kōseishō, *Jinkō dōtai tōkei*, vol. 1 (1997), 421.

45. François Caron in Cooper, *They Came to Japan*, 61–62.

46. *Manners and Customs of the Japanese, in the Nineteenth Century: From the Accounts of Dutch Residents in Japan and from the German Work of Philipp Franz von Siebold* (1841; reprint, Rutland, Vt.: Charles E. Tuttle, 1977), 123.

47. Alcock, *Capital of the Tycoon*, 192.

48. William Conn, *Japanese Life, Love, and Legend: A Visit to the Empire of the "Rising Sun." From "Le Japon pittoresque" of Maurice Dubard* (London: Ward & Downey, 1886), 70, 75.

49. Walter Weston, *Japan* (London: A. & C. Black, 1926), 221–22.

50. Calculated from "Kosekikyoku nenpō," in *Kokusei chōsa izen Nihon jinkō tōkei shūsei, 1872–1912*, additional vol. 4, ed. Hayami Akira (Hara shobō, 1993).

51. Hayami, *Kokusei chōsa izen*, additional vol. 4.

52. See chapter 2, "For the Sake of the House."

53. Yamakawa, *Women of the Mito Domain*, 108–9.

54. Cited from Taisei Rei reprinted in Shihōshō chōsaka, *Tokugawa jidai minji kanreishū*, vol. 1, *Jinji no bu* (1934; reprint, Tachibana shoin, 1986), 1.

55. Shihōshō, *Jinji no bu*, 152–77.

56. Robert J. Smith, "Transformations of Commoner Households in Tennō-

ji-mura, 1757–1858," in *Family and Population in East Asian History*, ed. Susan B. Hanley and Arthur P. Wolf (Stanford: Stanford University Press, 1985), 251.

57. Yamakawa Kikue, *Nijūseiki o ayumu: aru onna no ashiato* (Daiwa shobō, 1981), 110.

58. For a detailed account of concubinage in the peerage, see Takie Sugiyama Lebra, *Above the Clouds: Status Culture of the Modern Japanese Nobility* (Berkeley: University of California Press, 1993), 214–26.

59. Haru Matsukata Reischauer, *Samurai and Silk: A Japanese and American Heritage* (Cambridge, Mass.: Harvard University Press, 1986), 103.

60. Ishii Ryōsuke, *Nihon kon'in hōshi* (Sōbundō, 1977), 428. Paul Heng-Chao Ch'en, *London Oriental Series*, vol. 35, *The Formation of the Early Meiji Legal Order* (Oxford: Oxford University Press, 1981).

61. Taimie L. Bryant, "For the Sake of the Country, for the Sake of the Family: The Oppressive Impact of Family Registration on Women and Minorities in Japan," *UCLA Law Review* 39, no. 1 (1991): 148.

62. But Article 62 of the enactment law to the Civil Code permitted concubines to remain at their husband's residence. See Fuse Akiko, *Kekkon to kazoku* (Iwanami shoten, 1993), 59.

63. Alice Schalek, *Japan: Das Land des Nebeneinander* (Breslau: Ferdinand Hirt, 1925), 65.

64. Compare the process of convergence described in Eugen Weber, *Peasants into Frenchmen: The Modernization of Rural France, 1870–1914* (Stanford, Calif.: Stanford University Press, 1976).

65. Marius B. Jansen, "The Ruling Class," in *Japan in Transition: From Tokugawa to Meiji*, ed. id. and Gilbert Rozman (Princeton, N.J.: Princeton University Press, 1986), 84.

66. Peerage population in *Kokusei chōsa izen* volumes for 1886–98. Divorce rate of the peerage calculated with the number for peer divorces in Tsubouchi Yoshihiro and Tsubouchi Reiko, "Nihon no rikon," in *Tōnan ajia kenkyū sōsho*, vol. 4, *Rikon* (Sōbunsha, 1970), 164, table 43.

67. Calculation based on Tsubouchi, "Nihon no rikon," 165, table 44.

68. The Kanazawa rates are based on the first family register of 1871 and the prefectural numbers for the 1880s on national vital statistics; Tsubouchi and Tsubouchi, "Nihon no rikon."

69. City 25.4 percent and prefecture 28.7 percent. *Ōsaka-fu* (1892).

70. See appendix table A.1, "Japanese Divorce Rate by City Size, 1910–1935."

71. Suzuki's report is reprinted in Nishida Taketoshi, ed., *Seikatsu koten sōsho*, vol. 2, *Meiji zenki no toshi kasō shakai* (Kōseikan, 1970), 123–52.

72. Nishida, *Seikatsu koten sōshō*, 2:139.

73. Yokoyama Gennosuke, *Nihon no kasō shakai* (1899; reprint, Iwanami bunko, 1994), 57.

74. Urako Takeji, "Sumiyaki no mura sanson no kazoku," in *Mura no kazoku*, ed. Himeoka Tsutomu, Tsuchida Hideo, and Hasegawa Akihiko (Mineruba shobō, 1973), 59.

75. Shikata Hisao, "'Tsumadoikon' ni okeru rikon," *Soshioroji* 11, no. 4 (June 1965): 91, table 1. Yuzawa Yasuhiko, "Rikonritsu no suii to sono haikei" in *Kōza kazoku*, vol. 4, *Kon'in no kaishō*, ed. Aoyama Michio et al. (Kōbundō, 1974), 338–43. In fishing villages, divorce was particularly high.

76. Both Cornell and Smith have higher numbers for divorcées returning to the village than for women who were divorced in the village.

77. Hayami Akira, "Another *Fossa Magna:* Proportion Marrying and Age at Marriage in Late Nineteenth-Century Japan," *Journal of Family History* 12, no. 1–3 (special issue 1987): 57–71.

78. The official crude divorce rate in this chapter is from *Nihon teikoku jinkō dōtai tōkei* or the *Nihon tōkei nenkan*. Several-year averages of official divorce rates for prefectures are also published in Tsubouchi, "Nihon no rikon," 153.

79. In fact, 28 *sai* (years); the number is counted as one at birth and increases at the passing of every new year. For a conversion of the proportion marrying to an exact age, see Hayami, "Another *Fossa Magna*," 57–71.

80. Yuzawa Yasuhiko, "Nihon no rikon: kindaika no naka no konmei," in *Sekai no rikon: sono fūdo to dōkō*, ed. Yasuhiko Yuzawa et al. (Yūhikaku, 1979), 172–81.

81. Tsubouchi, "Nihon no rikon," 222–23, 182–89.

82. Taryō Ōbayashi, "Traditionelle Gesellschaftstypen und Kulturprovinzen in Japan," *Japanstudien* 6 (1994): 178. Some scholars even trace the differences between northeastern and southwestern Japan back to the Middle Ages, when samurai colonized the north and gave the region a hierarchical house *(ie)* structure in contrast to the village *(mura)* structure of the economically more developed southwest. Discussed in Amino Yoshihiko, *Higashi to nishi no kataru nihon no rekishi* (Soshiete, 1994), 162.

83. Suzuki Hideo, *Fūdo no kōzō* (Kōdansha, 1988), 200–213.

84. Hayami Akira and Kurosu Satomi, "Regional Diversity in Demographic and Family Patterns in Preindustrial Japan," *Journal of Japanese Studies* 27, no. 2 (Summer 2001): 303–4.

85. My own calculation based on *Nihon teikoku jinkō dōtai tōkei*.

86. Mosk, *Patriarchy and Fertility*, 84.

87. Laurel Cornell, "Gender Differences in Remarriage after Divorce in Japan and the United States," *Journal of Marriage and the Family*, vol. 51, no. 2 (May 1989): 457–63.

88. Miyashita Michiko, "Nōson ni okeru kazoku to kon'in," in *Nihon joseishi*, vol. 3, *Kinsei*, ed. Joseishi sōgō kenkyūkai, 6th ed. (Tōkyō daigaku shuppankai, 1990), 50.

89. Cornell, "Peasant Women and Divorce in Preindustrial Japan," 710–32; Hiroshi Kito, "Remarriage and Reproduction in a Rural Japanese Village in the Late Seventeenth and Eighteenth Century," *Sophia Economic Review* 33, no. 2 (February 1988): 84–102. Many divorced people remarrying in the town of Takayama: Yōichirō Sasaki, "Urban Migration and Fertility in Tokugawa Japan: The City of Takayama, 1773–1871," in *Family and Population in East Asian History*, ed. Susan B. Hanley and Arthur P. Wolf (Stanford: Stanford

University Press, 1985), 143. Smith, *Nakahara*, 106. Although Yamakawa calls divorce and remarriage "the ultimate disgrace," they were very frequent among Mito Domain samurai: Yamakawa, *Women of the Mito Domain*, 104. Robert Smith explains the common occurrences of remarriage after divorce in Suye Mura by the fact that an adult couple was needed to perform the work duties in a peasant household, which were often gender specific: Robert J. Smith and Ella Lury Wiswell, *The Women of Suye Mura* (Chicago: Chicago University Press, 1982), 275.

90. Wakita Osamu, "Bakuhan taisei to josei," in *Nihon joseishi* (Tōkyō daigaku shuppankai, 1982).

91. Asakura Yūko, "Buke josei no kon'in ni kansuru tōkeiteki kenkyū, shiron," in *Edo jidai no joseitachi*, ed. Kinsei joseishi kenkyūkai (Yoshikawa: 1990), 56–57.

92. Ibid., 70–71. In 1965, the remarriage rate was 46 percent for divorcées and 89 percent for divorcés. Goode, *World Changes in Divorce Patterns*, 239. According to a 1968 estimate, 48 percent of the wives remarried after divorce in contrast to 84 percent of the husbands. Linhart, "Familie," 559.

93. Gustav Kreitner, *Im Fernen Osten: Reisen des Grafen Bela Szecheny in Indien, Japan, China, Tibet und Birma in den Jahren 1877–1880* (Vienna: Alfred Hölder, 1881), 235. Some Meiji intellectuals nonetheless voiced opposition to remarriage after divorce: Tamaki Hajime, *Nihon kazoku seidoron* (Hōritsu bunkasha, 1971), 187. The family sociologist Yuzawa Yasuhiko believes that little community pressure existed to prevent a divorcée's remarriage in 1885. Yuzawa Yasuhiko, "Nihon: kindaika no naka no konmei," 170–202.

94. There were two periods in her married life when the bride was expected to visit her natal home, at least temporarily. One of these was the ritual of the bride's return to her parents after celebrating the wedding. Edwards, *Modern Japan Through Its Weddings*, 40. Childbirth would be another acknowledged event for which a married wife sought at least temporary shelter in her natal home. These customs fostered the maintenance of a relationship with her parents, siblings, and other relatives, which could continue on a more day-to-day basis. Etsu Sugimoto, who was a daughter of an upper-level samurai of Nagaoka who lived in the Meiji and Taishō eras, mentions frequent visits by her elder sister to their parents. Etsu Inagaki Sugimoto, *A Daughter of the Samurai: How a Daughter of Feudal Japan, Living Hundreds of Years in One Generation, Became a Modern American* (1925; reprint, Rutland, Vt.: Charles E. Tuttle, 1990), 70. Despite the ideological emphasis on cutting the ties with one's natal family upon marriage, social interaction lasted. When a bride had married into a family that lived near her parents, the community expected a close relationship with her natal home. A proverb warned against taking cats or brides from the neighborhood, as they would run away. Margret Neuss-Kaneko, *Familie und Gesellschaft in Japan: Von der Feudalzeit bis in die Gegenwart* (Munich: C. H. Beck, 1990), 41.

95. Tōkeiin, *Kai kuni genzai ninbetsuchō* (1882), 14, 43.

96. Sugimoto, *Daughter of the Samurai*, 12.

97. Weston, *Japan*, 215.

98. Exner, *Japan: Skizzen von Land und Leuten*, 36. Lafcadio Hearn, *Glimpses of Unfamiliar Japan* (Boston: Houghton, Mifflin, 1894), 429, also says that a "loving" widow "in the old days" cut her hair to put it in her husband's coffin.

99. Jichikan, *Jinji kanrei zenshū*, 360–61.

100. Ibid., 180.

101. John E. Knodel, *Demographic Behavior in the Past: A Study of Fourteen German Village Populations in the Eighteenth and Nineteenth Centuries* (Cambridge: Cambridge University Press, 1988), 449.

102. See appendix table A.2, Prior Status of Newlywed Brides by Age in Japan, 1919.

103. *Jinkō dōtai tōkei*, various years.

104. Goode, *World Changes in Divorce Patterns*, 239.

Chapter 4: Unsuitable to the Family Tradition?

1. Proverbs on divorce have been studied to shed light on customary values, but the limitation of this method is that the time and place of those sayings is hard to trace: Amano Takeshi, "Rikon no shūzoku," *Kōza kazoku*, vol. 4, *Kon'in no kaishō*, ed. Aoyama Michio et al. (Kōbundō, 1974), 313–18.

2. Actual divorce decisions depended on individual conditions, of course, as the 1875 survey recognized, noting, for example, that implementation of the child custody rules for Shinano Province, Takai District "depended on the parents."

3. Shihōshō, "Zenkoku minji kanrei ruishū," in *Meiji bunka zenshū*, vol. 9, *Hōritsu*, ed. Meiji Bunka Kenkyūkai (1929; reprint, Nihon hyōronsha, 1992). Translations from the 1875 survey are mine, unless indicated otherwise. The names of the province *(kuni)* and district (a Chinese character pronounced *kōri* until 1878, but known today as *gun*) for the examples cited in the text are given in notes: here, e.g., Musashi: Toshima.

4. Nagato: Abu.

5. Kai: Yamanashi.

6. Shinano: Hashina; for another example, see Rikuzen: Tōda.

7. Kai: Yamanashi.

8. Shinano: Hashina; for another example, see Rikuzen: Tōda.

9. Suō: Tsuno.

10. Sagami: Kamakura.

11. Kai: Yamanashi; Shinano: Hashina.

12. Kai: Yamanashi; Shinano: Hashina; and see for adultery *(kan)* Shinano: Chiisagata; Mikawa: Atsumi; Rikuzen: Miyagi; Suō: Yoshiki.

13. Although adultery of the husband was not commonly accepted grounds for divorce, wives divorced adulterous husbands even before World War II, and, of course, not every adulterous wife was divorced. In a village survey of the reasons for divorce between 1931 and 1935, Shikata Hisao found several instances of divorce due to the husband's adultery: Shikata Hisao, "Tsumadoikon ni okeru rikon," in *Mura no kazoku*, ed. Himeoka Tsutomu,

Tsuchida Hideo, and Hasegawa Akihiko (Mineruba shobō, 1973), 169. For the recollections of a wife who ran away from her husband after her best friend bore him a child: Jane Anne O. Freed, *The Changing Worlds of Older Women in Japan* (Manchester, Conn.: Knowledge, Ideas and Trends, 1992), 151–57. For a vivid narrative of the village gossip on illicit love affairs and divorces: Robert J. Smith and Ella Lury Wiswell, *The Women of Suye Mura* (Chicago: Chicago University Press, 1982), 186–98.

14. Kaibara Ekken, *Greater Learning for Women*, translated in Basil H Chamberlain, *Things Japanese* (1905; reprinted as *Japanese Things*, Tokyo: Charles E. Tuttle, 1971), 503–4.

15. Kaga: Nomi, for a government regulation that adopted sons were to be chosen among relatives; also for preference in adopting relatives and people with the same surname among Mito samurai: Yamakawa Kikue, *Women of the Mito Domain: Recollections of Samurai Family Life,* trans. Kate Wildman Nakai (Tokyo: University of Tokyo Press, 1992), 110.

16. Tsushima: Shimoagata; Tosa: Aki.

17. Horiuchi Misao and Katō Mihoko, "Meiji zenki ni okeru rikonhō," in *Kōza kazoku*, vol. 4, *Kon'in no kaishō* (Kōbundō, 1974), 240. Zennosuke Nakagawa, "A Century of Marriage Law," *Japan Quarterly* 10, no. 2 (April–June 1963): 184. Dominique T. Wang, "Le Divorce en Chine et au Japon," *Zeitschrift für Schweizerisches Recht* 93 (1974): 613. Yōzō Watanabe, "The Family and the Law: The Individualistic Premise and the Modern Japanese Family Law," in *Law in Japan,* ed. Arthur von Mehren (Cambridge, Mass.: Harvard University Press, 1963), 367. Friedrich Tappe, *Soziologie der japanischen Familie: Grundanschauungen, Ethik und Recht des japanischen Familiensystems* (Münster: Aschendorffsche Verlagsbuchhandlung, 1955), 91.

18. Sagami: Kamakura.

19. Uzen: Tagawa; Bingo: Mitsugi; Kii: Nagusa/Ama.

20. Shinano: Hashina.

21. Takagi, *Mikudarihan*, 82–83.

22. Ibid., 69–71.

23. Kaga: Nomi; Tango: Kasa.

24. Mikawa: Atsumi.

25. Chikugo: Mitsuma or Mii.

26. Tanba: Kuwata.

27. Hizen: Takaku; Higo: Akita.

28. A wife could not remarry as long as her husband was missing, and she did not get a divorce notice. Shinano: Saku; Kamakura: Ashigara.

29. Shihōshō, *Tokugawa jidai minji kanreishū,* vol 1, *Jinji no bu* (1934; reprint, Tachibana shoin 1986), 6–7.

30. Iga: Abe; Sagami: Ashigara.

31. Shihōshō, "Zenkoku minji kanrei ruishū," 161–374.

32. Ōmi: Sakata; Kii: Nagusa and Ama; Buzen: Kiku.

33. Mino: Ahachi; Ugo: Akita; Echigo: Koshi; Sado: Sawata; Iwashiro: Aizu. Neither was the divorce notice limited to a special social status. In Izumo Province, it was confined to the principal families in towns and villages. In Ugo

Province, only distinguished families *(gōzoku meimon)* exchanged divorce notices. By contrast, in Bingo Province, the practice was common among the poor *(senmin)*. In Kii Province, too, it was a lower-class *(katō jinmin)* wife who obtained a divorce notice.

34. For marriage and divorce by registration in the Edo period: Ishii Ryōsuke, *Nihon kon'inhōshi* (Sōbundō, 1977), 426.

35. On the cessation of endorsement in the early Meiji era: Hozumi Shigetō, *Rienjō to enkiridera* (Nihon hyōronsha, 1942), 175; Numa Masaya, "Hōgaku ni okeru kasetsu to kenshō," *Hōshakaigaku*, vol. 11, *Hōshakaigaku no shosō*, ed. Nihon hōshakai gakkai (Yūhikaku, 1961), 97. On the decline in divorce notices in the 1880s: Takayanagi Shinzō, "Meiji minpō izen no rikonhō," in *Kazoku mondai to kazokuhō*, vol. 3, *Rikon* (Sakai shoten, 1958), 117. Last divorce notice: Takagi, *Mikudarihan*, 308.

36. Takagi, *Mikudarihan*, 306.

37. Ibid., 306–8.

38. Shihōshō, "Zenkoku minji kanrei ruishū," 202.

39. Uzen: Oitama. André Bellesort, *La Société japonaise* (Paris: Perrin, 1926), 317, notes in his description of a trousseau that the clothes the bride brought with her were for all seasons and meant to last her entire life, since there was little change in fashion and usage.

40. See, e.g., Etsu Inagaki Sugimoto, *A Daughter of the Samurai: How a Daughter of Feudal Japan, Living Hundreds of Years in One Generation, Became a Modern American* (1925; reprint, Rutland, Vt.: Charles E. Tuttle, 1990), 46.

41. Smith and Wiswell, *Women of Suye Mura*, 165.

42. Nagahara Kazuko, "Minzoku no tenkan to josei no yakuwari," in *Nihon josei seikatsushi*, vol. 4, *Kindai*, ed. Joseishi sōgō kenkyūkai, 2d ed. (Tōkyō daigaku shuppankai, 1991), 78.

43. Kawachi: Mamuda; Shimotsuke: Kōchi.

44. Shihōshō, "Zenkoku minji kanrei ruishū," 202. In Iyo Province, a bride brought "property [*zaisan*] as a dowry when she was ugly [*menbō minikui*] or her entire body was deformed [*gotai fugu*]." Iyo: Onsen.

45. Edo-period literature also portrayed husbands or adoptive fathers who accepted dowry land and money as debased and greedy. For example, in *Tōsei keisei katagi*, written in 1771 by Masuya Tairyō, a groom calculates that with the interest earned by his dowry payment, he will be able to indulge himself in the pleasure quarters all year round, and he therefore does not object to his wife being one-eyed or lame. Cited in Nakada Kaoru, *Tokugawa jidai no bungaku ni mietaru shihō* (Meijidō shoten, 1925), 153.

46. Noto: Suzu.

47. Mino: Atsumi, Kagami, and Kagata.

48. Ise: Ano, Hōki: Aimi.

49. Mutsu: Tsugaru.

50. Kii: Nagusa and Ama.

51. Yamato: Sōnokami.

52. Kai: Yatsushiro.

53. Kai: Yamanashi.

54. Rikuchū: Izawa; reference missing in 1877. A *yōshi* or *muko yōshi* usually succeeded to the headship in Ugo Province. Ugo: Hiraga.

55. W. Heine, *Japan: Beiträge zur Kenntniss des Landes und seiner Bewohner* (1873; reprint, Dresden: Selbstverlag des Verfassers, 1880), 5; E. Lamairesse, *Le Japon: Histoire, Religion, Civilisation* (Paris: Librairie Coloniale, 1892), 13.

56. A. H. Exner, *Japan: Skizzen von Land und Leuten* (Leipzig: Weigel Nachfolger, 1891), 39; Arthur Lloyd, *Every-Day Japan: Written After Twenty-five Years' Residence and Work in the Country* (London: Cassell, 1909); 297–98. Daigoro Goh, "The Family Relations in Japan," *Transactions and Proceedings of The Japan Society, London* 2 (1892–93): 135, 147–48.

During the late Edo period, domains interfered with dowry practices in the same way, because they often limited the partitioning of inheritances. In order to enforce the law against wasteful expenditures, in Uzen Province, the bride's dowry was inspected. In Chikugo Province, a town official came to supervise the wedding celebration and to examine the dowry to prevent extravagance. In Buzen Province, the village headman had to be present at every wedding, which was also a way to enforce government regulations. The regulations also gave local officials the opportunity to participate in a lavish feast.

Another way of diminishing the value of the dowry was to limit it by outright prohibitions. In Hitachi Province, the dowry could not contain money and thus it was said to be "never used." In Mino Province, local regulations limited dowry money to ten *ryō* for every hundred *koku* of rice-producing land held by the bride's family. Special permission by the village office was necessary in Kazusa Province when the dowry included cultivated land *(denpata)*. The regulations against sumptuous dowries, however, revealed that the population must have attempted to transfer much more in the way of clothes, land, and money than the domains approved.

57. Exner, *Japan: Skizzen von Land und Leuten*, 39.

58. Cited in Dan F. Henderson, *Village "Contracts" in Tokugawa Japan* (Seattle: University of Washington Press, 1972), 141.

59. Shinano: Saku. Delay of dowry money or land: Sado: Sawata.

60. Suō: Kuga.

61. Sagami: Kamakura; Echigo: Kanbara.

62. Izumo: Nogi.

63. Suō: Yoshiki.

64. Mutsu: Tsugaru.

65. Awaji: Tsuna.

66. Yamashiro: Otagi and Kadono; Mikawa: Atsumi; Awaji: Tsuna; Chikugo: Mii; Higo: Tamana; Echigo: Kariha.

67. Mikawa: Atsumi.

68. There is also a promissory note dated 1833 from Jōemon to his sister Shizu to the effect that he will deliver thirteen *hyō* of rice per year, which suggests continued responsibility by the natal family after marriage: Henderson, *Village "Contracts,"* 140–41, 147.

69. Henderson, *Village "Contracts,"* 147–48, says that the document was the basis for a complicated dispute in the court of the Owari daimyo, which referred it to the go-between for settlement. It started with Omura wanting a divorce, and the grandmother submitted the suit, hoping to recover the 1,000 *ryō* promised in the event of divorce. Omura was divorced, but because she had committed adultery, she did not receive any money.
70. Uzen: Oitama.
71. Shinano: Saku.
72. Suō: Yoshiki.
73. Rikuzen: Tōda.
74. Awaji: Tsuna.
75. Chikugo: Mii.
76. Suō: Yoshiki.
77. Shihōshō, *Jinji no bu*, 2.
78. Exception: Shinano: Kogake.
79. Rikuzen: Miyagi.
80. Kaga: Ishikawa.
81. Chikugo: Mitsuma.
82. Mikawa: Atsumi.
83. Shinano: Takai.
84. Wigmore, ed., *Law and Justice*, pt. 7: 75, translates it as adultery, but there is no reason why *furachi* may not be limited to sexual misconduct. It was more common to designate adultery by the term *kan*. Wigmore also renders *furachi* as adultery for Suō: Yoshiki, which could lead to a prohibition of remarriage.
85. Rikuzen: Miyagi.
86. Shinano: Saku.
87. Etchū.
88. Suruga: Shida and Mashizu.
89. Shinano: Chiisagata. It is unclear whether the goods she had previously received *(sude ni kō furu buppin wa tsuma ni fu suru futsū)* referred only to the goods she brought into marriage or included those given to her during marriage. Wigmore interprets it as the husband "must allow her to take all that his family has given her." In the context of *yuinō* and dowry return, however, it is more likely to mean only dowry, not additional presents: See Wigmore, *Law and Justice*, pt. 7: 103 vs. Meiji Bunka Kenkyūkai, ed., *Meiji bunka zenshū*, 9: 217.
90. Shinano: Saku.
91. Shinano: Takai.
92. Iwami: Nema.
93. From *Kajō ruiten*, compiled in 1767 by the shogunate as a supplement to the *Kujikata osadamegaki* of 1742. Shihōshō, *Jinji no bu*, 38.
94. From *Kakitome*. Shihōshō, *Jinji no bu*, 40.
95. Rikuzen: Izawa. Attributed to the 1880 version by Wigmore *Law and Justice*, pt. 7: 67, but missing in Meiji Bunka Kenkyūkai, ed., *Meiji bunka zenshū*, vol. 9.
96. Buzen: Kiku.

97. Chikugo: Sansho.
98. For Japan: Joyce C. Lebra, "Women in an All-Male Industry: The Case of Sake Brewer Tatsu'uma Kiyo," in *Recreating Japanese Women*, ed. Gail L. Bernstein (Berkeley: University of California Press, 1991), 136. Lebra bases her interpretation on Miyamoto Mataji, *Ōsaka bunka shiron* (Bunken shuppan, 1979), 306–7. Also Margret Neuss-Kaneko, *Familie und Gesellschaft in Japan: Von der Feudalzeit bis in die Gegenwart* (Munich: C. H. Beck, 1990), 37, 41. For other societies: Gary S. Becker, *A Treatise on the Family* (Cambridge, Mass.: Harvard University Press, 1981), 28, 87. William J. Goode, *World Revolution and Family Patterns* (New York: Free Press, 1963), 155.
99. In medieval Jewish families, a divorced wife likewise recovered her dowry. Moreover, medieval Jews also had a high divorce rate. Some foreign visitors to Japan saw a parallel. The Japanese had "adopted with polygamy and concubines, other parts of the Jewish Law, and write letters of divorce," Rutherford Alcock noted (*Capital of the Tycoon*, 194). Hugh Cortazzi, *Victorians in Japan: In and Around the Treaty Ports* (Atlantic Highlands, N.J.: Athlone Press, 1987), 279, cites Albert Tracy as speaking of easy divorce according to Jewish customs.
100. Kai: Yamanashi; but this statement had been reserved for the samurai *(shizoku)* in the 1877 edition.
101. Alice M. Bacon, *Japanese Girls and Women* (Boston: Houghton, Mifflin, 1891), 61. Chamberlain, *Japanese Things*, 310. Naomi Tamura, *The Japanese Bride* (New York: Harper & Bros., 1893).
102. Higo: Tamana.
103. Shinano: Takai.
104. Hizen: Sonoki.
105. Musashi: Iruma.
106. Shinano: Saku; Settsu: Nishinari for marriage contract.
107. Shihōshō, "Zenkoku minji kanrei ruishū," 206.
108. Yamakawa, *Women of the Mito Domain*, 93.
109. Wolfgang Humbert-Droz, *Das Ehescheidungsrecht in Japan* (Cologne: Carl Heymanns KG, 1985), 72.
110. Chikamatsu Tokuzō, *Adakurabe kashiku no benigaki*, cited in Nakada, *Tokugawa jidai no bungaku*, 145.
111. Shihōshō, *Jinji no bu*, 64.
112. Nakada, *Tokugawa jidai no bungaku*, 145–46.
113. The Chamber of Decisions (temple, town, and finance magistrates) gathered the *Chōseidan* manual of 370 articles based on their precedents, but the more comprehensive *Kuji kata osadamegaki* replaced it after 1742: Wigmore, *Law and Justice*, pt. 1: 164; Nakada, *Tokugawa jidai no bungaku*, 144–47. On decline of split divorce custody in general: Nakayama, *Nihon kon'inshi*, 969.
114. From *Shin harigami*, which was compiled in 1844 and includes precedents between 1816 and 1844. Together with the *Ko harigami*, the *Shin harigami* was an essential reference manual for shogunate officials. Shihōshō, *Jinji no bu*, 64.

115. Shihōshō, "Zenkoku minji kanrei ruishū," 161–374.
116. Echigo: Uonuma.
117. Awaji: Tsuna.
118. Uzen: Oitama.
119. Shimotsuke: Tsuga.
120. Shinano: Chiisagata.
121. Echizen: Tsuruga.
122. Inaba: Ōmi; Mino: Atsumi, Kagami, and Kagata.
123. Ōmi: Shiga.
124. Shinano: Ogata.
125. Kaga: Ishikawa.
126. Harald Fuess, "A Golden Age of Fatherhood? Parent-Child Relations in Japanese Historiography," *Monumenta Nipponica* 52, no. 3 (Autumn 1997): 381–97.
127. Iwami: Naka.
128. Mino: Atsumi, Kagami and Kagata.
129. Suō: Kuga.
130. Sagami: Kamakura.
131. Izumo: Nogi.
132. Etchū: Imizu.
133. Etchū: Imizu.
134. Shinano: Ogata.
135. Chikugo: Sansho.
136. Shinano: Takai; Shinano: Saku; Musashi: Toshima.
137. Murakami Kazuhiro, *Meiji rikon saiban shiron* (Hōritsu bunkasha, 1994), 185–206.
138. Mikawa: Atsumi.
139. Iga: Amoo; Sagami: Ashigara.
140. Uzen: Chishi.
141. Yamakawa, *Women of the Mito Domain*, 96.
142. Bacon, *Japanese Girls and Women*, 73–74.
143. Hani Motoko, "Stories of My Life," *Japan Interpreter* 12, no. 3/4 (Summer 1979): 330–54; translated by Chieko Irie Mulhern.

Chapter 5: Between French Law and Japanese Customs

1. Decree no. 162 cited in Takayanagi Shinzō, "Meiji minpō izen no rikonhō," *Kazoku mondai to kazokuhō*, vol. 3, *Rikon* (Sakai shoten, 1958), 110.
2. Ōta Takeo, *Rikon gen'in no kenkyū—hanrei no hensen o chūshin to shite* (Yūhikaku, 1956), 5; Ishii Ryōsuke, *Nihon kon'in hōshi* (Sōbundō, 1977), 440.
3. Horiuchi Misao and Katō Mihoko, "Meiji zenki ni okeru rikonhō," in *Kōza kazoku*, vol. 4, *Kon'in no kaishō* (Kōbundō, 1974), 237.
4. Tamaki Hajime, *Nihon kazoku seido no hihan* (Minyūsha, 1948), 63. Horiuchi, "Meiji zenki ni okeru rikonhō," 247.
5. Hozumi Shigetō, *"Kazoku kon'in" kenkyū bunken senshū*, vol. 4, *Rikon seido no kenkyū*, ed. Yuzawa Yasuhiko (1924; reprint, Kuresu shuppan, 1989),

695. Ishii Ryōsuke, a famous postwar legal scholar, praised it as an unprecedented reformation. Ishii, *Nihon kon'in hōshi*, 431.

6. Kokushi daijiten henshū iinkai, *Kokushi daijiten* vol. 6 (Yoshikawa Kōbunkan), 219–20.

7. Takayanagi, "Meiji minpō izen no rikonhō," 111.

8. Mori Arinori, "On Wives and Concubines, Part One," *Meiroku Zasshi* (May 1874), in William Reynolds Braisted, trans., *Meiroku Zasshi: Journal of the Japanese Enlightenment* (Cambridge, Mass.: Harvard University Press, 1976), 104.

9. Mori Arinori, "On Wives and Concubines, Part Five," *Meiroku Zasshi* 27 (February 1875), in ibid., 332.

10. "Minpō hensei no kotae" *Kojun zasshi* 43 (5 April 1881), cited in Arichi Tōru, *Kindai nihon no kazokukan: Meijihen* (Kōbundō, 1977), 32–33.

11. Fukuzawa Yukichi, "Rikon no gen'in," *Jiji shinpō* (29 July 1886), in *Fukuzawa Yukichi on Japanese Women: Selected Works*, trans. and ed. Eiichi Kiyooka (Tokyo: University of Tokyo Press, 1988), 128–30.

12. *Jōgaku zasshisha*: see Nishida Nagakazu, "'Kon'inron kaidai," in *Meiji bunka zenshū*, vol. 16, *Fujin mondai*, ed. Meiji bunka kenkyūkai (Nihon hyōronsha, 1959), 7–9.

13. Yokoyama Masao, "Kon'inron," in *Meiji bunka zenshū*, vol. 16 *Fujin mondai*, ed. Meiji bunka kenkyūkai (Nihon hyōronsha, 1959), 76.

14. Ibid., 78–86.

15. Ibid., 86.

16. Hozumi Nobushige, "Rikon no hikakuron," *Hōritsu kyōkai zasshi*, no. 25/26 (May–July 1885), reprinted in *Hozumi Nobushige ibunshū*, ed. Hozumi shōgaku zaidan shuppan (Iwanami Shoten, 1932), 389–404.

17. Ishii, *Nihon kon'in hōshi*, 434.

18. May 1873 draft in Meiji bunka zenshū kenkyūkai, ed., *Meiji bunka zenshū*, vol. 9, *Hōritsu* (1929; reprint, Nihon hyōronsha, 1992), 589–98. October 1873 draft in Tetsuka Yutaka, *Meiji shonen no minpō hensan: Etō Shinpei no hensan jigyō to sono sōan* (Shihō daijin kanbō hishoka, 1944).

19. Tetsuka, *Meiji shonen no minpō hensan*, 52–55.

20. With respect to inheritance, however, the Japanese rejected French ideas. Etō Shinpei overruled his young French advisor Georges H. Bousquet, who proposed that estates be divided among all sons (ignoring daughters), in favor of legally instituting primogeniture as practiced by the Japanese samurai class. Robert Epp, "The Challenge from Tradition: Attempts to Compile a Civil Code in Japan, 1866–78," *Monumenta Nipponica* 22, no. 1–2 (1967): 29–30.

21. The liberty of divorce introduced during the French Revolution had already become restricted in 1803. Roderick Phillips, *Untying the Knot: A Short History of Divorce* (Cambridge: Cambridge University Press, 1991), 60–62.

22. Aoyama Michio, "Rikon no shiteki shokeitai to sono keitai," *Kazoku mondai to kazokuhō*, vol. 3, *Rikon* (Sakai shoten, 1958), 60–61.

23. Phillips, *Untying the Knot*, 120–23.

24. Isobe Shirō, *Dainihon shinten minpō shakugi* (Nagashima shobō, 1891), 288–90.

25. Epp, "Challenge," 36–44.
26. See chapter 4, "Unsuitable to the Family Tradition?"
27. Ishii Ryōsuke, ed., *Meiji bunka shiryō sōsho, hōritsu hen, jō* (1959), III, 4.
28. Epp, "Challenge," 45–46.
29. Phillips, *Untying the Knot,* 131.
30. The Napoleonic Code banned divorces in the case of marriages that had lasted less than two or more than twenty years and limited divorce to husbands over twenty-five and wives between twenty and forty-five.
31. Yamahana Masao, "Meiji minpō igo no rikonhō," *Kazoku mondai to kazokuhō,* vol. 3, *Rikon* (Sakai shoten, 1958), 154–55.
32. *Riyūsho, jō,* 1–2. Cited in Yamahana, "Meiji minpō igo," 155.
33. Isobe, *Dainihon,* 294.
34. *Kodansha Encyclopedia of Japan* (Kodansha, 1983), 1: 317.
35. Tetsuka Yutaka, "Meiji 23 nen minpō ni okeru yōshi seido," *Hōgaku kenkyū,* no. 28, 766, 919.
36. Ishii Ryōsuke, "Kyūminpō jinjihen genrōin teishutsuan, chōsakaian, giteian oyobi naikaku shūseian," *Kokka,* no. 71, 606.
37. Robert Epp, "Threat to Tradition: The Reaction to Japan's 1890 Civil Code" (Ph.D. diss., Harvard University, 1964), 88.
38. Hikaku kazokushi gakkai, ed., *Jiten kazoku* (Kōbundō, 1996), 788–89. Hans Peter Marutschke, *Einführung in das japanische Recht* (Munich: C. H. Beck, 1999), 87–92.
39. Hōmu daijin kanbō shihō hōsei chōsabu, ed., *Nihon kindai rippō shiryō sōsho,* vol. 6, *Hōten chōsakai: Minpō gijisoku kiroku* (Shōji hōmu kenkyūkai, 1984), 364. The legislation provided as reference to the committee members in the case of consensual divorce was for Japan the Council of State decree of 15 May 1873 permitting wives to divorce and an ordinance *(shirei)* of the Home Ministry of 20 October 1882; French "Old Law" (Article 233), Holland (Article 263), Italy (Article 148), Belgium (Article 227), German First Draft (Article 1440, 1), and German [Civil Code] Second Draft (Article 1459, 1).
40. These are among the seven Confucian grounds for divorce, discussed in chapter 1.
41. Hōmu daijin, ed., *Hōten chōsakai,* 6: 374.
42. Hozumi Nobushige's amendment cited Austria's Article 115, Sweden's laws of 27 April 1810 and 24 December 1874, no. 47, and France's Article 1, draft 718.
43. Hōmu daijin, ed., *Hōten chōsakai,* 6: 382.
44. Ibid., 382–85.
45. Ibid., 390.
46. Ibid., 391.
47. Ibid., 379.
48. Hōmu daijin kanbō shihō hōsei chōsabu, ed., *Nihon kindai rippō shiryō sōsho,* vol. 14, *Minpō seirikai gijisoku kiroku* (Shōji hōmu kenkyūkai, 1988), 412, 414, cited in Uramoto Kanyu, *Rikonhō no hendō to shisō* (Kyoto: Hōritsu bunkasha, 1999), 49.

49. Ueno Chizuko, *Kindai kazoku no seiritsu to shūen* (Iwanami shoten, 1994), 69. See also *The Invention of Tradition,* ed. Eric Hobsbawm and Terence Ranger (New York: Cambridge University Press, 1983, 1992).
50. See, e.g., Goode, *World Changes in Divorce Patterns,* 220.
51. Phillips, *Untying the Knot,* 60–61.
52. Hōmu daijin, ed., *Hōten chōsakai,* 6: 405–6.
53. Meiji Civil Code Article 819.
54. Hōmu daijin, ed., *Hōten chōsakai,* 6: 372, 409.
55. Phillips, *Untying the Knot,* 174–76.
56. Hōmu daijin, ed., *Hōten chōsakai,* 6: 375.
57. Lenore J. Weitzman, *The Divorce Revolution: The Unexpected Social and Economic Consequences for Women and Children in America* (New York: Free Press, 1985).
58. Tomii Masaaki, for example, believed the potential for abuse could be restricted through instituting formal registration requirements.

Chapter 6: When Marriage Was on the Rise

1. Roderick Phillips, *Putting Asunder: A History of Divorce in Western Society* (Cambridge: Cambridge University Press, 1988), 583.
2. Takeyoshi Kawashima and Kurt Steiner, "Modernization and Divorce Rate Trends in Japan," *Economic Development and Cultural Change* 9, 1 part II (October 1960): 213–39.
3. Laurel L. Cornell, "Peasant Women and Divorce in Preindustrial Japan," *Signs: Journal of Women in Culture and Society* 15, no. 4 (1990): 710–32.
4. Kitō Hiroshi, *Nihon nisennen no jinkōshi* (Kyoto: PHP kenkyūjo, 1983), 105.
5. Although the census defined a married couple by cohabitation, not by registration, the percentage of married people in the population declined. Rising marriage age and an increase in children could have contributed to the decrease in the percentage of married people in Yamanashi.
6. Nagahara Kazuko, "Minzoku no tenkan to josei no yakuwari," in *Nihon josei seikatsushi,* vol. 4, *Kindai,* ed. Joseishi sōgō kenkyūkai, 2d ed. (Tōkyō daigaku shuppankai, 1991), 75.
7. Yamakawa Kikue, *Women of the Mito Domain: Recollections of Samurai Family Life,* trans. Kate Wildman Nakai (Tokyo: University of Tokyo Press, 1992), 115.
8. Mary Crawford Fraser, *A Diplomat's Wife in Japan,* ed. Hugh Cortazzi (1899; abridged, New York: Weatherhill, 1982).
9. Rein visited Japan between 1874 and 1875. His interpretation of the effects of the Meiji Civil Code could thus not have been based on personal observations: J[ohan] J[ustus] Rein, *Japan nach Reisen und Studien im Auftrage der königlich preussischen Regierung dargestellt,* 2d ed. (Leipzig: Wilhelm Engelmann, 1905), 586.
10. J. E. de Becker, *Annotated Civil Code of Japan* (London: Butterworth; Yokohama: Kelley & Walsh, 1909–10), 2: 69–71.

11. Takano Iwasaburō, "Honpō rikon tōkei ippan (1)," *Tōkei shūshi* (1909): 45. Most scholars subsequently ignored the Meiji divorce slump problem either by deleting figures before 1899, such as in Okamatsu Michi, "Honpō rikon tōkei ippan (1)," *Tōkei shūshi* 383 (1913): 3–8, and Kōseishō, *Jinkō dōtai tōkei* (1990), 66–67, or by simply ignoring them, as in Kawashima and Steiner, "Modernization and Divorce Rate Trends in Japan."

12. Wolfgang Humbert-Droz, *Das Ehescheidungsrecht in Japan* (Cologne: Carl Heymanns KG, 1985), 114. For the same argument, see also René König, *Die Familie der Gegenwart: Ein interkultureller Vergleich* (Munich: C. H. Beck, 1974), 109; Oshio Shunsuke, "Rikon no imi," in *Kindai kazoku*, vol. 5, *Rikon*, ed. Eiichi Isomura, Takeyoshi Kawashima, and Takashi Koyama (Kawade, 1956), 39–57; Nagahara, "Minzoku no tenkan," 73; Kumagai Fumie, "Changing Divorce in Japan," *Journal of Family History* 8, no. 1 (Spring 1983): 91.

13. Official marriage rate: Kōseishō, *Rikon tōkei* (Kosei tōkei kyōkai, 1984), 34–36; Honseki married as a percentage of honseki population: Hayami, ed., *Kokusei chōsa izen Nihon jinkō tōkei shūsei*, 1992–93.

14. Tamaki Hajime, "Kon'in, rikon, tōkeiron," in *Kazoku seido zenshū*, vol. 2, *Rikon* (Kawade shobō, 1937), 332.

15. This population was recorded according to the legal place of residence *(honseki)*, in contrast to population according to the actual place of residence *(genjū)*.

16. Toda Teizō, *Kazoku to kon'in* (Chūbunkan, 1934), 52.

17. See chapter 5, "Between French Law and Japanese Custom."

18. The shift from legal to residential registration accounting in 1899 could also have contributed to the sharp Meiji-era decline. The annual numbers for marriages and divorces assessed by either method should have been equal, and in fact they matched. This contrasts with the differences between legal and residential populations. The number of divorces was 66,626 for both legal and residential populations in 1899. Kaida Kinjūrō, "Hokkaidō oyobi fuken genjūnin seisan, shisan, shibō, kon'in, rikon," *Tōkei shūshi* 257 (1902): 415, 417. Yasu Iwasaki attributes the fall in the divorce rate partly to the above change in the locality of registration. He notes that overseas Japanese were excluded from the national statistics after 1899. Yasu Iwasaki, "Divorce in Japan," *American Journal of Sociology* 36, no. 3 (November 1930): 436. According to the statistics bureau, only 99,039 Japanese lived overseas in 1899, 15,068 of them in Korea, out of a population of 43 million, a figure hardly large enough to be significant in a 50 percent drop in the divorce rate. Naikaku Tōkeikyoku, *Nihon teikoku tōkei tekiyō* (Naikaku tōkeikyoku, 1901): 12. The fact that 1903 population statistics record only 68 divorces of Japanese nationals in Taiwan and "foreign countries" further shows that exclusion of overseas Japanese was not an important factor in the precipitous fall in the divorce rate. Naikaku Tōkeikyoku, *Nihon teikoku jinkō dōtai tōkei* (1903), 1.

19. Scholars who support this hypothesis are Tsubouchi Yoshihiro and Tsubouchi Reiko, *Tōnan ajia kenkyū sōsho*, vol. 4, *Rikon* (Sōbunsha, 1970), 148–49; Horiuchi Misao and Katō Mihoko, "Meiji zenki ni okeru rikonhō," in *Kōza kazoku*, vol. 4, *Kon'in no kaishō* (Kōbundō, 1974), 244.

20. See, e.g., Sepp Linhart, "Familie," in *Japan-Handbuch,* ed. Horst Hammitzsch (Wiesbaden: Franz Steiner, 1981), 558.

21. J. E. de Becker, *Annotated Civil Code of Japan,* 47.

22. Increased requirements for registration were no absolute guarantee for ascertaining mutual consent of the parties involved. Article 811 declared that a registered divorce remained valid even if parents or relatives had not known about it or expressed discontent. A divorce was also binding when the registration formalities (Article 775) had been violated. The rules on consent and registration procedures should have guaranteed that the spouses and their immediate relatives acted on their own accord. By showing a way of ignoring the rules, the drafters of the code provided a way for neglecting its explicit demand for mutual consent.

Verifying mutual consent was also not absolutely demanded in practice. A 1917 reply *(kaitō)* by the head of the Ministry of Justice's legal affairs bureau prohibited officials from rejecting a divorce notification, even if there was doubt whether both spouses agreed to it. See Toshitani Nobuyoshi and Ishii Michiko, "Nihon no rikon," *Rikon no hōshakaigaku* (Tōkyō daigaku shuppankai, 1988), 68.

23. Barbara Molony, "Afterword," in *Facing Two Ways: The Story of My Life* (1935; reprint, Stanford University Press, 1984), xxii–xxiii.

24. Kawashima and Steiner, "Modernization and Divorce Rate Trends in Japan," 216–17.

25. See appendix table A.5, "Court Divorces, 1900–1940."

26. Yamahata Masao, "Meiji minpō ikō no rikonhō," in *Kazoku mondai to kazokuhō,* vol. 3, *Rikon* (Sakai shoten, 1958), 167.

27. See appendix table A.5, "Court Divorces, 1900–1940."

28. In the postwar period, the role of judicial divorce may have had a similar function, because in 60 percent of the court divorces, one of the spouses was absent in 1982: Taimie L. Bryant, "Marital Dissolution in Japan: Legal Obstacles and Their Impact," *Law in Japan* 17 (1984): 77.

29. On the Supreme Court decision: Kano Masanao, *Senzen "ie" no shisō* (Sōbunsha, 1983), 161. On other court precedents: Ikeda Ryūji, "Meiji minpō to josei no kenri," *Nihon joseishi,* vol. 4, *Kindai,* ed. Joseishi sōgō kenkyūkai (Tōkyō daigaku shuppankai, 1982), 67–72.

30. Margit Nagy, "Middle-Class Working Women During the Interwar Years," in *Recreating Japanese Women, 1600–1945,* ed. Gail L. Bernstein (Berkeley: University of California Press, 1991), 210–11.

31. About the establishment of Japanese family courts: Margit Nagy, "'How Shall We Live?': Social Change, the Family Institution and Feminism in Prewar Japan" (Ph.D. diss., University of Washington, 1981), 204–5; Kano, *Senzen "ie" no shisō,* 156–62. For primary sources on the committee: Horiuchi Misao, *Kaji shinpan seido no kenkyū,* 2 vols. (Chūō daigaku shuppankai, 1970–76).

32. Isono Seichi and Isono Fujiko, *Kazoku seido* (Iwanami shinsho, 1958), 113; Yanagita Kunio, *Japanese Manners and Customs in the Meiji Era,* trans. Charles S. Terry (Tokyo: Ōbunsha, 1957), 169; Toda Teizō, "Divorce—A

Comparative Study," *Contemporary Japan* (September 1933): 298–301; Robert J. Smith, "Making Village Women into 'Good Wives and Wise Mothers' in Prewar Japan," *Journal of Family History* 8, no. 1 (Spring 1983): 79; Robert J. Smith and Ella Lury Wiswell, *The Women of Suye Mura* (Chicago: Chicago University Press, 1982), 274; Yamakawa, *Women of the Mito Domain*, 111.

33. Shimazaki Toson, *The Family*, trans. Cecilia Segawa Seigle (Tokyo: Tokyo University Press, 1976).

34. Nakano Makiko, *Makiko's Diary: A Merchant Wife in 1910 Kyoto*, trans. Kazuko Smith (Stanford: Stanford University Press, 1995), 2–5.

35. Cornell, "Peasant Women and Divorce in Preindustrial Japan," 724.

36. Toda, "Divorce," 298–301.

37. Chie Nakane, "An Interpretation of the Size and Structure of the Household in Japan over Three Centuries," in *Household and Family in Past Time: Comparative Studies in the Size and Structure of the Domestic Group over the Last Three Centuries in England, France, Serbia, Japan and Colonial North America, with Further Materials from Western Europe*, edited by Peter Laslett (Cambridge: Cambridge University Press, 1972); Sōmuchō tōkeikyoku, *Kokusei chōsa*, listed at http:/www.stat.go.jp/data/Kokusei/2000, 29 July 2003.

38. Smith and Wiswell, *Women of Suye Mura*, 274.

39. Honma Hisao, *Yomiuri shinbun*, 28 April 1916, cited in *Shinbun shūroku Taishōshi* (hereafter *SSTS*) vol. 4 (Taishō, 1978), 144.

40. Shufu no Tomosha, ed., *Renai seikō no hiketsu hyakajō* (Shufu no tomosha, 1929); Saburō, ed., *Kekkon hiten* (Shufu no tomosha, 1938).

41. Linhart, "Familie," 552; Yuzawa Yasuhiko, *NHK bukkusu*, vol. 531, *Gendai Nihon no kazoku mondai* (Nihon hōsō shuppan kyōkai, 1987), 55.

42. *Kokumin shinbun*, 9 March 1916, cited in *SSTS*, 4: 97.

43. Konosuke Matsushita, *Quest for Prosperity: The Life of a Japanese Industrialist* (Kyoto: PHP Institute, 1988), 36–37.

44. Robert J. Smith, "Making Village Women," 80.

45. Hani Motoko, *Yomiuri*, 17 October 1916, cited in *SSTS*, 4: 348.

46. Yuzawa, *Gendai Nihon no kazoku mondai*, 172–73.

47. *Jinkō dōtai tōkei*, various years.

48. See appendix table A.3. Index of Divorce by Age Group in Japan, 1919–40.

49. Higher dissolution rates in Tōhoku are partly due to greater prevalence of in-marrying husbands. Yuzawa Yasuhiko, "Nihon no rikon: kindaika no naka no konmei," in *Sekai no rikon: sono fūdo to dōkō*, ed. Yasuhiko Yuzawa et al. (Yūhikaku, 1979), 172–81. Other statistical and ethnographic sources also show high divorce for early modern marriages of *muko yōshi*. For an Edo village: Cornell, "Peasant Women and Divorce in Preindustrial Japan," 732. A foreign observer writes that divorces of *muko yōshi* are not uncommon, because "in such marriages, the woman has the greater power, and the man has to remember what he owes her": Bacon, *Japanese Girls and Women*, 104. By contrast, Tamaki Hajime doubts that *muko yōshi* marriages dissolved more often than normal marriages: Tamaki Hajime, "Meiji ikō no rikon mondai," cited in Shikata Hisao "'Tsumadoikon' ni okeru rikon," *Soshioroji* 11, no. 4 (June

1965): 91. Since only a man could serve as head of a samurai house, divorcing a *muko yōshi* would make both sides worse off. The man would lose his stipend, and the family's position in the domain would be jeopardized without an heir. Yamakawa thus deduces that there must have been a low rate of divorce of *muko yōshi* marriages among samurai. Younger sons in the Shōwa period, however, could seek employment and establish their own independent households. Since the position of a *muko yōshi* become much less necessary and desirable, the *muko*'s inclination toward divorce increased. Yamakawa, *Women of the Mito Domain*, 103–4.

50. See appendix table A.4, "In-Marrying Husbands Among Newlyweds and Spouses Departing After Divorce, 1905–1935."

51. Other explanations that have been advanced for the gradual decline in the divorce rate seem implausible. One suggests that an oversupply of women of marriageable age abated once more younger sons had independent incomes to support families and thus were able to marry, but as has been noted, by the Meiji period, there already is little evidence of a difference between the rates at which men and women married.

52. William H. Erskine, *Japanese Customs: Their Origin and Value* (Tokyo: Kyo Bun Kwan, 1925), 7–8.

53. Ibid., 8.

54. Ibid., 9.

55. Walter Weston, *Japan* (London: A. & C. Black, 1926), 221–22.

56. Harold S. Williams, *Tales of the Foreign Settlements in Japan* (Rutland, Vt.: Charles E. Tuttle, 1958), 132–34.

57. Sotozaki Mitsuhiro, *Ueki Emori, katei kaikaku, fujin kaihōron* (Hōsei daigaku shuppankyoku, 1971), 181–84.

58. Arichi Tōru, *Kindai nihon no kazokukan: Meijihen* (Kōbundō, 1977), 142–43.

59. Minami Hiroshi, ed., *Kindai shomin seikatsushi*, vol. 9, *Renai, kekkon, kazoku* (San'ichi shobō, 1986).

60. *To (Kyōto no to)*, 7 December 1913, in *SSTS*, 1: 457.

61. *Yomiuri*, 13 October 1914, in *SSTS*, 2: 375.

62. *Chūō*, 1 June 1916, in *SSTS*, 4: 179.

63. Tanaka Akira, *Konrei gahō* (Shufu no tomosha, 1931), 36–45.

64. Smith and Wiswell, *Women of Suye Mura*, 168.

65. Robert J. Smith, "Making Village Women," 78.

66. Goh, "Family Relations in Japan," 135, 147–48. The Japanese anthropologist Ema Tsutomu believes that for convenience, money was more often included in a dowry from the Meiji period on. Ema Tsutomu chosaku kankōkai, ed., "Kekkon no rekishi," in *Ema Tsutomu chosakushō 7* (Chūō kōronsha, 1976), 368.

67. Thomas Elsa Jones, "Mountain Folk in Japan: A Study in Method" (Ph.D. diss., Columbia University, 1926), 74.

68. Smith and Wiswell, *Women of Suye Mura*, 274.

69. Carl Mosk, *Patriarchy and Fertility: Japan and Sweden, 1880–1960* (New York: Academic Press, 1983), 99–100.

70. Margret Neuss-Kaneko, *Familie und Gesellschaft in Japan, Von der Feudalzeit bis in die Gegenwart* (Munich: C. H. Beck, 1990), 37.
71. *Jiji*, 29 October 1916, in *SSTS*, 4: 364–65.
72. *Yomiuri*, 27 February 1917, in *SSTS*, 5: 77.
73. *Chūō*, 2 June 1918, in *SSTS*, 6: 190.

Chapter 7: Forward to the Past

1. *Nihon keizai shinbun*, chōkan, 1 January 1999, 38. The article compared the estimated divorce rate of Japan in 1998 (1.94) with that of France in 1996 (1.90). Exactly a year later, the same newspaper simply reported a record in the number of divorces "for the ninth consecutive year"; meanwhile, another historically low birthrate made headlines. Ibid., 1 January 2000, 38.
2. *Asahi shinbun*, 1 January 1999, 3; *Tōkyō yomiuri shinbun*, 1 January 1999, morning edition, 1; *Mainichi shinbun*, 1 January 1999, 30. After some delay, the same news also appeared in the English-language *Japan Times*, 9 January 1999.
3. *Asahi shinbun*, 1 January 1999, 3.
4. Kōseishō, *Jinkō dōtai tōkei* (Kōsei tōkei kyōkai, 1997), 1: 82–83. Japan: 1.60, Spain: 0.84, Italy: 0.48 (1994), Yugoslavia: 0.73, France: 2.01, Germany: 2.07, Netherlands: 2.21, United States: 4.44, and Russia: 4.51.
5. Kōseirōdōshō, *Heisei 14nen jinkō dōtai tōkei*, listed at http://www.mhlw.go.jp/toukei/, 29 July 2003. A record 289,838 couples divorced in 2002, compared with 757,331 marriages, that is 38.27 percent.
6. In English by date of publication: Kawashima Takeyoshi and Kurt Steiner, "Modernization and Divorce Rate Trends in Japan," *Economic Development and Cultural Change* 9, no. 1, part II (October 1960): 213–39; Fumie Kumagai, "Changing Divorce in Japan," *Journal of Family History* 8, no. 1 (Spring 1983): 85–107; Taimie L. Bryant, "Marital Dissolution in Japan: Legal Obstacles and Their Impact," *Law in Japan* 17 (1984): 73–98; Laurel L. Cornell, "Gender Differences in Remarriage After Divorce in Japan and the United States," *Journal of Marriage and the Family* 51, no. 2 (May 1989), 457–64; Taimie L. Bryant, "'Responsible' Husbands, 'Recalcitrant' Wives, Retributive Judges: Judicial Management of Contested Divorce in Japan," *Journal of Japanese Studies* 18, no. 2 (Summer 1992): 407–43; William J. Goode, *World Change in Divorce Patterns* (New Haven: Yale University Press, 1993), ch. 8.
7. Maria Nagy, "'How Shall We Live?': Social Change, the Family Institution and Feminism in Prewar Japan" (Ph.D. diss., University of Washington, 1981), 198–218.
8. Kurt Steiner, "The Revision of the Civil Code of Japan: Provisions Affecting the Family," *Far Eastern Quarterly* 9, no. 2 (February 1950), 179.
9. Meiji Civil Code, Article 772.
10. New Civil Code, Article 737, 3. For the text, see Yokoi Hideaki, *Minpō* (Jiyū kokuminsha, 1996).
11. New Civil Code, Article 731.
12. Ibid., Article 753. Attaining majority at marriage was in accordance

with the German principle: "Heirat macht mündig." Steiner, "Revision of the Civil Code," 179.

13. New Civil Code, Article 770.

14. Ibid., Article 768.

15. Yasuhide Kawashima, "Americanization of Japanese Family Law, 1945–1975," *Law in Japan* 16 (1983): 62.

16. Ibid., 68.

17. New Civil Code, Articles 763–69.

18. Toshitani Nobuyoshi and Ishii Michiko, "Nihon no rikon," in *Rikon no hōshakaigaku* (Tōkyō daigaku shuppankai, 1988), 67–71, 97–99.

19. There were 336 suits for the invalidation of divorce in 1954.

20. Mutual consent divorces constituted 91.5 percent of all divorces in 2000.

21. A merger of the "family council," created in 1948 as a branch of the district court, and the "juvenile council," created in 1923 as an executive agency under the Ministry of Justice.

22. Kawashima, "Americanization," 60–61.

23. Bryant, "Marital Dissolution in Japan," 79–81.

24. Kōseirōdōshō, *Jinkō dōtai tōkei Heisei 12nen* (Kōsei tōkei kyōkai, 2002), 1: 436.

25. Wolfgang Humbert-Droz, *Das Ehescheidungsrecht in Japan* (Cologne: Carl Heymanns KG, 1985), 43–44.

26. Bryant, "Marital Dissolution in Japan," 78–81.

27. New Civil Code, Article 770.

28. Judicial divorces constituted 0.8 percent of all divorces in 2000.

29. Toshitani and Ishii, "Nihon no rikon," 66, 72–79.

30. Ezra F. Vogel, *Japan's New Middle Class* (Berkeley: University of California Press, 1963).

31. Andrew Gordon, *The Evolution of Labor Relations in Japan: Heavy Industry, 1853–1955* (Cambridge, Mass.: Harvard University Press, 1988), 368–411.

32. Ann Waswo, *Modern Japanese Society, 1868–1994* (Oxford: Oxford University Press, 1996), 105–18.

33. In surveys conducted by the Prime Minister's Office in the 1990s, 57.8 percent of Japanese respondents continued to approve the sexual division of labor in which the husband goes out to work and the wife does the housekeeping. Sōrifu, *Danjo kyōdō sankaku shakai ni kan suru seron chōsa* (January 1998), item 3.

34. Lenore J. Weitzman, "The Divorce Law Revolution: No-Fault in America," in *The Divorce Revolution: The Unexpected Social and Economic Consequences for Women and Children in America* (New York: Free Press, 1985), 15–51; Herbert Jacob, *Silent Revolution: The Transformation of Divorce Law in the United States* (Chicago: University of Chicago Press, 1988).

35. Roderick Phillips, *Untying the Knot: A Short History of Divorce* (Cambridge: Cambridge University Press, 1991), 215–23.

36. Ibid., 248.

37. Eva Marie von Münch, *Ehescheidung nach neuem Recht* (Munich: C. H Beck, 1996), 35–105.
38. Lawrence Stone, *Road to Divorce: A History of the Making and Breaking of Marriage in England* (Oxford: Oxford University Press, 1995), 409–22.
39. Yozo Watanabe, "Family and Law in Modern Japan," *Annals of the Institute of Social Science* 15 (1974): 36–37.
40. *Hataraku josei no jitsujō* cited in Foreign Press Center, *Facts and Figures of Japan* (Tokyo: Foreign Press Center, 1995), 56. In 1985, 9.1 percent of female employees were widowed or divorced.
41. Defined in labor surveys by the Japanese government as under 35 or fewer hours per week.
42. Women constituted 40.7 percent of the total labor force in 1997.
43. Sumiko Iwao, *The Japanese Woman: Traditional Image and Changing Reality* (New York: Free Press, 1993), 114.
44. Sōrifū, *Danjō kyōdō*, items 7 and 8.
45. Kōseishō, *Jinkō dōtai tōkei*. This trend continued: in 2000, 17.7 percent of husbands and 15.4 percent of wives had previously been married. Kōseirōdōshō, *Heisei 14nen jinkō dōtai tōkei*.
46. Watanabe, "Family and Law in Modern Japan," 30.
47. According to a 1977 NHK survey. Percentages of love/arranged marriages: 16/74 (1947), 29/68 (1957), 47/52 (1967), 58/40 (1977), cited in Kamiko Takeji and Masuda Kōkichi, *Nihonjin no kazoku kankei* (Yūhikaku, 1985), 41.
48. Stone, *Road to Divorce*, 411.
49. *Nihon teikoku jinkō dōtai tōkei* and Kōseishō, *Jinkō dōtai tōkei*, 1: 437.
50. Kōseirōdōshō, *Jinkō dōtai tōkei Heisei 12nen*, 1: 119.
51. Gary S. Becker, *Treatise on the Family*, 221–23.
52. Stone, *Road to Divorce*, 413.
53. David R. Hall, "Marriage as a Pure Relationship: Exploring the Link Between Premarital Cohabitation and Divorce in Canada," *Journal of Comparative Family Studies* 27, no. 1 (Spring 1996): 3.
54. Walter Edwards, *Modern Japan Through Its Weddings: Gender, Person, and Society in Ritual Portrayal* (Stanford: Stanford University Press, 1989), 123.
55. Kindai bungeisha, ed., *Watashi ga rikon shita riyū* (Kindai bungeisha, 1996).
56. Ikeuchi Hiromi, *Risutora rikon: Tsuma ga otto o suteru toki* (Sōyō, 1996).
57. Kōseirōdōshō, *Heisei 13nen jinkō dōtai tōkei*, 1: 499.
58. Percentage of divorcing couples with children: 57.3% in 1950, rising to 68.2% in 1985, then declining to 59.5% in 2000. Ibid.
59. Aoyama Michio, *Nihon kazoku seido no kenkyū* (Iwamatsudō shoten, 1947), 131.
60. Single-parent households have ranged from 4 to 5 percent of all households since the 1960s, but the number of such households rose from about 515,300 in 1967 to around 789,900 in 1993.

61. Meiji Civil Code, Articles 812, 819.
62. New Civil Code, Article 819.
63. Kōseirōdōshō, *Heisei 14nen jinkō dōtai tōkei*, 1: 450.
64. Mary Ann Mason, *From Father's Property to Children's Rights* (New York: Columbia University Press, 1994), xiii–xvi.
65. New Civil Code, Article 768.
66. Goode, *World Changes in Divorce Patterns*, 235.
67. In 1982, there was no monetary award in 3,248 (64.3 percent) of the 5,054 divorce cases handled by district courts. Bryant, "Marital Dissolution in Japan," 81.
68. *Heisei 4 nendo shihō tōkei nenpō* cited in *Minpō no kaisetsu*, ed. Minpō kyōiku shidō kenkyūkai (Ichibashi shuppan 1995), 19.
69. Ralph Lützeler, "Zur Regionalen Dimension Sozialer Probleme in Japan," *Japanstudien* 5 (1990): 229–73.
70. Bryant, "Marital Dissolution in Japan," 86–88.
71. The national single-mother household survey of 1993 by the Ministry of Health and Welfare estimates a household income level of 31 percent of ordinary households. Ebihara Yumi, "Tsuma no jiritsu no tame ni nani ga hitsuyō ka," *Jiyū to seigi* (August 1999): 152. An unspecified 1992 survey recorded an annual income of 5.13 million yen for two-parent households, 2.42 million yen for widowed mother households (47 percent), and 1.85 million yen (36 percent) for divorced mothers with children. "Equality in Marriage, Not Divorce," *Daily Yomiuri*, 14 July 1994, 3. Divorced father households similarly have a lower annual level of income than two-parent families and widowed fathers. As expected, their income is initially higher than that of divorced mothers, but their earning capacity begins to decline after divorce. Several surveys indicate about one quarter to a third of those fathers have to change jobs after divorce. Moreover, until the 1980s welfare services were mainly designed for lone mothers. Satoshi Minamikata, "Custodial Fathers in Japan," in *Economic Consequences of Divorce: The International Perspective*, ed. Lenore J. Weitzman and Mavis Maclean (Oxford: Clarendon Press, 1992), 381–89.
72. Phillips, *Untying the Knot*, 1–27.
73. Observed in England. Stone, *Road to Divorce*, 420.
74. Bryant, "'Responsible' Husbands, 'Recalcitrant' Wives," 413–15. Saikō saibansho, Grand Bench, judgment of 2 September 1987, *Minshū*, no. 41, 1423, and Toshitani and Ishii, "Nihon no rikon," 79–82.
75. Bryant, "'Responsible' Husbands, 'Recalcitrant' Wives," 409.
76. Ibid., 408–10, 415.
77. Tōkyō bengoshikai, ed., *Kore kara no sentaku fūfu bessei* (Nihon hyōronsha, 1990).
78. Harald Fuess, "Die japanische BGB-Reformkontroverse (1996): Japanische Identität und die Rolle der Frau," *Japanstudien* 9 (1997): 255–86.
79. Hōmushō pamphlet, *Minpō no ichibu o kaisei suru hōritsuan yōkō*, 26 February 1996, 6–7.
80. The Justice Ministry decided not to publish the deliberations, but ministry officials contended that these details belonged in separate laws and not in a

civil code. Interview with civil code committee member Yoshioka Mutsu, 16 July 1996.

81. Hōmushō pamphlet, *Minpō no ichibu o kaisei*, 5–6.

82. Hōmushō, *Kon'in seido nado ni kan suru minpō kaisei yōkō shian oyobi shian no setsumei* (Nihon kajo shuppan, 1994).

83. Tokotani Fumio, "Saikon kinshi kikan wa seisabetsu ka," in *Kon'inhō kaisei*, ed. Kon'inhō kaisei o kangaerukai (Nihon hyōronsha, 1995), 30–40.

84. In a poll on family law reform in the summer of 1996, only 18.0 percent of respondents thought that a fixed period of separation was not sufficient grounds for divorce. While there was no overall difference in opposition between sexes, young women between twenty and twenty-nine and men over sixty held the strongest opposing views, in marked contrast to the other sex of the same age group, as if they felt especially vulnerable to divorce. Sōrifu, *Seron chōsa: Kazokuhō* (January 1997), 26–29.

85. That separate spousal surnames would weaken the feeling of family unity *(kazoku no ittaikan)* was believed by 46.5% of respondents and seen as having no effect by 48.7% of respondents. Sōrifu, *Seron chōsa*, 18.

86. "Japan Rushes into Divorce," *Japan Times*, 11 January 1998.

87. Hōmu daijin kanbō shihō hōsei chōsabu, ed., *Nihon kindai rippō shiryō sōsho*, vol. 6, *Hōten chōsakai: Minpō gijisoku kiroku* (Shōji hōmu kenkyūkai, 1984), 390.

88. "Aru hi gūzen, tsuma kara no mikudarihan," *Forbes Nihongoban* (December 1999), 152–61.

89. "30 dai josei riyū naki rikon: Otto no uwaki de mo bōryoku de mo okane no mondai de mo nai aite no donkansa ga yurusenai" (*"Women in Their Thirties Divorcing Without Grounds: Even Absent the Husband's Adultery, Violence, or Money Trouble, They Do Not Condone Their Mate's Insensitivity"*), *Aera* 12, no. 1 (28 December 1998–4 January 1999): 6–9.

90. "Otoko no rikon wa itai: rikon shita otoko wa shokku de heikin jumyō ga 10nen chichimaru" (the subtitle reads: "The Shock Shortens Divorced Men's Life Expectancy by Ten Years"), *Aera* 12, no. 25 (14 June 1999): 10–14.

91. "Rikon shita no wa watashi no wagamama, dakedo watashi ni wa kare ga hitsuyō," *Aera* 12, no. 7 (15 February 1999): 10–14.

92. "'Tsuma' ni suterareru 'otto' ga kyūzōchū," *Shūkan bunshū*, 18 June 1998, 58–60.

93. See, e.g., "Jukunen rikon wa, genjitsuteki ni mo hōritsuteki ni mo otoko ga naku" ("Divorce in Maturity: In Reality and in Law, Men Are Crying"), *Yomigaeru* (October 1999): 18–22, and "Chūkōnen ni oiuchi 'risutora rikon' no kaze," *Shūkan yomiuri*, 13 January 1998, 131–33.

94. *Mainichi Daily News*, 10 June 1997.

95. "Egao de rikon," *Fujin kōron*, 7 April 1998, 64–67. "Rikon shite, shiawase ni naru,"ibid., 7 October 1998, 23–57.

96. Kameyama Sanae, *Pojitibu rikon* (Nesuko, 1997).

Bibliography

Japanese-Language Sources

NOTE: Unsigned magazine and newspaper articles are not included here. Where Tokyo is the place of publication of a Japanese-language book, the place-name is omitted.

Amano Takeshi. "Rikon no shuzoku." In *Kōza kazoku*, vol. 4, *Kon'in no kaishō*, edited by Aoyama Michio et al. Kōbundō, 1974.
Amino Yoshihiko. *Higashi to nishi no kataru nihon no rekishi*. Soshiete, 1994.
Aoyama Michio. *Nihon kazoku seido no kenkyū*. Iwamatsudo shoten, 1947.
———. "Rikon no shiteki shokeitai to sono keitai." In *Kazoku mondai to kazokuhō*, vol. 3, *Rikon*. Sakai shoten, 1958.
Arichi Tōru. *Kindai nihon no kazokukan: Meijihen*. Kōbundō, 1977.
———. *Nihon no oyako nihyakunen*. Shinchōsha, 1986.
Asakura Yūko. "Buke josei no kon'in ni kansuru tōkeiteki kenkyū, shiron." In *Edo jidai no joseitachi*, edited by Kinsei joseishi kenkyūkai. Yoshikawa, 1990.
Chikamatsu Monzaemon. "Shinjū yoigōshin." In *Kabuki kanshō jiten*, edited by Mizuochi Kiyoshi. Tōkyōdō shuppan, 1993.
Ebihara Yumi. "Tsuma no jiritsu no tame ni nani ga hitsuyō ka." *Jiyū to seigi*, August 1999, 152.
Ema Tsutomu chosaku kankōkai, ed. "Kekkon no rekishi." In *Ema Tsutomu chosakushō 7*. Chūō kōronsha, 1976.
Emori Itsuo. *Nihon kisō bunka no minzoku gakuteki kenkyū*, vol. 2, *Nihon no kon'in—sono rekishi to minzoku*. Kōbundo, 1986.
Fuse Akiko. *Kekkon to kazoku*. Iwanami shoten, 1993.
Go Bunsō. "Bankoku ichi no rikon koku." *Chūō kōron*, February 1902, 45–46.
Hasegawa Akihiko. "'Tsumadoikon' to 'yomeiri.'" In *Mura no kazoku*, edited by Himeoka Tsutomu, Tsuchida Hideo, and Hasegawa Akihiko. Mineruba shobō, 1973.
Hashiura Yasui. *Nihon hōri sōsho*, vol. 11, *Kazoku seido no kenkyū 2*. Sotsudō shoten, 1941.

Hayami Akira, ed. *Kokusei chōsa izen Nihon jinkō tōkei shūsei.* 22 vols., with additional vol. 4. Hara shobō, 1992–93.
Hikaku kazokushi gakkai, ed. *Jiten kazoku.* Kōbundō, 1996.
Hōmu daijin kanbō shihō hōsei chōsabu, ed. *Nihon kindai rippō shiryō sōsho,* vol. 6, *Hōten chōsakai: Minpō gijisoku kiroku.* Shōji hōmu kenkyūkai, 1984.
Hōmushō. *Kon'in seido nado ni kan suru minpō kaisei yōkō shian oyobi shian no setsumei.* Nihon kajo shuppan, 1994.
———. *Minpō no ichibu o kaisei suru hōritsuan yōkō.* Pamphlet. 26 February 1996.
Horiuchi Misao, ed. *Kaji shinpan seido no kenkyū.* 2 vols. Chūō daigaku shuppankai, 1970–76.
———, ed. *Meiji zenki mibunhō daizen,* vol. 2, *Kon'inhen* 2. Chūō daigaku shuppankai, 1974.
Horiuchi Misao and Katō Mihoko. "Meiji zenki ni okeru rikonhō." In *Kōza kazoku,* vol. 4, *Kon'in no kaishō.* Kōbundō, 1974.
Hozumi Nobushige. *Hozumi Nobushige ibunshū.* Edited by Hozumi shōgaku zaidan shuppan. Iwanami shoten, 1932.
Hozumi Shigetō. *"Kazoku kon'in" kenkyū bunken senshū,* vol. 4, *Rikon seido no kenkyū.* Edited by Yuzawa Yasuhiko. 1924. Reprint. Kuresu shuppan, 1989.
———. *Rienjō to enkiridera.* Nihon hyōronsha, 1942.
Igarashi Tomio. *Kakekomidera.* Hanawa shinsho, 1989.
Ikeda Ryūji. "Meiji minpō to josei no kenri." In *Nihon joseishi,* vol. 4, *Kindai,* edited by Joseishi sōgō kenkyūkai. Tōkyō daigaku shuppankai, 1982.
Ikeuchi Hiromi. *Risutora rikon: tsuma ga otto o suteru toki.* Sōyō, 1996.
Ishii Ryōsuke. *Edo no rikon: mikudari-han to enkiridera.* Nihon keizai shinbunsha, 1965.
———. "Kyūminpō jinjihen genrōin teishutsuan, chōsakaian, giteian oyobi naikaku shūseian." *Kokka* no. 71 (1962), 606.
———. *Nihon kon'in hōshi.* Sōbundō, 1977.
———, ed. *Meiji bunka shiryō sōsho, hōritsu hen, jō.* Kasama shobō, 1959.
Isobe Shirō. *Dainihon shinten minpō shakugi.* Nagashima shobō, 1891.
Isono Seichi and Isono Fujiko. *Kazoku seido.* Iwanami shinsho, 1958.
Jichikan, ed. *"Kazoku kon'in" kenkyū bunken senshū,* additional vol., *Jinji kanrei zenshū,* edited by Yuzawa Yasuhiko. 1911. Reprint. Kuresu, 1990.
Kaida Kinjūrō. "Hokkaidō oyobi fuken honsekinin seisan, shisan, shibō, kon'in, rikon." *Tōkei shūshi* 257 (1902): 412–17.
Kameyama Sanae. *Pojitibu rikon.* Nesuko, 1997.
Kamiko Takeji and Masuda Kōkichi. *Nihonjin no kazoku kankei.* Yūhikaku, 1985.
Kamishima Jirō. *Nihonjin no kekkonkan.* Kōdansha gakujutsu bunko, 1992.
Kano Masanao. *Senzen "ie" no shisō.* Sōbunsha, 1983.
Kindai bungeisha, ed. *Watashi ga rikon shita riyū.* Kindai bungeisha, 1996.
Kitō Hiroshi. *Nihon nisennen no jinkōshi.* Kyoto: PHP kenkyūjo, 1983.
Kokuseiin. *Nihon teikoku jinkō dōtai tōkei.* Kokuseiin, 1922.

Kokushi daijiten henshū iinkai. *Kokushi daijiten*, vol. 6. Yoshikawa Kōbunkan, 1979–1997.
Kōseirōdōshō. "Heisei 14 nen jinkō dōtai tōkei," http://www.mhlw.go.jp/toukei/.
———. *Jinkō dōtai tōkei Heisei 12nen*, vol. 1. Kōsei tōkei kyōkai, 2002.
Kōseishō. *Jinkō dōtai tōkei*, vol. 1. Kōsei tōkei kyōkai, 1997.
———. *Rikon tōkei*. 1984.
Masato Takase. "1890 nen–1920 nen no wagakuni no jinkō dōtai to jinkō seitai." *Jinkōgaku kenkyū* 14 (May 1991): 21–34.
Meiji bunka zenshū kenkyūkai, ed. *Meiji bunka zenshū*, vol. 9, *Hōritsu*. 1929. Reprint. Nihon hyōronsha, 1992.
Minami Hiroshi, ed. *Kindai shomin seikatsushi*, vol. 9, *Ren'ai, kekkon, kazoku*. San'ichi shobō, 1986.
Minpō kyōiku shidō kenkyūkai, ed. *Minpō no kaisetsu*. Ichibashi shuppan, 1995.
Miyamoto Mataji. *Osaka bunkashiron*. Bunken shuppan, 1979.
Miyashita Michiko. "Nōson ni okeru kazoku to kon'in." In *Nihon joseishi*, vol. 3, *Kinsei*, edited by Joseishi sōgō kenkyūkai. Tōkyō daigaku shuppankai, 1990.
Murakami Kazuhiro. *Meiji rikon saibanshiron*. Hōritsu bunkasha, 1994.
Nagahara Kazuko. "Minzoku no tenkan to josei no yakuwari." In *Nihon josei seikatsushi*, vol. 4, *Kindai*, edited by Joseishi sōgō kenkyūkai. Tōkyō daigaku shuppankai, 1991.
Naikaku Tōkeikyoku. *Kokusei chōsa hōkoku: Fuken no bu. Taishō 9nen*, vol. 17. Tōkyō tōkei kyōkai, 1924.
———. *Kokusei chōsa hōkoku: Fukenhen. Shōwa 10nen*, vol. 2. Tōkyō tōkei kyōkai, 1937.
———. *Nihon teikoku jinkō dōtai tōkei*. Naikaku tōkeikyoku, 1903.
———. *Nihon teikoku tōkei tekiyō*. Naikaku tōkeikyoku, 1901.
Nakada Kaoru. *Tokugawa jidai no bungaku ni mietaru shihō*. Meijidō shoten, 1925.
Nakayama Tarō. *Nihon kon'inshi*. Shunyōdō, 1928.
Nishida Nagakazu. "'Kon'inron kaidai." In *Meiji bunka zenshū*, vol. 16, *Fujin mondai*, edited by Meiji bunka kenkyūkai. Nihon hyōronsha, 1959.
Nishida Taketoshi, ed. *Seikatsu koten sōsho*, vol. 2, *Meiji zenki no toshi kasō shakai*. Kōseikan, 1970.
Numa Masaya. "Hōgaku ni okeru kasetsu to kenshō." *Hōshakaigaku*, vol. 11, *Hōshakaigaku no shosō*, edited by Nihon hōshakai gakkai. Yūhikaku, 1961.
Okamatsu Michi. "Honpō rikon tōkei ippan 1." *Tōkei shūshi* 383 (1913): 3–8.
Oshio Shunsuke. "Rikon no imi." In *Kindai kazoku*, vol. 5, *Rikon*, edited by Eiichi Isomura, Takeyoshi Kawashima, and Takashi Koyama. Kawade, 1956.
Ōta Takeo. *Naien no kenkyū*. Yūhikaku, 1965.
———. *Rikon gen'in no kenkyū—hanrei no hensen o chūshin to shite*. Yūhikaku, 1956.
Saburō, ed. *Kekkon hiten*. Shufu no tomosha, 1938.
Saikō saibansho. *Minshū*, no. 49 (1987): 1423.

Saitō Osamu. "Meiji shonen nōka setai no shūgyō kōzō." *Mita gakkai zasshi* 78, no. 1 (1985): 14–32.
Segawa Kiyoko. *Kon'in oboegaki*. Kōdansha, 1957.
———. *Wakamono to musume o meguru minzoku*. Miraisha, 1972.
Shihōshō. *Tokugawa jidai minji kanreishū*, vol. 1, *Jinji no bu*. 1934. Reprint. Tachibana shoin, 1986.
———. "Zenkoku minji kanreiruishū." In *Meiji bunka zenshū*, vol. 9, *Hōritsu*, edited by Meiji bunka kenkyūkai. 1929. Reprint. Nihon hyōronsha, 1992.
Shikata Hisao. "'Tsumadoikon' ni okeru rikon." *Soshiorojii* 11, no. 4 (June 1965): 87–116.
———. "Tsumadoikon ni okeru rikon." In *Mura no kazoku*, edited by Himeoka Tsutomu, Tsuchida Hideo, and Hasegawa Akihiko. Mineruba shobō, 1973.
Shufu no tomosha, ed. *Ren'ai seikō no hiketsu hyakkajō*. Shufu no tomosha, 1929.
Sōmuchō tōkeikyoku. *Heisei 2 nen kokusei chōsa hōkoku*, vol. 2. Nihon tōkei kyōkai, 1992.
———. *Kokusei chōsa*, listed at http://www.stat.go.jp/data/kokusei/2000, 29 July 2003.
Sōrifu. *Danjo kyōdō sankaku shakai ni kan suru seron chōsa*. January 1998.
———. *Seron chōsa: Kazokuhō*. January 1997.
Sotozaki Mitsuhiro. *Ueki Emori, katei kaikaku, fujin kaihōron*. Hōsei daigaku shuppankyoku, 1971.
Suzuki Hideo. *Fūdo no kōzō*. Kōdansha, 1988.
Takagi Tadashi. *Enkiridera Mantokuji no kenkyū*. Seibundō, 1990.
———. *Mikudarihan Edo no rikon to joseitachi*. Heibonsha, 1987.
———. *Mikudarihan to enkiridera*. Kōdansha, 1992.
Takahashi Shin'ichi, ed. *Kokusei chōsa ikō Nihon jinkō tōkei shūsei*. 7 vols. Hara shobō, 1994.
Takano Iwasaburō. "Honpō rikon tōkei ippan 1." *Tōkei shūshi* 336 (1909): 45–48.
Takayanagi Shinzō. "Meiji minpō izen no rikonhō." In *Kazoku mondai to kazokuhō*, vol. 3, *Rikon*, edited by Nakagawa Zennosuke. Sakai shoten, 1958.
Takei Masaomi. *Naienkon no genjō to kadai*. Kyoto: Hōritsu bunkasha, 1991.
Tamaki Hajime. "Kon'in, rikon, tōkeiron." In *Kazoku seido zenshū*, vol. 2, *Rikon*, edited by Hozumi Shigetō and Nakagawa Zennosuke. Kawade shobō, 1937.
———. *Nihon kazoku seido no hihan*. Minyūsha, 1948.
———. *Nihon kazoku seidoron*. Hōritsu bunkasha, 1971.
Tamura Gorō. *Katei no saiban—fūfu*. Nihon hyōronsha, 1985.
Tanaka Akira. *Konrei Gahō*. Shufu no tomosha, 1931.
Tetsuka Yutaka. "Meiji 23 nen minpō ni okeru yōshi seido." *Hōgaku kenkyū*, no. 28 (1955).
———. *Meiji shonen no minpō hensan: Etō Shinpei no hensan jigyō to sono sōan*. Shihō daijin kanbō hishoka, 1944.
Toda Teizō. *Kazoku kōsei*. Kōbundō, 1937.

———. *Kazoku to kon'in.* Chūbunkan, 1934.
Tōkeiin, ed. *Kai kuni genzai ninbetsuchō.* Tōkeiin, 1882.
Tokotani Fumio. "Saikon kinshi kikan wa seisabetsu ka." In *Kon'inhō kaisei,* edited by Kon'inhō kaisei o kangaerukai. Nihon hyōronsha, 1995.
Tōkyō bengoshikai, ed. *Kore kara no sentaku fūfu bessei.* Nihon hyōronsha, 1990.
Toshitani Nobuyoshi and Ishii Michiko. "Nihon no rikon." In *Rikon no hōshakaigaku.* Tōkyō daigaku shuppankai, 1988.
Toyoda Tamotsu and Yokoe Katsumi. "Fūfu kankei keizoku kikanbetsu rikon no kenkyū ka." *Tōkei shūshi* 659 (1936): 14–33.
Tsubouchi Yoshihiro and Tsubouchi Reiko. "Nihon no rikon." In *Tōnan azia kenkyū sōsho,* vol. 4, *Rikon,* edited by Tsubouchi Yoshihiro and Tsubouchi Reiko. Sōbunsha, 1970.
Uematsu Akashi. "Kon'inshi no shomondai." In *Kōza Nihon no minzoku,* vol. 3, *Jinsei girei,* edited by Inoguchi Shōji. Yūseidō, 1978.
Ueno Chizuko. *Kindai kazoku no seiritsu to shūen.* Iwanami shoten, 1994.
Urako Takeji. "Sumiyaki no mura sanson no kazoku." In *Mura no kazoku,* edited by Himeoka Tsutomu, Tsuchida Hideo, and Hasegawa Akihiko. Mineruba shobō, 1973.
Uramoto Kanyu. *Rikonhō no hendō to shisō.* Kyoto: Hōritsu bunkasha, 1999.
Wakita Osamu. "Bakuhan taisei to josei." In *Nihon joseishi,* edited by Joseishi sōgō kenkyūkai. Tōkyō daigaku shuppankai, 1982.
Yamahana Masao. "Meiji minpō igo no rikonhō." In *Kazoku mondai to kazokuhō,* vol. 3, *Rikon,* edited by Nakagawa Zennosuke. Sakai shoten, 1958.
Yamakawa Kikue. *Nijūseiki o ayumu: aru onna no ashiato.* Daiwa shobō, 1981.
Yokoi Hideaki. *Minpō.* Jiyū kokuminsha, 1996.
Yokoyama Gennosuke. *Nihon no kasō shakai.* 1899. Reprint. Iwanami bunko, 1994.
Yokoyama Masao. "Kon'inron." In *Meiji bunka zenshū,* vol. 16, *Fujin mondai,* edited by Meiji bunka kenkyūkai. Nihon hyōronsha, 1959.
Yuzawa Yasuhiko. "Nihon no rikon: kindaika no naka no konmei." In *Sekai no rikon: sono fūdo to dōkō,* edited by Yasuhiko Yuzawa et al. Yūhikaku, 1979.
———. *NHK bukkusu,* vol. 531, *Zusetsu: Gendai Nihon no kazoku mondai.* Nihon hōsō shuppan kyōkai, 1987.
———. "Rikonritsu no suii to sono haikei." In *Kōza kazoku,* vol. 4, *Kon'in no kaishō,* edited by Aoyama Michio et al. Kōbundō, 1974.

Western-Language Sources

Alcock, Rutherford. *The Capital of the Tycoon: A Narrative of a Three Years' Residence in Japan.* 2 vols. 1863. Reprint. New York: Greenwood Press, 1969.
Aoki, Michiko, and Margret Dardess. "The Popularization of Samurai Values—A Sermon by Hosoi Heishū." *Monumenta Nipponica* 31, no. 4 (Winter 1976): 393–413.

Araki, Torataro. *Japanisches Eheschließungsrecht*. Göttingen: Univ.-Buchdruckerei von W. Fr. Kästner, 1893.
Bacon, Alice M. *Japanese Girls and Women*. Boston: Houghton, Mifflin, 1891.
Baumann, Felix. *Japaner Mädel*. Berlin: Langenscheidt, 1908.
Becker, Gary S. *A Treatise on the Family*. Cambridge, Mass.: Harvard University Press, 1981.
Becker, J. E. de. *Annotated Civil Code of Japan*. 4 vols. London: Butterworth; Yokohama: Kelley & Walsh, 1909–10.
Bellesort, André. *La Société japonaise*. Paris: Perrin, 1926.
Bird, Isabella. *Unbeaten Tracks in Japan*. 1880. Reprint. Rutland, Vt.: Charles E. Tuttle, 1973.
Braisted, William Reynolds, trans. *Meiroku Zasshi: Journal of the Japanese Enlightenment*. Cambridge, Mass.: Harvard University Press, 1976.
Bryant, Taimie L. "For the Sake of the Country, for the Sake of the Family: The Oppressive Impact of Family Registration on Women and Minorities in Japan." *UCLA Law Review* 39, no. 1 (1991): 109–68.
———. "Marital Dissolution in Japan: Legal Obstacles and Their Impact." *Law in Japan* 17 (1984): 73–98.
———. "'Responsible' Husbands, 'Recalcitrant' Wives, Retributive Judges: Judicial Management of Contested Divorce in Japan." *Journal of Japanese Studies* 18, no. 2 (Summer 1992): 407–43.
Chamberlain, Basil H. *Things Japanese*. 1890. 5th ed. rev. 1905. Reprinted as *Japanese Things: Being Notes on Various Subjects Connected with Japan, for the Use of Travelers and Others*. Rutland, Vt.: Charles E. Tuttle, 1971.
Ch'en, Paul Heng-Chao. *The Formation of the Early Meiji Legal Order: The Japanese Code of 1871 and Its Chinese Foundation*. London Oriental Series, vol. 35. Oxford: Oxford University Press, 1981.
Chikamatsu, Monzaemon. "Love Suicides at Amijima." In *Major Plays of Chikamatsu Monzaemon*, translated by Donald Keene. New York: Columbia University Press, 1961.
Commission européenne. *Les Femmes et les hommes dans l'union européenne*. Luxembourg: Office des publications officielles des communautés européennes, 1995.
Conn, William. *Japanese Life, Love, and Legend: A Visit to the Empire of the "Rising Sun." From "Le Japon pittoresque" of Maurice Dubard*. London: Ward & Downey, 1886.
Cooper, Michael, ed. *They Came to Japan: An Anthology of European Reports on Japan, 1543–1640*. Berkeley: University of California Press, 1981.
Cornell, Laurel L. "Gender Differences in Remarriage After Divorce in Japan and the United States." *Journal of Marriage and the Family* 51, no. 2 (May 1989): 457–64.
———. "Peasant Women and Divorce in Preindustrial Japan." *Signs: Journal of Women in Culture and Society* 15, no. 4 (1990): 710–32.
———. "Why Are There No Spinsters in Japan?" *Journal of Family History* 9, no. 4 (Winter 1984): 326–39.

Cornell, Laurel L., and Hayami Akira. "The Shūmon Aratame Chō: Japan's Population Registers." *Journal of Family History* 11, no. 4 (1986): 311–28.
Cortazzi, Hugh. *Victorians in Japan: In and Around the Treaty Ports*. Atlantic Highlands, N.J.: Athlone Press, 1987.
Edwards, Walter. *Modern Japan Through Its Weddings: Gender, Person, and Society in Ritual Portrayal*. Stanford: Stanford University Press, 1989.
Emiko, Ochiai. "Familie und Geschlechterbeziehung in Japan seit Ende des Zweiten Weltkrieges bis zur Gegenwart." In *Monographien*, vol. 22, *Das Bild der Familie in den japanischen Medien*, edited by Hilaria Gössmann. Munich: Iudicium, 1998.
Epp, Robert. "The Challenge from Tradition: Attempts to Compile a Civil Code in Japan, 1866–78." *Monumenta Nipponica* 22, no. 1/2 (1967): 15–48.
———. "Threat to Tradition: The Reaction to Japan's 1890 Civil Code." Ph.D. diss., Harvard University, 1964.
Erskine, William H. *Japanese Customs: Their Origin and Value*. Tokyo: Kyo Bun Kwan, 1925.
Exner, A. H. *Japan: Skizzen von Land und Leuten*. Leipzig: Weigel Nachfolger, 1891.
Foreign Press Center. *Facts and Figures of Japan*. Tokyo: Foreign Press Center, 1995.
Fraser, Mary Crawford. *A Diplomat's Wife in Japan*. 1899. Abridged ed. Edited by Hugh Cortazzi. New York: Weatherhill, 1982.
Freed, Jane Anne O. *The Changing Worlds of Older Women in Japan*. Manchester, Conn.: Knowledge, Ideas and Trends, 1992.
Fuess, Harald. "A Golden Age of Fatherhood? Parent-Child Relations in Japanese Historiography." *Monumenta Nipponica* 52, no. 3 (Autumn 1997): 381–97.
———. "Die japanische BGB-Reformkontroverse (1996): Japanische Identität und die Rolle der Frau." *Japanstudien: Jahrbuch des Deutschen Instituts für Japanstudien* 9 (1997): 255–86.
Fukuzawa, Yukichi. *The Autobiography of Yukichi Fukuzawa*. Translated by Eiichi Kiyooka. 1934. 1st American ed. New York: Columbia University Press, 1966.
———. *Fukuzawa Yukichi on Japanese Women: Selected Works*. Translated and edited by Eiichi Kiyooka. Tokyo: University of Tokyo Press, 1988.
———. *Kyūhanjō*. Translated by Carmen Blacker. *Monumenta Nipponica* 9 (1953): 304–29.
Goh, Daigoro. "The Family Relations in Japan." *Transactions and Proceedings of the Japan Society, London* 2 (1892–93): 117–53.
Goode, William J. *World Changes in Divorce Patterns*. New Haven, Conn.: Yale University Press, 1993.
———. *World Revolution and Family Patterns*. New York: Free Press, 1963.
Gordon, Andrew. *The Evolution of Labor Relations in Japan: Heavy Industry, 1853–1955*. Cambridge, Mass.: Harvard University Press, 1988.

Hall, David R. "Marriage as a Pure Relationship: Exploring the Link Between Premarital Cohabitation and Divorce in Canada." *Journal of Comparative Family Studies* 27, no. 1 (Spring 1996): 1–12.
Hani, Motoko. "Stories of My Life." *Japan Interpreter* 12, no. 3/4 (Summer 1979): 330–54. Translated by Chieko Irie Mulhern from "Hansei o kataru," in *Hani Motoko chosakushō*, vol. 14 (Fujin no tomosha, 1974), 1–93.
Hanley, Susan B. "Family and Fertility in Four Tokugawa Villages." In *Family and Population in East Asian History,* edited by Susan B. Hanley and Arthur P. Wolf. Stanford: Stanford University Press, 1985.
Hayami, Akira. "Another *Fossa Magna*: Proportion Marrying and Age at Marriage in Late Nineteenth-Century Japan." *Journal of Family History* 12, special issue, no. 1/3 (1987): 57–71.
———. "Illegitimacy in Japan." In *Bastardy and Its Comparative History,* edited by Peter Laslett, Karla Oosterveen, and Richard M. Smith. Cambridge, Mass.: Harvard University Press, 1980.
Hayami Akira and Kurosu Satomi. "Regional Diversity in Demographic and Family Patterns in Preindustrial Japan," *Journal of Japanese Studies* 27, no. 2 (Summer 2001): 295–321.
Hearn, Lafcadio. *Glimpses of Unfamiliar Japan.* Boston: Houghton, Mifflin, 1894.
Heine, W. *Japan: Beiträge zur Kenntniss des Landes und seiner Bewohner.* 1873. Reprint. Dresden: Selbstverlag des Verfassers, 1880.
Henderson, Dan F. *Conciliation and Japanese Law,* vol. 1. Seattle: University of Washington Press, 1965.
———. *Village "Contracts" in Tokugawa Japan.* Seattle: University of Washington Press, 1972.
Hobsbawm, Eric, and Terence Ranger, eds. *The Invention of Tradition.* New York: Cambridge University Press, 1983, 1992.
Hozumi, Nobushige. *Lectures on the New Japanese Civil Code: As Material for the Study of Comparative Jurisprudence.* Tokyo: Maruzen, 1912.
Humbert-Droz, Wolfgang. *Das Ehescheidungsrecht in Japan.* Cologne: Carl Heymanns, 1985.
Iwao, Sumiko. *The Japanese Woman: Traditional Image and Changing Reality.* New York: Free Press, 1993.
Iwasaki, Kojiro. *Das japanische Eherecht.* Leipzig: Roßberg'sche Verlagsbuchhandlung, 1904.
Iwasaki, Yasu. "Divorce in Japan." *American Journal of Sociology* 36, no. 3 (November 1930): 568–83.
Jacob, Herbert. *Silent Revolution: The Transformation of Divorce Law in the United States.* Chicago: University of Chicago Press, 1988.
Jansen, Marius B. "The Ruling Class." In *Japan in Transition: From Tokugawa to Meiji,* edited by Marius B. Jansen and Gilbert Rozman. Princeton, N.J.: Princeton University Press, 1986.
Jones, Thomas Elsa. "Mountain Folk in Japan: A Study in Method." Ph.D. diss., Columbia University, 1926.
Kaibara, Ekken [Ekiken]. *Greater Learning for Women.* Translated by Basil H.

Chamberlain in *Things Japanese*. 1890; 5th ed. rev., 1905. Reprinted as *Japanese Things: Being Notes on Various Subjects Connected with Japan, for the Use of Travelers and Others*. Rutland, Vt.: Charles E. Tuttle, 1971.
Kawashima, Takeyoshi, and Kurt Steiner. "Modernization and Divorce Rate Trends in Japan." *Economic Development and Cultural Change* 9, no. 1, pt. 2 (October 1960): 213–39.
Kawashima, Yasuhide. "Americanization of Japanese Family Law, 1945–1975." *Law in Japan* 16 (1983): 54–68.
Keene, Donald. *Chūshingura: The Treasury of Loyal Retainers*. New York: Columbia University Press, 1971.
Kito, Hiroshi. "Remarriage and Reproduction in a Rural Japanese Village in the Late Seventeenth and Eighteenth Century." *Sophia Economic Review* 33, no. 2 (February 1988): 84–102.
Knodel, John E. *Demographic Behavior in the Past: A Study of Fourteen German Village Populations in the Eighteenth and Nineteenth Centuries*. Cambridge: Cambridge University Press, 1988.
Kodansha Encyclopedia of Japan. Vol. 1. Tokyo: Kodansha, 1983.
König, René. *Die Familie der Gegenwart: Ein interkultureller Vergleich*. Munich: C. H. Beck, 1974.
Kreitner, Gustav. *Im Fernen Osten: Reisen des Grafen Bela Szecheny in Indien, Japan, China, Tibet und Birma in den Jahren 1877–1880*. Vienna: Alfred Hölder, 1881.
Küchler, L. W. "Marriage in Japan. Including a Few Remarks on the Marriage Ceremony, the Position of Married Women, and Divorce." *Transactions of the Asiatic Society of Japan* 13 (1885): 114–40.
Kumagai, Fumie. "Changing Divorce in Japan." *Journal of Family History* 8, no. 1 (Spring 1983): 85–107.
Lamairesse, E. *Le Japon: Histoire, religion, civilisation*. Paris: Librairie coloniale, 1892.
Lebra, Joyce C. "Women in an All-Male Industry: The Case of Sake Brewer Tatsu'uma Kiyo." In *Recreating Japanese Women*, edited by Gail L. Bernstein. Berkeley: University of California Press, 1991.
Lebra, Sugiyama. *Above the Clouds: Status Culture of the Modern Japanese Nobility*. Berkeley: University of California Press, 1993.
Linhart, Sepp. "Familie." In *Japan-Handbuch*, edited by Horst Hammitzsch. Wiesbaden: Franz Steiner, 1981.
Lloyd, Arthur. *Every-day Japan: Written After Twenty-five Years' Residence and Work in the Country*. London: Cassell, 1909.
Lützeler, Ralph. "Zur Regionalen Dimension Sozialer Probleme in Japan." *Japanstudien* 5 (1990): 229–73.
Manners and Customs of the Japanese, in the Nineteenth Century: From the Accounts of Dutch Residents in Japan and from the German Work of Philipp Franz von Siebold. 1841. Reprint. Rutland, Vt.: Charles E. Tuttle, 1973.
Marutschke, Hans Peter. *Einführung in das japanische Recht*. Munich: C. H. Beck, 1999.

Mason, Mary Ann. *From Father's Property to Children's Rights.* New York: Columbia University Press, 1994.
Matsukata Reischauer, Haru. *Samurai and Silk: A Japanese and American Heritage.* Cambridge, Mass.: Harvard University Press, 1986.
Matsukawa, Tadaki. *La Famille et le droit au Japon.* Paris: Economica, 1991.
Matsushita, Konosuke. *Quest for Prosperity: The Life of a Japanese Industrialist.* Kyoto: PHP Institute, 1988.
Minamikata, Satoshi. "Custodial Fathers in Japan." In *Economic Consequences of Divorce: The International Perspective,* edited by Lenore J. Weitzman and Mavis Maclean. Oxford: Clarendon Press, 1992.
Molony, Barbara. "Afterword." In *Facing Two Ways: The Story of My Life.* 1935. Reprint. Stanford: Stanford University Press, 1984.
Morris, Dana, and Thomas C. Smith. "Fertility and Mortality in an Outcaste Village in Japan, 1750–1869." In *Family and Population in East Asian History,* edited by Susan B. Hanley and Arthur P. Wolf. Stanford: Stanford University Press, 1985.
Mosk, Carl. *Patriarchy and Fertility: Japan and Sweden, 1880–1960.* New York: Academic Press, 1983.
Münch, Eva Marie von. *Ehescheidung nach neuem Recht.* Munich: C. H. Beck, 1996.
Nagy, Maria. "'How Shall We Live?' Social Change, the Family Institution and Feminism in Prewar Japan." Ph.D. diss., University of Washington, 1981.
Nakagawa, Zennosuke. "A Century of Marriage Law." *Japan Quarterly* 10, no. 2 (April–June 1963): 182–92.
Nakane, Chie. "An Interpretation of the Size and Structure of the Household in Japan over Three Centuries." In *Household and Family in Past Time: Comparative Studies in the Size and Structure of the Domestic Group over the Last Three Centuries in England, France, Serbia, Japan and Colonial North America, with Further Materials from Western Europe,* edited by Peter Laslett. Cambridge: Cambridge University Press, 1972.
Nakano, Makiko. *Makiko's Diary: A Merchant Wife in 1910 Kyoto.* Translated by Kazuko Smith. Stanford: Stanford University Press, 1995.
Neuss-Kaneko, Margret. *Familie und Gesellschaft in Japan: Von der Feudalzeit bis in die Gegenwart.* Munich: C. H. Beck, 1990.
———. "Scheidung auf Japanisch." In *Japanologentag,* edited by Ernst Lokowandt. Munich: Iudicium, 1990.
Ōbayashi, Taryō. "Traditionelle Gesellschaftstypen und Kulturprovinzen in Japan." *Japanstudien* 6 (1994): 165–203.
Omachi, Tokuzō. "Ashiire-Kon, Putting-One's-Feet-in-Marriage." In *Studies in Japanese Folklore,* edited by Richard Dorson. Bloomington: Indiana University Press, 1973.
Phillips, Roderick. *Putting Asunder: A History of Divorce in Western Society.* Cambridge: Cambridge University Press, 1988.
———. *Untying the Knot: A Short History of Divorce.* Cambridge: Cambridge University Press, 1991.
Rein, J. J. *Japan nach Reisen und Studien im Auftrage der königlich preus-*

sischen Regierung dargestellt. 1881–86. 2d ed. Leipzig: Wilhelm Engelmann, 1905.
Riley, Glenda. *Divorce: An American Tradition.* Oxford: Oxford University Press, 1991.
Sakamoto, Saburo. *Das Ehescheidungsrecht Japans.* Berlin: Georg Pintus, 1903.
Sasaki, Yōichirō. "Urban Migration and Fertility in Tokugawa Japan: The City of Takayama, 1773–1871." In *Family and Population in East Asian History*, edited by Susan B. Hanley and Arthur P. Wolf. Stanford: Stanford University Press, 1985.
Schalek, Alice. *Japan: Das Land des Nebeneinander.* Breslau: Ferdinand Hirt, 1925.
Shively, Donald H. "Bakufu Versus Kabuki." In *Studies in the Institutional History of Early Modern Japan*, edited by John W. Hall and Marius B. Jansen. Princeton, N.J.: Princeton University Press, 1968.
Smith, Robert J. "Making Village Women into 'Good Wives and Wise Mothers' in Prewar Japan." *Journal of Family History* 8, no. 1 (Spring 1983): 70–84.
———. "Transformations of Commoner Households in Tennōji-mura, 1757–1858." In *Family and Population in East Asian History*, edited by Susan B. Hanley and Arthur P. Wolf. Stanford: Stanford University Press, 1985.
Smith, Robert J., and Ella Lury Wiswell. *The Women of Suye Mura.* Chicago: University of Chicago Press, 1982.
Smith, Thomas C. *Nakahara: Family Farming and Population in a Japanese Village, 1717–1830.* Stanford: Stanford University Press, 1977.
Steiner, Kurt. "The Revision of the Civil Code of Japan: Provisions Affecting the Family." *Far Eastern Quarterly* 9, no. 2 (February 1950).
Stone, Lawrence. *Road to Divorce: A History of the Making and Breaking of Marriage in England.* Oxford: Oxford University Press, 1995.
Sugimoto, Etsu Inagaki. *A Daughter of the Samurai: How a Daughter of Feudal Japan, Living Hundreds of Years in One Generation, Became a Modern American.* 1925. Reprint. Rutland, Vt.: Charles E. Tuttle, 1990.
Tamura, Naomi. *The Japanese Bride.* New York: Harper & Bros., 1893.
Tappe, Friedrich. *Soziologie der Japanischen Familie: Grundanschauungen, Ethik und Recht des japanischen Familiensystems.* Münster: Aschendorffsche Verlagsbuchhandlung, 1955.
Taeuber, Irene B. *The Population of Japan.* Princeton, N.J.: Princeton University Press, 1958.
Toda, Teizo. "Divorce—A Comparative Study." *Contemporary Japan*, September 1933, 294–302.
Toson, Shimazaki. *The Family.* Translated by Cecilia Segawa Seigle. Tokyo: Tokyo University Press, 1976.
Ueno, Chizuko. "The Position of Japanese Women Reconsidered." *Current Anthropology* 28, no. 4 (August–October 1987): S75–S85.
Varner, Richard E. "The Organized Peasant: The *Wakamonogumi* in the Edo Period." *Monumenta Nipponica* 32, no. 4 (Winter 1977): 459–83.

Vogel, Ezra F. *Japan's New Middle Class*. Berkeley: University of California Press, 1963.
Wang, Dominique. "Le Divorce en Chine et au Japon." *Zeitschrift für Schweizerisches Recht* 93 (1974): 609–39.
Waswo, Ann. *Modern Japanese Society, 1868–1994*. Oxford: Oxford University Press, 1996.
Watanabe, Yōzo. "Family and Law in Modern Japan." *Annals of the Institute of Social Science* 15 (1974): 36–37.
———. "The Family and the Law: The Individualistic Premise and the Modern Japanese Family Law." In *Law in Japan*, edited by Arthur von Mehren. Cambridge, Mass.: Harvard University Press, 1963.
Weber, Eugen. *Peasants into Frenchmen: The Modernization of Rural France, 1870–1914*. Stanford: Stanford University Press, 1976.
Weitzman, Lenore J. *The Divorce Revolution: The Unexpected Social and Economic Consequences for Women and Children in America*. New York: Free Press, 1985.
Weston, Walter. *Japan*. London: A. & C. Black, 1926.
Wigmore, John H., ed. *Law and Justice in Tokugawa Japan: Materials for the History of Japanese Law and Justice Under the Tokugawa Shogunate 1603–1867*. 9 vols. Tokyo: University of Tokyo Press, 1969–86.
Williams, Harold S. *Tales of the Foreign Settlements in Japan*. Rutland, Vt.: Charles E. Tuttle, 1958.
Wöhr, Ulrike. *Frauen zwischen Rollenerwartung und Selbstdeutung: Ehe, Mutterschaft und Liebe im Spiegel der japanischen Frauenzeitschrift Shin shin fujin von 1913 bis 1916*. Wiesbaden: Harrassowitz, 1997.
Wright, Diana E. "Severing the Karmic Ties That Bind: The 'Divorce Temple' Mantokuji." *Monumenta Nipponica* 52, no. 3 (Autumn 1997): 357–80.
Yamakawa, Kikue. *Women of the Mito Domain*. Translated by Kate Wildman Nakai. Tokyo: University of Tokyo Press, 1992.
Yanagita, Kunio. *Japanese Manners and Customs in the Meiji Era*. Translated by Charles S. Terry. Tokyo: Obunsha, 1957.
Yōichirō Sasaki. "Urban Migration and Fertility in Tokugawa Japan: The City of Takayama, 1773–1871." In *Family and Population in East Asian History*, edited by Susan B. Hanley and Arthur P. Wolf. Stanford: Stanford University Press, 1985.

Index

Adopted husband, see In-marrying husband
Adoption, 14, 78
Adultery, 77, 105, 162; sexual double standard, 77, 87, 102, 108, 117, 130, 146–47, 191–92
Alimony, 35, 88, 98, 116
Alternate attendance, 22
American Occupation, 145–49
Ariga (Aruga) Kizaemon, 140
Asakura Yūko, 22
Ashikaga family, 41

Bacon, Alice Mabel, 4, 97
Becker, Gary, 154–55
Becker, Joseph Ernest, 124
Betrothal present, 41, 89
Bird, Isabella, 11
Blakemore, Thomas L., 147
Boissonade de Fontarabie, Gustave-Emile, 107
Bourbon dynasty, 106
Bousquet, Georges Hilaire, 198
Bridewealth (*yuinō*), 41, 89
British Parliament, 138

Catholicism, 106
Census, 11. *See also* Yamanashi census
Chamberlain, Basil Hall, 2
Charter Oath, 48
Chikamatsu Monzaemon, 27
Child custody, 91–96, 116, 148, 156–59
Child support, 94–95, 98, 148, 158
Child visitation rights, 95
Christianity, 20, 103, 110, 138, 141–42
Chōsokabe Motochika, 12
Civil Codes, *see* Old Civil Code, Meiji Civil Code, *and* New Civil Code

Common-law marriage (*naien*), 11, 48, 51, 53, 66–67, 72, 112, 125, 154–55
Concubinage, 17, 54–57, 78, 180, 188
Confucianism, 24–25, 36, 44–45, 55, 67, 75. *See also* Grounds for divorce, Confucian
Consensual divorce (*kyōgi rikon*), 1, 4, 101, 105, 110, 124, 147, 149. *See also* Customary consent divorce
Constitution, 146
Cornell, Laurel, 8, 12
Council of State Decree No. 162, *see* Decree No. 162
Court divorce (*saiban rikon*), 4–5, 9, 38, 102, 105, 108, 128–31, 149–51; origins and function, 101, 110f, 113, 147. *See also* Grounds for divorce, no-fault court divorce
Courtesan, 25, 34
Criminal Codes, 48, 51, 56
Custody, *see* Child custody
Customary consent divorce, 1, 9, 25–28, 76–96, 106; simple procedure, 4–5, 28, 98, 102–3, 115. *See also* Unilateral divorce
Customs survey of 1875, 15, 49, 51, 64, 68, 75, 77, 87, 91–92, 116, 125, 179

Daigoro, Goh, 84, 140
Daimyo divorce, 22, 58, 180–81
Decree No. 162, 100–101, 105, 178, 199
Division of matrimonial assets, 102, 105, 116, 147, 158
Divorce by adjustment (*shinpan rikon*), 149
Divorce by agreement, *see* Consensual divorce *and* Customary consent divorce
Divorce by conciliation (*chōtei rikon*), 149

Divorce by registration, *see* Consensual divorce *and* Customary consent divorce
Divorce law, 7, 8, 11, 18, 44, 101, 147, 184; legal definition, 11, 14–15 , 48, 126–27, 146–48, 178. *See also* Meiji Civil Code *and* New Civil Code
Divorce notice, 4, 28, 35, 78–81, 192–93
Divorce rate, 2–4, 22, 24–25, 120–21, 145; change, 119, 145; class difference, 22, 45, 57–59; decline, 3, 7, 10, 65, 72–73, 115, 140–41; local variation, 22–24, 58–64, 72–73
Divorce revolution, 1, 10, 150, 152
Divorce temple, 20, 30, 39–44, 183. *See also* Mantokuji *and* Tōkeiji
Divorce, 1, 7–10, 14, 20, 23, 29–36, 45, 47, 57–65, 74, 95, 100, 115, 119, 160, 166; corporal punishment, 33, 37–38, 80, 183; debate, 4–5, 102–4, 108, 112, 120, 141; frequency, 1–3, 47, 54, 65, 110, 121; life cycle, 50–51, 66, 73, 122, 135–36, 153–54; social variation, 36–37, 39, 49, 102–3, 121, 159. *See also* Consensual divorce *and* Customary consent divorce
Double suicide, 25
Dowry, 82–91, 137, 140–41, 193–94; return, 29, 41, 85–91
Dual divorce system, 101, 105, 109, 114, 147

1875 survey, *see* Customs survey of 1875
England, 104, 138, 151
Erskine, William, 4, 137–38
Etō Shinpei, 105, 198
Europe, 1, 110, 116, 119, 151, 159
Exner, A. H., 70, 84

Family courts, 6, 130–31, 146, 149, 151
Family registration laws, 3, 11, 48, 124–28 *passim*
Family structures, 59–65, 67, 189
Family, 6–7, 146, 160. *See also* Household
Father-in-law, 33
Female employment, 8, 152
Female heads of households, 65, 184
Female plaintiffs, 128–31, 161. *See also* Wife demands divorce
Filial piety, 20
Foreign views of divorce, 1–2, 19, 54, 68, 84, 124, 141, 150, 196. *See also* individual observers by name
France, 105–8, 115, 144
Fukuzawa Yukichi, 21, 103, 123

Gender equality and divorce, 44–46, 102, 108, 114, 118, 164–65

Germany, 104, 117, 144, 151
Giddens, Anthony, 154–55
Go-between, 12, 41, 58, 81, 90–91
Greater Learning for Women (Onna daigaku), 19–20, 55, 68, 78
Grounds for divorce: customary, 20, 45, 76–78, 82; Confucian, 19, 45, 111; legal, 101, 105, 129–30, 150, 159, 162; no-fault court divorce, 101, 111, 114–15, 117, 151–52, 161–63
Guilty party, 45, 159

Hani Motoko, 97
Heine, Wilhelm, 84
Honma Hisao, 133
Hosoi Heishū, 20
Household, 8, 28, 62–63, 150. *See also* Family
Hozumi Nobushige, 104, 109, 110–13
Hozumi Shigetō, 5, 100
Hozumi Yatsuka, 109, 114
Husband's prerogatives, 30, 42, 109, 124
Hōjō Tokimune, 41

Igarashi Tomio, 43
Illegitimate childbirth, *see* Out-of-wedlock childbirth
In-marrying husband, 13–14, 32–36, 45–46; divorce of, 27, 32–36, 117, 130, 136–37, 160, 166, 181, 183, 203–4; rates, 63, 83–84, 87
Ishii Ryōsuke, 7
Ishimoto Shidzue, 127–28
Isobe Shirō, 107, 109
Iwasaki, Yasu, 5

Japan as high divorce society, 1, 6, 10, 47, 100, 142, 145, 166
Jones, Thomas Elsa, 140
Judicial divorce, *see* Court divorce

Kaibara Ekiken (Ekken), 19
Kitō Hiroshi, 23
Konosuke Matsushita, 134
Kreitner, Gustav, 68
Kumano Toshizō, 107, 109
Küchler, L.W., 5

Law of Legal Procedure, 100
Letter of divorce, *see* Divorce notice
Liberal Democratic Party, 150, 161
Life cycle, 10, 154
Lifetime employment, 150, 165
Lloyd, Arthur, 84

Madoka Yoriko, 166

Mantokuji, 31–32, 39–44
Marriage, 7, 8–9, 11, 13, 16, 19, 21, 47–51, 72, 75, 102–3, 137–41, 180; arranged marriage, 12, 103, 153; demographic parameters, 62, 71, 125–26, 135–36, 180; duration, 24, 65, 128, 137, 141, 153; legal definition, 11–13, 146–47; love marriage, 12, 27, 112f, 133–35. *See also* Common-law marriage, *and* Trial marriage
Marriage ceremony, *see* Wedding
Marriage notification, *see* Marriage registration
Marriage registration, 11, 47, 49, 51
Meiji Civil Code (of 1898); divorce, 3, 5, 10–11, 13, 16, 48, 52–53, 57, 77, 101, 129–30; and divorce rate, 123–28; draft, 110, 114; position of women, 114–18, 123–24, 129–30; revision of, 145–46, 156, 158, 160
Meiji Restoration, 10, 121
Mikudarihan, *see* Divorce notice
Ministry of Education, 6
Ministry of Health and Welfare, 144
Ministry of Justice, 15, 70, 101, 107, 109, 148, 162–64, 179
Mistress, *see* Concubinage
Mitford, Algernon Bertram, 2
Mitsukuri Rinshō, 107
Monogamy, 57
Mori Arinori, 57, 102
Morris, Dana, 24
Mortality, 24, 153, 156
Mosk, Carl, 16
Mother-in-law, 20, 32, 34–35, 45, 77, 131–33, 160
Motherhood, 158
Muko yōshi, *see* In-marrying husband
Murata Tamotsu, 109
Mutual consent divorce, *see* Consensual divorce

Napoleonic Code, 105–6, 108, 115, 148, 199
Naquet Law, 107
New Civil Code (of 1947), 14, 48, 117, 145–48; revision, 148, 153–64 *passim*
Numa Masaya, 81

Ochiai Emiko, 24
Okano Keijirō, 130
Old Civil Code (of 1890), 114
Osaka, 52, 58, 158, 183
Ōki Takatō, 107
Out-of-wedlock childbirth, 51–54, 112, 154–55, 187; rate, 52–53, 66–67

Ozaki Yukio, 57

Peerage, 57–58
Pleasure quarter, 25, 35
Popular divorce customs, *see* Customary consent divorce
Prenuptial contract, 86
Private settlement (*naisai*), 29, 31, 38, 42, 184
Property division, *see* Division of matrimonial assets
Prussia, 112

Rein, Johann Justus, 124, 200
Religious affiliation survey (*shūmon aratame*), 9, 48–49, 177
Remarriage, 5, 8, 41, 47, 67–71, 80, 98–99, 129; waiting period, 41–42, 116, 164, 183, after spousal death, 15, 70–71, 127, 191
Russia, 144
Rutherford, Alcock, 4, 196

Sakai Toshihiko, 123
Samurai, 21, 107, 114, 141; divorce, 18, 68, 81, 83, 96–97, 136, 190
Satsuma rebellion, 107
Sayo divorce case, 30–32, 43
Secondary wife, *see* Concubinage
Segawa Kiyoko, 178
Sexual relations, 51, 141–42
Siebold, Philipp Franz von, 54
Single mothers, 208
Smith, Robert, 8
Smith, Thomas, 24
Social stigma after divorce, 5, 143, 152–53, 161
Split custody, *see* Child custody
Spousal relations, 7–8, 10, 14, 109
State and divorce, 45; divorce by magistrates, 29–39, 40–42, 44, 184. *See also* Divorce law, Old Civil Code, Meiji Civil Code, *and* New Civil Code
Steiner, Kurt, 7
Supreme Court, 130, 150, 161–62, 164, 185
Survey of religious affiliation, *see* Religious affiliation survey
Suye Mura, 134, 139–40, 190
Suzuki Umeshirō, 58
Sweden, 151

Taihō Code, 19, 113
Taishō emperor, 139
Takagi Tadashi, 39
Takeyoshi Kawashima, 7

Tamaki Hajime, 126
Temple divorce, *see* Divorce temple
Theater, 25
Toda Teizō, 5, 126, 132
Tōkeiji, 39–42, 44
Tokyo, 58–59, 97
Tokyo Statistical Association, 103
Tomii Masaaki, 110, 117–18
Trial marriage, 2, 47, 49f, 54, 61–62, 72–74, 137, 160, 185–86

Ueki Emori, 138
Ueno, Chizuko, 177
Ume Kenjirō, 110, 114
Unilateral divorce, 78–79, 113, 148, 162, 165. *See also* Divorce *and* Divorce law
United States, 1, 119, 144, 151, 157, 159
Universal marriage, 12, 74

Valignano, Alessandro, 1
Values, 75

Virtue, 19, 26–28

Waiting period, *see* Remarriage, waiting period
Wedding, 49–50, 137–40, 155
Western legal systems, 103–4, 151–52
Weston, Walter, 54, 70, 138
Wife demands divorce, 65, 76, 79–80, 88, 96–101; wife's right to demand divorce, 44–45, 77, 100–101, 113. *See also* Female plaintiffs
Wife's protection against divorce, 114
Wiswell, Elsa, 139
Wright, Diane, 8

Yamakawa Kikue, 55, 123
Yamanashi census, 15, 55, 121–23, 160, 178
Yokoyama Gennosuke, 58–59
Yokoyama Masao, 103–4
Yuzawa Yasuhiko, 190